Productive Trout Flies for Unorthodox Prey

THE ODDBALLS

Jeff Morgan

Photos by Arlen Thomason

Productive Trout Flies for *Unorthodox Prey*

Jeff Morgan
Photos by Arlen Thomason

THE ODDBALLS

Frank Amato Publications

©2012 Jeff Morgan

ALL RIGHTS RESERVED. No part of this book may be reproduced in any means (printed or electronic) without the written consent of the publisher, except in the case of brief excerpts in critical reviews and articles.

All inquiries should be addressed to:
Frank Amato Publications, Inc.
P.O. Box 82112
Portland, Oregon 97282
www.amatobooks.com
(503) 653-8108

All subject/scenic photos by Arlen Thomason unless otherwise noted
Fly pattern photos by Jim Schollmeyer
Illustrations by Bill Marshall
Cover and book design by Tony Amato

ISBN-13: 978-1-57188-426-8   UPC: 0-81127-00260-3

Printed in China

1 3 5 7 9 10 8 6 4 2

Contents

Introduction 6

Chapter I
How Understanding "Oddball" Trout Prey Will Improve Your Angling ... 8

Chapter II
Why Have We Overlooked Oddballs? ... 10

Chapter III
A Case Study of Oddballs: The Ecology of Terrestrials ... 16

Chapter IV
How To Use This Book ... 20

Chapter V
The Prey ... 22

Ants	23	*Daphnia*	87
Aphids	27	**Dragonflies**	91
Baitfish	29	**Grasshoppers**	96
Trout and Salmon Fry	30	**Horse Flies and Deer Flies**	102
Sticklebacks	36	**Honeybees**	106
Tui Chub	39	**Leeches**	107
Sculpins	41	**Mosquitoes**	111
Rainbow Smelt	44	**Moths**	113
Shad and Alewives	46	**Net-Winged Midges**	115
Beetles	48	**Phantom Midges**	117
Black Flies	55	**Scuds**	121
Centipedes and Millipedes	60	**Aquatic Snails**	126
Chironomids	61	**Sow Bugs**	130
Crayfish	72	**Water Boatmen and Backswimmers**	133
Crane Flies	76		
Damselflies	81		

Index 136

Introduction

This book explores the concept of "Oddball" trout prey writ large. It includes most of the important North American trout foods, sans the triumvirate of conventional "trout bugs": mayflies, caddis, and stoneflies. Some of these prey items may seem mainstream—particularly hoppers, chironomids, damselflies, or scuds. However, most of these foods have not been subjected to any full-length entomological evaluation by anglers. Many anglers have assumed rather than proven their relative importance. Other insects—from black flies and *Daphnia* to snails and phantom midges—have been omitted from both introductory lessons, guided instruction, and most standard American angling monographs.

Do not conflate the term "Oddball" with "marginal." Oddball refers to trout prey that anglers have either underestimated or ignored over the past three decades. The reasons for the omission of these foods are many. Anglers miss the importance of inchworms or snails because they are only locally important in specific ecological niches. Other anglers overlook certain prey items, like sow bugs and crane fly larvae, because they elude most "bottom samples" that do not also probe the upper levels of the substrate. Anglers never encounter other prey, like *Daphnia*, phantom midges, and juvenile fish, because they concentrate their angling efforts in the wrong habitats during the wrong season. Finally, anglers confuse some prey with others. For decades, anglers have commonly conflated "microcaddis larvae" with black fly larvae.

The greatest reason for the devaluation of most of these Oddballs has been their inability to produce visible "hatches." Anglers have long held an anthropocentric bias towards foods they can directly observe trout feeding on.

Despite their omission in standard texts, Oddball foods compose a major, in not central, portion of the trout diet. On the "average water," the annual trout diet may be 30% mayflies, 30% caddis, 10% stoneflies, and 30% "other." However, we never fish *average* waters and we certainly never fish them on an *annual* basis. We fish *particular* waters on a *daily* basis.

When both scientists and angler entomologists break down these "annual diet" estimations into their seasonal and local factors, a high degree of randomness appears. It is this variability that creates "mystery hatches," "non-biting fish," and frustrated anglers. During summer and fall on most lakes, the trout diet shifts almost entirely away from the traditional Chironomid-Damsel-*Callibaetis* regime to mostly *Daphnia* and baitfish. The traditional stillwater foods make up less than ten percent of the average stillwater trout diet from mid-summer through late fall.

Because anglers focus intently on averages, we tend to overlook the influence of transitioning seasons and transitioning spaces on the trout diet. Take for example, the most controlled and stable of trout environments, the tailwater. During summer, tailwater and lake outlet-dwelling trout may eat some PMD's and net-spinning caddis. However, near riffle stretches those trout usually eat *more* black fly larvae. Some rivers also support dense concentrations of particular trout prey—such as sow bugs or crane fly larvae—immediately below a dam; even though those foods may not exist in other "blue ribbon" stretches just a couple miles downriver. In the wintertime, those same tailwater trout may eat a couple salmonfly nymphs, but fish eggs, fry, crane fly larvae, and aquatic worms kicked up in spate flooding contribute far more calories to their diet. On one river, depending on the

time and precise location, Oddballs can outshine all the "normal" foods combined.

This study also intends to put prey into their proper perspective. This includes explaining when and where foods are *not* important to trout. This book will not insist that every single food is a panacea for some "mystery hatch" situation. Some readers may recoil at the denigration of grasshoppers, adult dragonflies and adult damselflies in this text. However, if a food is not important to trout, and scientists have spent entire careers disinterestedly documenting the interactions, we should not insult both in order to mollify a huckster promoting his latest adult dragon pattern.

This book admittedly attributes a greater relative weight to professional scientific literature than fly fishing magazines and books. This is not to impugn the knowledge of fly anglers and writers, but we fly fishing writers often exist in an anecdotal world. Their samples only contain what they find where and when they choose to fish and sample. For example, American angling writers consistently overlook *Daphnia*. Why? Trout prey heavily upon *Daphnia* in the open water parts of lakes that North American fly anglers generally avoid. North American angling experts have understood and examined the various foods common to the paragon stillwater habitat—shallow, weedy flats. However, this wealth of information has come at the cost of overlooking essential foods in other important stillwater habitats.

Secure in their funding and forced through peer-review to note the limits of their sampling, scientific ecological studies rarely share the inherent (and unavoidable) biases of angling entomologies. In addition, their studies often are more comprehensive and detailed in terms of location, dates, and time. (The scientific citations of studies included in this book do not represent conclusive evidence of the universality of certain foods, but should demonstrate that under certain conditions, trout can feed heavily on each of the many foods that we normally overlook in the trout diet.)

Obviously, this study omits many forms of trout prey. Every region in North America has its local culinary style, and the trout of each region have different preferred prey. Alaskan anglers may be miffed at the omission of salmon flesh, Quebecois anglers may scream "Vous Dupez!" at the lack of mouse imitations, and Southeastern anglers chasing stocked rainbows may want some consideration of juvenile bass and bluegill. Obviously, every specific locality has its unique food resource, and this text cannot include them all.

More significantly, this book excludes many important, but overlooked mayfly, caddis, or stonefly species. While I would love to argue the value of Mahogany Duns versus Salmonflies in the annual diet of trout, it would open a Pandora's Box of debate that could never be resolved in a one hundred forty page text. Anglers have long debated these important foods, and it is time that we devote our time to many ignored, derided, yet still essential, prey in the trout diet.

This book owes much to the work and life of Gary LaFontaine. I had the opportunity to meet Gary near the end of his life, and he graciously offered to endorse my first book and gave me unrivaled advice on both writing and critical thinking. This book attempts to embody the last words of *Caddisflies*, "Skepticism is not only healthy—it is the only way new ideas can find room to stand."

—*Jeff Morgan*
San Francisco, CA

Chapter I:

How Understanding "Oddball" Trout Prey Will Improve Your Angling

Anyone who has spent time hanging around fly shops or teaching beginner classes knows the first rule of fly fishing: "The three most important things to catching trout are presentation, presentation, and presentation." Any well-placed fly will catch usually catch a few fish, but even the "perfect pattern" will fail if fished improperly. This is essential advice to the newcomer often more interested in stuffing his or her fly boxes with pretty patterns than worrying about how to execute a drag-free drift.

Small lakes offer unique microhabitats that make one or more Oddball prey forms essential to trout growth.

Jeff Morgan photo

However, apply this advice to the intermediate-skill angler and the naiveté of the rule becomes apparent. Without an understanding of bugs and fly selection, an intermediate-skilled angler may execute perfect dead drifts with a Royal Coachman Streamer or a nice wet-fly swing with a Parachute Adams, but only fool a fraction of the fish they would if they actually imitated what trout eat.

The problem with most angling entomologies and entomology classes is that they rarely push the angler beyond the basics. Too often angling entomologies rely on excellent photography or innovative fly patterns to distinguish themselves from the other entomologies that cover an identical cohort of mayflies, caddis, and stoneflies. These works treat other trout foods as an aside. Ants and beetles and sow bugs and crane flies all are treated matter-of-factly—"if you see them, imitate them." With little of the serious analysis devoted to the "major" trout foods, these "other" foods receive spare attention unless they occur on famous waters, such as the aquatic worms of the San Juan, the cicadas of the Green River, or the sow bugs of the Letort.

However, "Oddball" foods—a cosmopolitan lot ranging from ants and beetles to *Daphnia* and phantom midges to black flies and sow bugs—make up at least 30% of the diets of trout in most waters. Often one of these foods provides the majority of the Oddball component of the trout diet. In a region of clear cuts, flying ants may be crucial to summertime trout in both rivers and streams. A stream below a burned area with high nutrient levels and suspended sediments may be rich in black fly larvae. Trout in a deep medium-sized lake with warm summertime temperatures may turn nearly exclusively to *Daphnia* over the course of the two months when trout hang near the thermocline.

Despite the local essentiality of these prey items, they are discounted by angling entomologies when looking at the "average" trout diet across the nation. However, anglers don't fish for "average" trout. We fish for individual trout, and those individual trout on individual waters regularly feed heavily on one or more Oddballs.

For the advanced or expert angler, understanding Oddballs has significant advantages. It obviously allows them to deconstruct of the "mystery hatches" that perplex all of us at one time or another. And for advanced anglers—who can approach and present to fish, as well as carry a solid knowledge of entomology—the "mystery hatch" or "mystery prey" situation represents a proportionately larger barrier to consistent success than it does for the novice angler struggling through the roll cast.

More importantly, understanding Oddballs gives the advanced angler the ability to outmaneuver other anglers. While most Americans shun the idea of competitive fly fishing, we all participate in it nearly every time we hit the water. Guides vie for the "best" runs, stillwater anglers prefer to have monopoly on creek inlets or prime flats, and everyone likes to fish the early days of a hatch period before highly-pressured fish become more selective. A thorough knowledge of Oddball insects allows anglers to escape the traditional concentrations of pressure without sacrificing—indeed often improving—their productivity. Because Oddball insects thrive in "patchy environments," advanced anglers can find new niches on familiar waters all to themselves. When all the others congregate on flats in anticipation of the morning PMD spinner fall, the angler familiar with Oddballs will enjoy plenty of elbow-room in the riffles where trout gorge themselves on black fly larvae.

For the beginning angler, understanding Oddballs has its own rewards. We often dumb-down entomology for beginning anglers, making it seem like mastering the life-stages of the Big Three is the only key to understanding entomology. We teach them that everything else is either superfluous or a luxury examine far later in their training as anglers.

This oversimplification does not necessarily create an ecological problem, for the Big Three are generally important foods for trout, but it creates two countervailing pedagogical problems for the instructor. First, focusing on aquatic insects fights the natural tendency of humans to understand the trout world through their human experience. The beginning fly angler is significantly influenced by their pre-fly fishing experiences with terrestrial insects and anthropomorphized animals. In other words, most new anglers understand nature through the Nemo and Jiminy Cricket, rather than extensive personal experience. This means that they attribute undue importance to flying insects, large insects, and critters even familiar to the angler minimally exposed to the outdoors—such as crayfish, grasshoppers, and mosquitoes. A mayfly might as well be a type of WWII fighter plane to many beginning anglers, but the same anglers have observed and been aware of Oddball insects long before their fishing experiences began. Focusing on Oddballs makes entomology more understandable and absorbable to the greenhorn angler.

Secondly, focusing on aquatic prey items that emerge in neat "hatches," helps reinforce the terrestrial bias by discounting *fully* aquatic prey. Since the "rediscovery" of nymph fishing in the 1970's, anglers have paid far more attention to certain fully aquatic prey forms, like scuds or leeches. However, anglers have been much slower to recognize the situational importance of many others—from snails and *Daphnia* to sow bugs and aquatic beetles. Using Oddballs as a template to expose the diversity of aquatic prey will help beginners embrace the many possibilities that can occur on the stream.

A comprehensive understanding of Oddballs allows novices to note the relative importance of foods they are roughly acquainted with—ants, beetles, crane flies, sow bugs, baitfish, backswimmers, worms, etc. At the same of time, it offers them ability and incentive to seek out even the most obscure and least anthropocentric forms of trout prey, like phantom midges or *Daphnia*. Since on any given body of water Oddball prey forms constitute anywhere from 20-40% of the total consumed prey, using Oddballs as a beginning teaching tool can make for a more lasting, interesting, and successful introduction to aquatic entomology.

In summary, understanding Oddballs allows the anglers to solve "mystery hatches," gives anglers more opportunities during the "off-seasons," encourages anglers to spread out pressure to different habitats, and creates more open-minded and experimental anglers. While focusing attention to Oddballs will not solve all angling problems, I would be willing to wager that the average angler who fished only Oddball imitations would catch at least, if not more, trout over the course of a season than the angler who only fished imitations of mayflies, caddis, and stoneflies.

Chapter II:

Why Have We Overlooked Oddballs?

*I*f we accept the importance of Oddball prey, then we also must accept that trout predation is far more complex than the simple model of "trout either eat the nymphs on the bottom or rise to the adults on the surface." We should not attribute the diversity of trout feeding behavior to trout non-conformism. No trout is Wavy Gravy, nor do fish elect for behavioral patterns to simply infuriate anglers. Trout eat what they can. If a food will produce more calories for the trout than that fish must expend to acquire it, we can generally assume that trout will eat it. It is that simple.

Even big waters provide small niches, like this riffle edge, that support Oddballs that do not exist in the rest of the river.
Jeff Morgan photo

This chapter will discuss the many reasons why we have underestimated the complexity of trout feeding and how to better understand the ecology of trout predation. The reasons are myriad and often exacerbate each other. They range from the anthropocentric—terrestrial bias, angling tradition, or vagrancies of the fly fishing industry—to the ecological—habitat patchiness, trout prey selectivity, or relationships between prey that make some more available than others at different times. The angler should keep these factors all in mind when trying to reconcile the generalities they find in fishing reports and the realities they experience on the stream.

Mere Anthropocentrism

Why have we so commonly and consistently misunderstood the trout diet? While we could, and will, list a variety of reasons, many are connected by a common theme: anthropocentrism. Our perspective of the natural world is, of course, different than a fish's perspective. This, in itself, is not a problem. Only when we begin to give greater credence to things **we** see, rather than what the **fish** sees, do we run into trouble.

The anthropocentric bias refers to the anglers' attention to surface prey as opposed to subsurface prey. Anglers have long considered mayflies the most important trout insect because their regular, periodic, and sustained emergences bring trout to the surface. Caddis and stoneflies may not elicit the same consistent surface feeding, but they do have highly synchronous emergences and buzz noticeably around about the shoreline angler. Anglers will use imitations of these bugs simply because they see them flying about, not necessarily because they see fish feeding on them.

Conversely, consider how anglers value insects with a brief emergence period. Take black flies, one of the most common trout stream insects. They emerge instantly, without struggling from their pupal shucks, and elicit virtually no surface feeding. For their lack of visible surface predation, black flies have been forsaken by generations of trout anglers.

Of course, the anthropocentric bias does more than segregate trout feeding into surface and subsurface components. Take the case of terrestrial insects. Anglers fish hoppers because they see them hopping about the path from the car to the stream. Trout consume far more beetles and ants, but since they aren't noticeably bouncing off our waders on the way to the river, we ignore them. The same thing also occurs with large insects, which are readily visible from a distance, while smaller insects greatly outnumber them in sheer volume and availability.

In *Caddisflies*, Gary LaFontaine brought up a shrewd point about why, even in 1980, anglers still devoted little serious study to caddis. Gary suggested that, "the consistent failure of anglers to solve the problems caused by selective feeding on caddisflies has diminished their practical value to anglers." Anglers naturally respond to what works for them. This is partially why dry flies are so popular—people see fish rising, they usually can guess what trout eat, and they can see how the fish react to their imitations. When trout feed on Oddballs, even when we notice it, we rarely match the hatch well because we didn't expect them and were not prepared with the right imitations, frustrating those of us singularly planning on imitating a particular bug. This selective and irregular feeding on Oddballs has long troubled anglers, leaving Oddball creatures detested and ignored rather than embraced.

Anthropocentrism also arises in how anglers pursue their sport. Anglers seek out "optimal" conditions when possible—good weather, clear water, dense hatches. We fish on our terms. However, fish have their own agenda. When anglers do not catch anything during high water when using their standard mayfly, caddis, or attractor patterns, they often migrate to a clearer stream with more comfortable conditions. Though the anglers can leave, trout cannot. In turn, they dine on the newly abundant fish eggs, crane fly larvae, aquatic worms, and drowned terrestrials kicked up by the high water. During the dog days of summer, many stillwater anglers choose to take a long daytime siesta or fish cool tributary streams, since the fishing on the shallow flats "slows down." While the trout may also leave the flats, they do so to move into open water and feed heavily on clouds of *Daphnia* and phantom midges.

This natural tendency to locate the optimal fishing conditions works only as long as anglers are mobile. Most our "off-days" occur during sub-optimal conditions, when we do not or cannot leave for greener pastures. We may want to write it off and say, "the fish aren't biting." Unlikely. The fish probably are feeding, but in different places and on different foods than we expect. When we start to pay attention to what the fish tell us to do, we'll know that they're telling us to examine Oddballs.

Angling Tradition

Anyone who has fished or hunted respects the strength of tradition. No matter how strong our vagabond urges pull us to new waters, we still have our favorite streams, favorite seasons, and favorite hatches that bring us back to the same places season after season. A choking swarm of springtime Mother's Day Caddis on the Yellowstone, the early summer explosions elicited by the Deschutes' famed salmonflies, or a crisp fall evening BWO emergence on the Au Sable are the memories that keep us inspired during our off-seasons.

We love to go back to revisit those places and relive those memories, using the same flies and fishing the same runs. If the expected hatch fails to emerge and the fish utilize another prey item, we often tough it out a bit too long with patterns and techniques that worked in the past. If swinging a soft hackle worked before, we may start with and stick with that technique for an hour or two…longer if it scores the occasional fish. At the end of a lackluster day, we may blame the conditions or luck, but the problem really was one of imagination. We let traditions and expectations blind us to the trout feeding on something different.

Now, this example exaggerates things a bit. No angler would fish a green drake all day with a lack of naturals or rising trout. Yet, tradition often shapes where anglers start fishing, what they fish with, and the bugs they expect to face. This tendency causes anglers to increasingly focus on the "normal," while ignoring the irregular.

DIFFERENCES BETWEEN BLUE RIBBON WATERS AND WHERE YOU FISH

When we read about tactics for stillwaters or tailwaters or small streams, we often hear stories rooted in the context of ideal conditions. Stillwater, tailwater, and small stream experts often gain their expertise on the very best waters through rigorous experience of guiding these waters or operating fly shops near these waters. They are professionals and they know exactly what they talk about.

However, the productivity of "blue ribbon" waters exists at the expense of the biodiversity. Famous streams become famous via their ability to produce reliable hatches of a few insects each year. It is no coincidence that tailwater streams with constant releases, moderate temperatures, and homogenous insect regimes are so popular among anglers. If anglers can anticipate a hatch, then successfully fish that hatch, then the odds are good that they will return to chase that hatch in the future. If hatches are inconsistent and/or unduly complex, few anglers will be willing to fork over hundreds of dollars for a trip to that water.

Rarely does diversity elicit praise among the fly fishing establishment. Diversity in the natural world means uncertainty, and no economy thrives on uncertainty. It is the best interest of most in the fly fishing industry to keep things simple, understandable, and consistent in order to cater to the largest possible audience

Unfortunately, nature is complex, indecipherable, and variable. Most trout waters that average anglers fish have these same characteristics. Rarely do we fish a lake perfectly lined with eight-foot deep flats. Rarely do we find a stream with a wide, gentle run with reliable Trico spinner falls between nine o'clock and noon on every single day of the hatch cycle. When we lower the expectations for diversity by reducing complex ecosystems into the component parts that fly anglers most commonly fish, we make it much harder to look beyond the few ideal situations we actually encounter.

Many stillwater experts hammer home the essential nature of chironomids, leeches, *Callibaetis*, and damselfly nymphs, but often from a truncated interpretation on trout habitat. The waters they fish tend towards the ideal stillwater: uniformly shallow, flat, weedy, rich in calcium, and slightly alkaline. Under these conditions, it is unsurprising that this particular niche of insects dominates.

However, what about the angler whose stillwater options are limited to massive reservoirs, alpine lakes, or stocked lowland ponds? Certainly pulling Woolly Buggers, Seal Buggers, or hand-twisting chironomids will hook many trout in any of these waters. Yet, these tactics were developed for a very different ecotype. The large reservoir angler often lacks the weedy "shallow flat" conditions assumed by most stillwater anglers, yet these anglers often find enormous schools of migratory baitfish that large trout pursue with vigor. These anglers must also face the low-dissolved oxygen period of summertime where trout migrate to the thermocline and rely heavily on *Daphnia* and *Chaoborus* (Phantom Midge) larvae. The alpine lake angler rarely has the luxury of calcium-rich flats teeming with *Callibaetis* or damselflies, yet their small, rocky waters often support huge populations of long-lived dragonfly nymphs that can cope with short growing seasons. These waters also will harbor large numbers of terrestrial insects swept up by high-elevation wind patterns. Lowland stocked ponds often abound in nutrients, in turn supporting a diverse array of trout prey—from low-oxygen tolerating snails to summertime swarms of adult crane flies to fall migrations of backswimmers.

Stream anglers often experience a reality far different than that seen in fly club slide shows or books. The uniform "glamour" hatches of Golden Stones or Green Drakes usually are complicated on the stream by contemporaneous emergences of a variety of other insects. While most writers have long warned of "multiple hatch" situations on rivers, rarely do they explore these other insects in detail and ask why trout rely on them under certain circumstances. When anglers find trout feeding on an unknown "small brown caddis," "little red ant," or a "tiny black midge," most are taken by surprise because they never were warned of the biology, habitat, or behavior of these insects.

If the big-river angler rarely fishes over a simple glamour hatch, small stream anglers are lucky to find a glamour hatch per season. The angler raised on the common Western "*Baetis*-PMD-Green Drake-Salmonfly-spotted sedge" Cliff Notes is often perplexed when trout turn selective on small streams. Rarely, if ever, do small streams produce homogenous emergences. If one insect emerges, ten others species likely will flutter over it before it flies away. Since small streams contain a greater variety of microhabitats, they produce locally dense populations of insects that can turn trout in one pool into selective feeders, while trout in the pool below never see the same bug. The unique ecology of small streams—more leafy input, greater shoreline-to-surface area ratio, and a greater variability in flow—often supports an entirely different cohort of insect life than do larger streams. Unlike the ecological reductionism common on larger waters, "tactical reductionism" also masks small stream diversity. Anglers have long been taught that attractors and wet flies are "all you need" on a small stream, thus rarely look closely at hatches and how trout react to them.

The discrepancy between the "ideal" trout diet and the actual diet of individual trout should be attributed neither to the malevolence, nor the stupidity of "experts." It is simply the product of the progression and professionalization of the sport over the past three decades. Professional fly anglers target the best and most consistent fly waters with their guiding clients and fly shop customers. Even on these steadfast waters, we tended to focus on a handful of even more predictable runs, pockets, bays or shorelines with reliable fish and reliable hatches. I have guided myself, so I'm not knocking the emphasis on reliability. Guides would do their clients and themselves a disservice by behaving otherwise. However, these prime waters and prime

Jeff Morgan photo

"Blue-ribbon waters," like the Deschutes, have homogenous populations of well-known insects, but smaller waters usually offer far more biodiversity.

runs differ significantly from the waters that most everyday fly anglers stumble upon. Our waters exhibit diversity, complexity, and inconsistency, but they also provide us with that intangible that the glamour waters lack—mystery. It is this mystery, and its incorporated thrills of discovery and failure, that draws us to the places where Oddballs are important to trout.

REPETITION OF THEMES

In the research for my previous books, I was shocked by the repetition of the same entomological themes. Did you ever play "Pass It On" when you were young? One person says a sentence, whispers it to his or her neighbor, who then whispers the sentence into his or her neighbor's ear, on and on until the sentence makes it all the way around the room. When the sentence reaches the last person he or she says the sentence aloud and everyone has a good laugh at how much the sentence changed from the original.

This is what has happened with angling entomologies. The last twenty years has produced dozens, but they all take similar form. The newer texts read the same classic 1970's and 1980's canon—*Hatches, Nymphs, Caddisflies*, , etc—reword them, add a few new anecdotes, and miraculously a "new" entomological analysis emerges. The third generation borrowed from this second generation, and the cycle continued. Proven "facts" became blurred as individual anecdotes were incorporated into the collective body of angling knowledge. Rarely did these books consult any scientific works—journal articles, controlled studies, or entomology textbooks—that the original great works considered. The result is a body of knowledge that grew neither richer nor deeper; rather it has grown fuzzier and more speculative.

What was lost? The caveats and exceptions were lost. The iconoclastic tone of works like *Caddisflies* or *Western Hatches* was tempered into reverential treatments of past writing. Conventional wisdom overwhelmed entomological exploration when the sport grew more commercialized. Is it any coincidence that the production of "classic" entomologies ceased in the mid-1980's? During the fly fishing boom of the late 1980's and 1990's, cultivating new patterns, new technologies, and new angling clients became more expedient than challenging older entomological doctrine.

To be sure, the old entomological truths prove still prove useful. If not for Arbona's excellent work on mayflies, LaFontaine's breakthrough with caddis, or Leiser and Boyle's insight on stoneflies, we still might struggle through particular hatches. However, it is time that we shake things up, look at the scientific literature of the past thirty years, and paint a more inclusive picture of trout prey and its imitation.

ANGLER SAMPLING VERSUS PROFESSIONAL SAMPLING

The importance of Oddball prey lies in that disputed ground between angler experience and professional (peer-reviewed) research. This study relies heavily on professional research, simply because it is more comprehensive, replicable, documented, and systematic than the research of nearly all angler entomologies.

This is not to say that angler sampling is "wrong" it is simply limited by its results-based approach.

When anglers sample we generally do so when we aren't catching fish. Our goal is to catch fish, so we check the bottom to look for bugs when the "expected" results do not turn up. If we get lucky enough to catch a trout or two after a slow morning, we pump them to see what they have been eating. When we catch trout at a respectable pace, we usually do not bother to check what is going on or what might work better.

While the tendency to sample only during "slow times" creates a bias, relying too heavily on the samples taken from fly-caught fish creates a more pronounced one. Phillip Rowley's superb 2000 book *Fly Patterns for Stillwaters,* bases its "productive stillwater trout diet" on the samples he has taken from fish he has caught over the past ten years. There is no doubt that Rowley kept good records and he smartly warned readers to note that all fish were all from his region of British Columbia. However, by only sampling fish caught by anglers, we create a major collection bias. Rowley's conclusion that the stillwater trout diet is made up of 39% chironomids and 19% scuds likely resulted from catching most of his fish on chironomids and scuds. In that study, zooplankton, forage fish, and terrestrials contributed three, one, and one percent of the trout diet, respectively. However, one must ask how many fish did he catch on zooplankton, forage fish, and terrestrial imitations, or even how many fish did he catch in the regions of the lake where these foods predominate? Zooplankton, scuds, and terrestrials each inhabit different habitats, so it would not be surprising that "angler caught" samples would emphasize one of these foods, but not the others. Rowley's book is one of the best stillwater technique and fly pattern books on the market today, but also reflects the inherent biases of angler sampling.

Angler sampling has greatly increased the entomological awareness of the average angler over the past two decades. Bottom sampling has helped anglers focus more accurately on the nymph stages of aquatic insects and stomach sampling also helped many anglers discover the tiny size of most of the trout diet.

Patchiness and Microhabitats

Part of the problem of deciphering the diet of trout is the concept of "patches": colloquially discussed as "microhabitats." The idea behind "patchiness" holds that within an insect's general distribution area there are certain streams that are more likely to support that insect, and on those streams, there are certain "patches" that harbor far more of the insect than other parts of the stream. Though one can trace the concept of patches back to the origins of ecological thought in the 1930's, even ecologically aware anglers have been loathe to utilize the idea when discussing entomology and devising fishing strategies.

For example, brown drake mayflies (*Ephemera simulans*) may be found in sparse numbers on a particular stream, but their numbers are highly concentrated in the fine gravel that settles behind fallen logs. Another example is Grannom (*Brachycentrus*) caddis, which congregates near areas of small springs that trickle into a stream. Fish holding downstream of these habitats will obviously be more receptive to imitations of these insects than trout in other sections of the river.

Anglers have long overlooked many Oddballs because of their patchy habitat preferences. Egg-laying black flies usually congregate on large, flat rocks near riffles and lay their eggs right at the water's surface or just below it. Trout on the edges of this riffle water may eat dozens, but mid-river trout may never see one over the course of the season. On lakes, trout inhabiting stump-strewn flats may eat a crayfish every day, while the trout on weedy flats may not distinguish a crayfish from a turtle.

Understanding patches holds impressive potential for the fly angler, as they can allow fishers to target specific lies and anticipate feeding without waiting for a hatch to reveal itself. Rather than seeking a general "flying ant swarm" on a lake, anglers will position themselves downwind from the clear-cuts that have concentrated populations of ants. Instead of fishing sow bugs throughout the entirety of a stream, anglers might just focus their imitation at the base of riffles that halt upstream migrations and create congregations of sow bugs. Further scientific research by anglers holds great promise by further refining our knowledge of Oddballs and their availability to trout.

Prey Selectivity

Trout simply don't act like random number machines, picking out particular prey in direct proportion to their numbers in the bottom or in the drift. This is clear to any burgeoning entomologist who examines "availability-preference" studies that compare what is in the water and what trout actually eat. For reasons as diverse as prey color, size, opacity, abundance, drift depth, angling pressure, or availability, trout consume certain prey items more than others.

Often these factors create a matrix of prey selectivity. Salmon flies are a classic example of the subtleties of the prey selectivity phenomenon. During the earliest phase of a hatch, trout do not know what to make of such large prey, occasionally nibbling at them but allowing many to drift by unscathed. After a couple hours or days of experimentation, trout attack salmonflies with vigor due to their size and caloric value, and almost every salmonfly that drifts over a fish elicits a rise. As the hatch goes on, the abundance of the adults wanes until egg laying activity peaks, and many trout have grown gorged and possibly fooled by imitations. In this situation, maybe only one in eight or ten salmonflies drifted over a given trout elicits a rise, as trout turn to the safer and abundant smaller food forms.

Oddballs often have characteristics that make them highly desirable prey, despite their occasionally small populations. Large, calorie-rich foods like crayfish, crane fly larvae, grasshoppers, and leeches may not make up a huge portion of the trout diet due to their lack of availability, but trout rarely pass up an opportunity for such a big morsel. Other Oddballs stand out due to their flashiness. The glistening oxygen and plastron carried by backswimmers makes them a conspicuous target for a hungry, open-water trout. Trout desire other Oddballs because of angler pressure. Anglers have long known that tiny ant imitations will fool selective trout during a mayfly emergence, since the less-imitated ants are a safer food item than a less-than-perfect-looking mayfly.

Clearcuts provide dead wood for carpenter ants, young foliage for aphids, and endless nooks and crannies for beetles to hide.

Jeff Morgan photo

COMPLEX ECOLOGICAL RELATIONSHIPS

Anglers have rarely focused on more than the direct predatory relationship between trout and their prey. If trout eat a certain prey item, anglers will try to figure out where that bug lives and then try to imitate them in that section of a stream or lake. A common generalization goes like this: "since *Baetis* feed on algae, a stream with algae should have bumper crops of *Baetis*."

However, reality is not nearly that simple. Prey and trout do not have a binary relationship. Myriad factors—from the presence or absence of other insects to water conditions, from life cycles to parasitic infections—alter the relative availability of prey items to trout.

For examine, let's consider the previous statement regarding *Baetis* and algae. Say this algae-rich stream has an abundance of sculpins. Here, *Glossosoma* caddis, an algae-grazing competitor of *Baetis,* would be more abundant as their rocky cases allow them to feed without being preyed upon by sculpin. The relative importance of *Baetis* to trout drops significantly, while the relative importance of *Glossosoma* rises. Now assume instead of sculpins, aggressive predatory insects like perlid stoneflies or *Rhyacophila* caddis dominate the predatory regime. These critters patrol the undersides and protected portions of the substrate, where they can find food without exposing themselves to the current, thus not risking becoming trout food themselves. In this situation, *Baetis* become extremely abundant in the drift, as they must roam the tops of the rocks to escape the predators dwelling at the bottom of the rocks. Of course, if you keep an eye on the riparian rocks, you may just see birds feasting on *Baetis* females preparing for their egg-laying descent to the bottom of the stream, an egg-laying behavior that makes them highly available to trout. These are just a few of the ecological relationships of one type of trout prey! However, this is a level of analysis we normally don't apply to fly fishing. If we did, we would start to better understand the role of Oddballs.

Many anglers know an ant when they see them, but what habitats do ants prefer? Ants love clear-cut areas with dead wood and young deciduous vegetation. What else lives in that habitat? For one, aphids love the soft tissue of young deciduous plants and, indeed, they thrive in the same habitat as ants. What eats aphids? Ladybugs, of course! So simply finding a lot of ants can clue us into other potential food resources for trout.

Black flies and juvenile fish create another set of connections. Juvenile trout and rough fish love black fly larvae, in fact, some studies show that the larvae may make up 75% or more of juvenile trout diet on certain waters. Young fish preying on the larvae concentrate in riffle margins, rather than distributing themselves evenly in shallower water throughout the stream. Anglers that find dense black fly populations will often do far better with streamers around riffle water than they would on the rest of the stream.

Once anglers think about the connections that bind together the aquatic world, the role of Oddballs as both prey and indicator species will become far more apparent and useful for them.

Chapter III:

A Case Study of Oddballs: The Ecology of Terrestrials

Terrestrials are not supplemental components of the trout diet, worthy of a contemptuous nod after discussing the more important "hatches." On any given stream, terrestrials are as critical to trout as any single order of mayflies, caddis, or stoneflies over the course of a season. To anglers fond of fishing dry flies, they may be more important than all three combined. Indeed, many of the most popular dry flies imitate terrestrials more than mayflies or stoneflies. During periods without a concentrated emergence or spinner fall—most of our time on the water—either imitative or suggestive terrestrial patterns can bring more trout to the surface than any other kind of dry fly. In lieu of a massive ecological assessment of all trout feeding, lets consider the ecology of terrestrials in general as kind of a case study for how and why Oddball foods are so important to trout.

A long shoreline of low-hanging trees will provide a smorgasbord of random terrestrials.

Few anglers doubt that trout will eat terrestrials, but most consider terrestrials a special treat for trout raised on a meat-and-bones, mayfly-and-caddis diet. However, most stream ecologists consider terrestrials vital to trout production on most streams and smaller lakes. In 1951, one New Zealand researcher, K.R. Allen, found that total production of aquatic insects was insufficient to support the trout population in a particular stream—even if the trout ate every single insect! Terrestrial foods were essential to trout growth in this situation. Several other studies repeated the result where aquatic insects alone could not support the rest of the aquatic food chain, and eventually the term "Allen's Paradox" came to explain this phenomenon. Allen's research paved the way for fisheries biologists to study trout stream production as entire riparian systems rather than simply looking at bottom samples. Modern anglers should follow their lead!

The closer attention to terrestrials has produced a wealth of research supporting the essential relationship between terrestrials and trout. In only one chapter of the book *The Coupling of Land and Water Systems* there are over thirty references to terrestrial predation by salmonids, including papers which show that terrestrials can, at times, represent 90% of the trout diet. Another study from Scotland held that 50% and 80% of the annual brown trout diet on two streams was composed of terrestrial Diptera, Hemiptera, and Hymenoptera. In a summer study of a Wyoming trout stream, terrestrials were only 14% of the drift, while they composed 31% of the trout diet. It is widely accepted that on most trout streams, terrestrials form 35-40% of the trout diet in the hatchless days of August and September. Terrestrial feeding on small streams may often reach 60-80%. In fact, on small streams, terrestrials often make up over 30% of the total annual trout diet!

The relative importance of terrestrials over the course of summer results from a combination of waning hatches of aquatic insects and terrestrials growing even more abundant. One study saw the terrestrial component of brook trout diets grow from 2.9% in July to 36% in September. Terrestrials, especially ants and beetles, may be just as common in the spring and early summer, but anglers often overlook these foods amongst the buffet of early season hatches.

Why are terrestrials important to dry fly anglers? In the summer, with few emergences of aquatic insects, terrestrials may compose only 35% of the overall diet but 90% of the surface feeding! This leads me to the most pressing question I have for attractor pattern advocates: why tell summertime anglers to use attractor patterns (which trout feed on 0% of the time) when terrestrial imitations match things fed upon by rising trout 90% of the time?

Terrestrials peak as available prey during the afternoon, as cold morning temperatures greatly inhibit terrestrial activity. However, the abundance of drifting aquatic foods also plays a role in when trout feed on terrestrials. During mid-day, nymphs rarely drift and few hatches occur, which in effect, makes trout rise more opportunistically to terrestrial prey. In a study on brown trout in the Spanish Pyrenees, feeding on terrestrials peaked between noon and 3:00pm, when drift rates for aquatic insects were at their lowest. The trout turned to the more abundant drifting aquatic taxa later in the evening, though they still ingested some terrestrials until dusk.

Like all Oddballs, the importance of terrestrials to the angler lies in their local abundance. We often exaggerate the importance of mayflies, caddis, and stoneflies because we usually talk about trout prey in general terms. However, angling reality is not rooted in generalities, but in local specifics. Sure terrestrials may contribute 25% of the summer diet of trout, but usually one or two insects make up the majority of that 25%. Those particular terrestrial insects vary depending on the local ecological conditions—they may be the relatively common ants, beetles, crane flies, or grasshoppers, but sometimes they may be more obscure Oddballs. On some Canadian streams where coastal cutthroat trout fin under a broad canopy of old growth firs and spruces, Lepidoptera larvae (inchworms) are the single most important food source over the course of a summer. In one German study, aphids composed 10% of the total drift, and 5% of the total trout diet! Terrestrial spiders can also appear in modest numbers, they can even be the most common terrestrials after a spring rain. These random freak shows can make you love or hate terrestrial insects and the trout that prey on them.

While every burgeoning stream ecologist learns about the importance of shaded streams, "shaded" rarely equals "productive." In fact, the absence of tall riparian tree cover increases aquatic insect populations, because the sunlight sparks photosynthesis that fuels algae and plant growth. Streams with a dense, coniferous canopy often stay cold in the summer, but relatively sterile sinse the trees block the sun's rays. Young deciduous growth, however, allow a great deal of ambient sunlight. Willows, for example, also add leaf input in the fall and provide adequate shelter for adult caddis, stoneflies, crane flies, and a variety of terrestrial insects. On Tiritea Stream in New Zealand, terrestrials made up 7.1% of the drift in willowless sections and 61.7% of the drift in moderately willowed sections. When looking for ideal terrestrial habitat, look for shorelines with moderate amounts of willows or other short, deciduous vegetation.

The type of holding water determines the importance of terrestrial insects to trout. Fish holding along banks, under overhanging trees, near large boulders or fallen logs, or foamy eddies tend to consume more terrestrials than fish in other parts of the stream. On the Mohaka River in New Zealand, the brown trout are larger and more aggressive than rainbow trout. Consequently, brown trout bully rainbow trout out of prime backwater and shore lies, and in turn, the brownies consume nearly eight times the number of beetles.

Fortunately for anglers, juvenile trout consume far fewer terrestrials than adult trout do. This happens for two reasons: the larger size of many terrestrials makes them prohibitive targets and rising to surface terrestrials increases the vulnerability of small trout to predators. A small stream angler would be wise to rely heavily on large terrestrial imitations—like adult crane fly patterns—for they deter small fish and match the numerically dominant prey.

Anglers have stressed few ecological relationships more than the one that exists between undercut banks and terrestrial insects. While it is difficult for the angler to present to trout holding in undercuts, they certainly can harbor large trout. Besides offering a good place to present terrestrial…carve out that undercut" changes to "Remember that undercuts are not just places to throw terrestrials; the powerful upstream riffle that carves out the undercut provides its own array of food sources. Therefore a wise angler will throw larvae imitations of black flies, crane flies, green rock worms, net spinning caddis, or other common riffle-dwelling aquatic insects into undercut banks. Being a good terrestrial angler also means not slavishly sticking to them when ecological circumstances suggest otherwise.

So exactly how and where to trout feed on terrestrials? One of the most significant challenges facing anglers trying to learn more about terrestrial feeding by trout is the lack of research that pinpoints exactly how and where terrestrial insects end up in the water. It may be easier for anglers to simply assume that "they are blown in." Let the academics sort out the details. The problem is, the academics aren't sorting out the details. While we have dozens of studies how certain *Baetis* habits increase their availability to trout, few such studies investigate terrestrials. For example, certain behaviors may place terrestrial insects in precarious situations or certain riparian plants may attract particular insects. A wise angler, considering the reasons *why* certain terrestrial insects end up in the water, is more likely to be prepared to put the right fly in the right spot and see greater success.

Two factors positively correlate with terrestrial availability and trout predation: temperature and stream discharge. Warm air temperatures make terrestrials more active, and activity makes terrestrials more likely to wind up in the water. Hot weather increases the activity of winged terrestrials (grasshoppers, winged ants, winged termites, beetles) even more dramatically than wingless ones. Cold temperatures

A cool mountain morning will keep terrestrials lethargic and away from trout.

Jeff Morgan photo

characterized by the chilly September and October mornings that forewarn the end of terrestrial season, render most terrestrials immobile, and imitating them under these conditions is rarely productive.

Rising waters also influence terrestrial availability to trout. As flood waters inundate rock crevices and logs, they flush terrestrial insects out and into the water. Keep in mind that not all terrestrial food sources are the flying bugs that we see buzzing and biting us while we fish—many live below our radar. Tipulidae larvae (crane fly larvae) and terrestrial Oligochaeta (earthworms), not to mention the crawling ants, beetles, millipedes, spiders that compose a virtual Noah's Ark of random insects, all are available to trout after a period of high water sweeps them from their riparian homes.

Much is made about trout feeding on terrestrials during periods of high wind, but heavy rain may be just as important—especially on streams with abundant overhanging foliage. Several studies support this and it makes sense that insects would be more likely to slide off wet leaves than dry ones. In tropical and subtropical regions, fish depend most heavily on terrestrial insects during the "wet" seasons. Logically, the calm hours following a storm create the perfect condition for throwing both dry and sunken terrestrial patterns. It is also more enjoyable to fish terrestrials in the calm following a heavy rain rather than trying to whip a fly through the heavy winds that precede it.

Sure terrestrials may matter on streams, but do stillwater trout prey heavily on terrestrials? Like everything in fly fishing, it depends. On smaller lakes, especially those with deep water near the bank, terrestrials often are important if not essential for trout that take up cruising patterns along those margins that offer both food and deep-water security. Surface feeding is even more pronounced in the presence of low-branching trees like Englemann Spruce, which provide both terrestrial input and cover for bank-cruising trout. Winds blowing off marshes and wetlands often carry many terrestrial insects. In a couple Norwegian Lakes, terrestrial foods accounted for 63% and 64% of the diet of brown trout over the course of a season, even though there were numerous chironomids, caddis, and *Daphnia* available to trout. The researchers in this case attributed the heavy terrestrial input to the vast marshlands surrounding the lakes. On California's Eagle Lake, ants contributed 42% of the caloric input of rainbow trout, and beetles added another 10%. On a June study I made on Oregon's Timothy Lake, beetles made up roughly 70% of the diet! This study was shocking, as I was dredging Timothy's shallow stump fields with dragonfly nymphs and crayfish patterns to ascertain which was more important. Terrestrials rendered my other hypotheses irrelevant!

Doubtless terrestrials are important to trout, far more than most of us give them credit for. Professional studies and professional angler experience suggest their importance, but terrestrials remain one of the most mysterious of trout foods due to the structural limitations of both styles of research. Scientists devote little research to the interactions between trout and specific terrestrial foods due to narrow

Large woody debris in streams provides both trout and terrestrial habitat.

specialization in the fields of entomology and fish ecology—trout specialists in fish and wildlife look primarily at aquatic production, while the funding for terrestrial specialists steers them towards agricultural research. At the same time, angling experts often dismiss the contribution of terrestrial insects as a "bonus" for trout; of secondary importance to the predictable hatches that do the real leg-work of growing trout and providing angling opportunities. Few people who make a living fly fishing for trout accept the dangerous volatility required to track the importance of terrestrials on a variety of waters, season-after-season. It is a far better economic decision to rely on the researched, well documented "glamour hatches" that produce steady, if not maximizing, results.

The importance of terrestrials to trout is analogous to other Oddball insects. Anglers accept their importance without asking the same questions they would with "hatching" insects. Like scuds, crayfish, or leeches, they are assumed to either exist or not. No further inquiry required. If you see them, they are worth imitating; if not, they are of no concern. However, preparing oneself with the tools, knowledge, and imitations to match the entirety of the trout diet will make any angler far more successful.

Chapter IV:

How to Use this Book

My way is not the only way to do things. I hope that no one who reads this books walks away a converted fundamentalist. The mission of this piece is to explore the best ways to imitate the Oddball insects that slip through the cracks of traditional angling entomologies. It is neither a guide to the usual entomological suspects that one finds on a stream, nor a manual for the easiest way to imitate insects. Indeed, this book targets those situations where the "usual" and "easiest" tactics fail. It is also not intended to provide a comprehensive reference for patterns…or even a guide to standard imitations. In fact, many of the classic patterns that most anglers traditionally associate with particular insects will not appear in this book. There are many fine resources for standard patterns, most of which are listed in the bibliography of this book. The patterns included here are largely "new" flies that I hope will push anglers to try to construct their own new patterns that are easy to tie, entomologically appropriate, and most importantly, catch trout.

Experimentation on the water is the key to cultivating new angling knowledge.

Some of the criticisms contained herein may seem harsh to previous interpretations or skeptical of certain approaches. This should not be conflated with criticisms of particular people or their knowledge. Most of the writers and angling luminaries mentioned in this book are highly skilled and knowledgeable anglers, and have contributed greatly to the development of our sport. However, if we cannot critically evaluate long-held assumptions or engage in critical, respectful conversations on aspects of the sport, we forsake opportunities to expand our knowledge. Debate is healthy and needed in our sport, and in the end, it will only accelerate the learning curve of anglers. Most fly fishing professionals that I have met praise the virtues of free market economics. I concur. Consistently, I also praise the virtue of the free market in ideas.

The format of the chapters progress as follows:

The Prey: Before any rational discussion of fly patterns begins, we must have a common background on the particular organism we want to imitate. This section is derived from a number of sources including (in ascending order of importance): personal experience, personal research, correspondence with other anglers, correspondence with shops, and most importantly, scholarly (peer-reviewed) journals, books, reports, and M.S/ Ph.D. thesis projects. If I cannot document the information—i.e. industry magazine articles and, especially, fishing books without bibliographies—then its validity can be put in doubt, and I don't want to taint my writing with misinformation culled from elsewhere. If I screw up—which will happen more than once—I want it to be my fault. For that reason, what appears here about certain insects here may conflict with what has been written elsewhere, but at least I can show you where it came from.

Insects and other trout foods often appear far different in their natural medium than when we extricate them from it. Some critters experience a color change (leeches), others lose their trapped gasses (chironomids and backswimmers), and others change shape (snails and aquatic worms). The goal of "The Insect" section is to provide a clearer picture of how insects appear to *trout* rather than how they appear to *humans*. This information, in turn, may affect how you construct and fish your imitations.

Thoughts on Imitation: This section provides a thorough analysis on how to imitate the various trout prey. Sometimes, this analysis may drift into what may seem as superfluous detail. Yet, this strategy seeks to maximize the productivity of imitating that particular prey item. I consider *maximizing* a combination of minimizing tying time, expense, and difficulty while matching the size, shape, color, movement, and behavior of a natural as closely as possible.

Naturally, this section will emphasize fly pattern stylistics, but it will also provide plenty of information regarding presentation, reading water, and other factors that influence how and where to fish those patterns. This section will rely on knowledge garnered from the *Insect* section, so if you find yourself with a foreign term in the *Thoughts on Imitation* section, simply reread the preceding section.

Keys to Match: If you want a summary from the *Thoughts on Imitation*, here you go. This will cover the three things to keep in mind when imitating a particular insect.

Keys to Avoid: If we should match certain things, we should also avoid other things. This section may sound like a broken record after a while ("too thick" will pop up more than once), but most insects have some specific tying problems that tiers must avoid when imitating them. Like the *Keys to Match*, this section will also summarize from the *Thoughts on Imitation*.

Patterns: This section will list a handful (in the case of inchworms) to a bucketful (in the case of chironomids) of useful patterns for a particular insect. If an insect has multiple life stages (like larvae-pupae-adult), the patterns may be segregated into those categories. There will be a picture, recipe, and summary of each pattern. Because of space and repetition, tying instructions are not included.

While many patterns in this book may look unorthodox, others may appear familiar and renamed without "credit" to the designer. The "Trade marking" of patterns in recent years is one of the more disturbing innovations in the past decade of our sport. It is rather absurd to think that somebody "invented" a pattern that nobody else has, intentionally or accidentally, tied before. I have seen the many sides of fly-naming disputes in the past. I've been employed to design patterns for a shop owner, only to see his name go on the flies and their commercial contract sent overseas. I've given credit for the creation of particular flies to one tier, only to have others claim they are the "real" inventor. Some patterns I have "invented" on my own (without claiming credit for "invention"), only to get nasty letters saying I "stole" someone else's pattern. I have also been wrongly attributed credit for patterns created by others. In reality, fly tying it is akin to the "folk method" of traditional music: artists borrow from a variety of proven older tactics and add a few twists of their own. Woody Guthrie never wrote an "original" song and no pattern enjoyed an immaculate conception. For this reason, this book will refuse to give "Name Credits," but rather it will give absurd names to fly patterns ranging from professional wrestling jargon to hip hop slang, from Phil Hendrie characters to Bob Dylan lyrics.

As mentioned above, these flies should not be seen as an endgame, but rather an entrepot to matching particular prey items. I hope that you can find creative ways to improve them and adjust them for your fishing situations. Better yet, the provided biological information will spark memories of your personal experiences that will lead you to come up with new patterns of your own. These flies should help highlight the intersection of ecology and creativity.

Chapter V:
The Prey

Ants (Hymenoptera)

The Insect

Like hoppers, ants are familiar to non-anglers. Ants are tolerated by many who don't like insects in general, so much so that they have even been the subject for that most anthro-friendly medium, a cartoon movie (*Ants*, 1999). However, unlike hoppers jumping wildly about, making themselves visible to even the most inattentive angler, hordes of ants crawl about stream banks with little fanfare or angler recognition. Yet, there is no doubt that ants are a significant factor in the diets of stream-dwelling trout. In one study, they comprised only two percent of the drift, but eight and ten percent of the total feeding activity of rainbow trout and brown trout, respectively.

Especially during their migrations, ants will dominate the trout diet for days or weeks at a time. On a small pond sampled by a Smithsonian entomologist, ants were second only to Diptera (doubtless including many aquatic forms) in a surface feeding experiment. In a study of Eagle Lake in California, ants made up 42% of the total food items ingested by trout.

Ants can be easily overlooked in studies that quantify the total mass of ingested foods. They are small and light, and so anglers should also consider ants in terms of numbers of individuals ingested rather than total caloric value. Typical of this differential approach, one study found that ants composed 16.3% of individual prey items ingested, but only 8% of caloric input.

Despite this importance, we have long considered ants a "second-tier" terrestrial, somewhere well below hoppers. This view has lead to a sort of "fly box tokenism"—we carry a couple ant patterns because we know we should, but we rarely turn to them first or give them much technical thought. Anglers who use ant patterns occasionally as attractor patterns are awestruck at how selective trout will become during an ant fall. I usually compare heavy ant feeding activity to heavy mayfly activity, and a close approximation is essential to consistent success.

A hideous swarm of flying ants will quickly tutor the angler in how selective fish can turn to ants. When ants are dense in the air, they are doubtless common on the water's surface. Sometimes "dense" is an understatement. In September 1983, a swarm washed up on Dewey Beach, Delaware, where 100 ants per inch of beach coated a six-mile stretch, with an estimated total of 38 million drowned ants rotting on the shore. Mating flights and migrations are the major impetus of these swarms and they can come out of nowhere with little warning on almost any trout water in the United States. For this reason, being prepared with at least a half dozen ant patterns in various sizes is essential to coping with an "ant hatch" situation.

Ants, like beetles, exhibit extreme variations in size and color, making imitation during a dense hatch problematic. I have fished hatches on Timothy Lake and Sparks Lake in Oregon, where a size 8 Cascade Flying Ant pattern was just a shade smaller than the naturals! Conversely, I have fished on a small stream in Alberta where there was a swarm of winged brown ants in the size 24 range. I first thought they were tricos, and like with tricos, trout became snotty over the slightest inconsistency (a #24 brown worked, the #20 black was snubbed repeatedly). Be prepared for a variety of colors, as ant shades can also range widely from the common blacks to the less common browns to the less common "two-tone" (black and reddish) to the even less common (in temperate habitats) full-blown red.

Even if you don't see ants around, look on riparian plants for the presence of aphids. The relationship between ants and those

The shiny exoskeleton and fine abdominal hairs make ants one of the "flashier" terrestrials.

Chapter V: The Prey

Alpine and canyon habitats experience diurnal winds that push ant swarms up and down in elevation throughout the day.

little green bugs is well-known and the presence of aphids almost universally equates to good ant populations. Both, for example, have been shown to be extremely abundant (23 times more abundant) following clear-cutting activity.

What a great point to transition to ants and clear-cuts! The real question is, do you really need any dry flies other than ant patterns when fishing in a heavily clear-cut region? On a small stream, you probably don't. In Oregon and Washington, where clear-cuts are as common as self-help specials on Oprah, flying ant patterns are far and away one of the most productive small stream flies. Why are clear cuts so great for ants and termites? The dead timber on the ground makes excellent nesting and foraging sites, as does the abundance of lush deciduous plants that take over when the big trees are cut out. Like dams, you may not like clear-cuts, but don't ignore the benefits they can offer the angler.

Ants, of course, are social, colony-based insects. When populations get too large for the nest, a generation of winged reproductive adults is produced, and they fly off in large swarms to establish a new site. Swarming takes place most often in the late morning of warm calm days, with peak ant numbers appearing between 10:00am and noon, though activity may trickle over into early afternoon. Swarming takes place in the warmer months of the year: May-September, with a pronounced peak in June and July. Major swarming behavior seems to be more pronounced at high elevations (4,000-8,000 feet), with some of the most amazing swarms congregating at the summits of mountain peaks. This results from daytime thermal updrafts that carry the bugs to high elevations, as mating swarms gather during the warming part of the day. Alpine lakes are especially prone to flying ant falls. Anybody fishing high-elevation lakes during the summertime is certainly handicapping themselves by not packing winged-ant imitations.

Most anglers, whether they know it or not, imitate carpenter ants (*Camponotus* spp.). Carpenter ants are the largest common ant that anglers encounter, with workers in the 6-10mm range, winged males to 13mm and winged females to larger than 17mm. Most are black or black and red in color. They thrive in areas of fallen timber, and thus are a no-brainer to imitate on woodland trout streams.

I make a special note to look closely at any large mounds built up in the riparian zones of streams. These are most often ant mounds, filled with tens of thousands of ants that are most likely to be encountered by the very trout you plan on presenting to. Also look for tiny, closely configured holes in high cut-banks. These are often underground nests. Quickly checking the environment in this manner can eliminate the guesswork that comes with fishing new waters. Sometimes looking for specific mounds is even unnecessary; just take a moment to look at the ground under your feet, the logs on the banks, and the plants hanging over the stream. You will be amazed at the number of ants that are crawling around as potential trout food, just waiting for the next wind gust or drop of rain to propel them into the water.

It would be amiss to conclude that ants are just "there or not," with no strong ecological connection with the environment around them. Ants and aspen groves are just one example of direct ecological connections. These groves, according to C.L. Hoff, contained a greater number of ant species, but also "significantly greater" population densities. The reason for this preference is multifold: greater sunlight penetration, greater soil moisture, and a greater diversity of life in general (i.e. more dead leaves and bugs to eat). Deciduous forests, in general, harbor greater ant populations than conifer stands, thanks to the moist, soft leaf mold on the forest floor. Of course, ants abound near paved roads and sidewalks, and the small (2-4mm long) brown and black pavement ants (*Tetramorium caespitum*) are regular immigrants to streams traced by roads and lined with picnic areas. In another case, canyon bottoms prove to also be magnets for some ants. According to one scholar, "the sheltered canyons may be regarded as the best place to collect *Formica*, and for that matter most ants in Colorado." These are just four examples of prime ant fishing locales, though there are certainly more out there to be discovered.

Ants are the perfect opportunistic dry fly of summer, only rivaled by beetle imitations. If I were restricted to one fly in July, regardless of water or location, I would be hard pressed to stray far from a size 14 Cascade Flying Ant. But it is important to remember to prepare for the diversity of ant imitation. While many of us may think, "it's just an ant," trout don't share our generalities.

Thoughts on Imitation

Back in my high school days, my calculus teacher, Mr. Brady, asked me to tie him some flying ant patterns for his trip to Idaho. Flying Ants? Why not an Iron Blue Wingless or a freaking Quill Gordon? Come on, he can't be serious, can he? At the time I was into CDC, beadheads, and all the innovative new materials and styles in American and European tying. I naïvely passed off his choice as the patterns of an "old guy." When I had a few extra patterns left over after his order, I tucked them away for several months before reluctantly tying them on. That was the biggest mistake of my angling life. I now use ant patterns in about 20% of my dry fly fishing.

Ants, like grasshoppers, initially receive a great deal of attention from anglers who encounter them sporadically throughout their day-to-day activities. It is hard to pretend that trout never see an insect that will quickly colonize any food left out during a shoreline lunch. Beginning anglers use ant imitations, but those same patterns tend to quickly move to the back of their boxes as they become more advanced anglers. This discrimination has more to do with the growing fascination with other trout foods (and their imitations) rather than with a lack of productivity of the ant patterns. For unlike hoppers, ants form a critical part of the midsummer trout's diet. In a month-long stomach sampling I did in 2000 in Yellowstone, ants were six times more prevalent than hoppers in stomach samples.

Ant patterns are simple, cheap, and easy (and fun) patterns to tie, so getting stocked up for a season of terrestrial fishing should be a joy not a burden. Even a novice tier can create flies that are quite realistic. They can be great searching patterns: realistic enough to fool picky trout, yet representative enough to elicit strikes from opportunists. They can also be the perfect curveball to throw at midsummer trout that have seen it all.

Creating the basic ant requires nothing more than two balls of dubbing and a wrap of hackle; this will give you the universal commercial pattern found in most fly shops. This fly, while it catches fish, has many shortcomings. It is difficult to see for many anglers, it is commonly recognized (and rejected) by pressured trout, and lacks realistic embellishments like flash and wings. It is also a poor floater in fast water, yet floats awkwardly in slow water where a true float is essential.

As always, experimentation is useful in creating a more effective ant pattern. The first things I would add to the standard ant pattern are wings. Be they hackle tip, Raffia, Z-Wing or CDC, the wing will give an added dimension to your pattern. Most ants encountered by trout, especially in lakes, are of the winged variety. Flying ants are more mobile and more easily blown around in the wind. Besides realism, the wing can add floatation and visibility to your fly.

The only exception to this rule is when you are tying tiny ant patterns intended for ultra-selective fish. Under those conditions, a standard ant pattern with dubbing or foam and deer hair legs usually works best. The smallest worker ants are often wingless anyhow.

Next, always use sparkle dubbing with ant patterns. Why? Ants have exoskeletons, and if you look closely, light reflects off an ant like a piece of living obsidian. They also have tiny hairs on their abdomens that recast light. This may not seem obvious to us, but to that big Letort Brown shadowing your pattern with a nose close enough to brush the hackle tips, this minor difference can sell your fake. When this kind of effect can be achieved by simply buying a different type of dubbing, why not utilize it?

Since lack of visibility is a common complaint with ant patterns, the use of contrasting colors can be useful in spotting these patterns at a distance. The Cascade Flying Ant pattern does this well by creating a "Trivisible" pattern that contrasts with itself under any light or water conditions. It has a black body, brown hackle, and grizzly hackle tip wing, each of which contrasts with other parts of the fly. While most anglers turn to over-used parachute patterns for visibility, this fly enhances visibility without utilizing the same visual clues that can turn off heavily-pressured trout.

If you need to use high-visibility materials on ant patterns, try to keep them as subdued as possible. I remember reading an article by George Harvey in an old *Fly Fisherman* magazine about how fluorescent materials on flies do not affect fish taking the flies. While that may be true, in many studies bright colors painted on trout prey has shown to reduce the number of prey ingested. Given a choice, avoid bright colors and simply follow a patch of water where you fly should be if you happen to lose sight of it.

Ants, especially those without wings, don't tend to remain on the surface long. A sunken ant pattern is perfect to imitate those ants that are knocked off trees and drown. Sunk ant patterns are superb in swift small streams where an ant that falls in is instantly submerged in rough water and drifts until it is eaten. A sunken ant is easily and effectively fished under a dry fly like a high-floating caddis or adult crane fly imitation. Sunken ants, while some occasionally swing them like wet flies, are best fished with a natural dead drift and no movement.

With ant patterns, most people only fish imitations in the size 12 to 14 range. I also use these patterns 75% of the time, but I also carry an enormous variety of sizes from size 6 down to size 22 or 24. The extreme sizes, both large and small, are excellent for fooling heavily pressured trout that have seen it all. The larger flying ant patterns are great for the big ants that take to the air in the Cascades and Sierra Nevada during May and June.

Ant patterns are not foolproof, however. Over-hackled ant patterns are a consistent problem facing fly tiers and fly buyers, as an ant pattern with too much hackle can roll over so that it rides with its ass in the air (or below the surface). Besides adversely affecting how the fly rides on the water, over-hackled dries, of any sort, just aren't as effective on selective trout. Like we mentioned above, ants can be prolific and trout can be selective to them. The greater variety in your box often translates to better odds on the water.

Another problem that faces the ant tier is loose dubbing, which after a fish or two, tends to "fuzz up" and wipe out the characteristic bulges of the ant pattern. This is something to be avoided. Sure, a shredded fly may still catch some fish, but fewer of the trout that are keying into ants. Make sure to dub your flies tightly and neatly to ensure the longest possible durability.

Once you seriously invest time into tying and fishing ant patterns, it'll be hard to go back to the standard old attractors. Perhaps it will turn you onto the brave new world of terrestrial fishing, where beetle, cricket, crane fly, inchworm, cicada, wasp, and black fly patterns finally start evicting Humpies, Wulffs, and Variants from their tenured seats in American fly boxes.

Finally, a Chernobyl Ant is *not* an ant imitation.

Patterns

Keys to Avoid
1. **Overhackled:** Ants only have 6 legs, not 329 of them.
2. **Loose Dubbing:** After four trout, a loosely dubbed black ant pattern takes on the proportions of a deer turd.
3. **Big Flashy Colors:** Proper construction will make it visible without making it look like a John Waters Film Festival.

Keys to Match
1. **Cornucopia of Size and Color:** You never know what you'll need, so be prepared
2. **Wings:** When trout are picky wings matter and when they are not, they don't hurt
3. **Sparkle Dubbing:** It can make a difference in slow water.

Cascade Flying Ant

Hook: Dai Riki #300, #8-18
Abdomen: Black Ice Dub
Wing: Grizzly hackle
Hackle: Brown hackle, two wraps
Thorax: Same as abdomen

This fly is so effective because it is both realistic and visible. With the black/brown/white (grizzly) coloration it is almost a "tri-visible"—the colors contrast with themselves under almost any light or water condition. It is consistently one of my five top dry flies each season, and often my first searching pattern when prospecting with terrestrials.

CDC High Vis Ant

Hook: Dai Riki #300, #8-18
Abdomen: Black Haretron Dubbing
Hackle: Black hackle, two wraps, trimmed on the bottom
Thorax: Same as abdomen
Wing: white CDC feather over black CDC feather

While I am not a fan of high-vis anything, some clients really needed something they could see better on the water and this pattern is a good solution for that predicament. The black CDC wing obscures the white CDC overwing from the trout, and the CDC wing stabilizes the fly and keeps it riding properly on the water.

Brown CDC Ant

Hook: Dai Riki #300, #8-18
Abdomen: Brown Haretron Dubbing
Wing: Tan CDC
Hackle: Brown hackle, two wraps
Thorax: Same as abdomen

A simple brown ant pattern that isn't an exact flying ant imitation, but the CDC adds some floatation and makes the fly a bit more visible to the angler.

Blacktail Ant

Hook: Dai Riki 305 or 310, #16-20
Abdomen: Reddish (maroon) sparkle dubbing
Wing: Tan Swiss straw, treated with Flexament
Hackle: Black, one or two turns
Thorax: Black sparkle dubbing

This is my preferred pattern for "selective" trout on flat water. Make sure to tie a sparse hackle so that the wing shows up clearly. Prepare the wing material with two coats of Flexament to ensure its durability through several fish. This pattern works best for me on Rocky Mountain states, which has an abundance of these bi-colored ants.

Cubist Ant

Hook: Dai Riki 320, #10-18
Body: Black peacock Ice Dub blended with black Haretron
Hackle: Black palmered
Post (Optional): White antron

This is both an "attractor" and "imitator" pattern. I have been experimenting with "busy" styled flies that look like an insect in motion, and the success that this pattern has had on smooth spring creeks suggests that trout may take it for a buzzing flying ant. The body provides a solid core silhouette, which is distorted by the full-body palmered hackle. Despite its effectiveness on flat water, it floats as well as any ant pattern in pocket water.

Aphids (Aphididae)

The Insect

When found in large numbers, Aphids, the little green bugs dreaded by home and commercial gardeners alike, actually may be a modest source of food for trout. That may be a surprise to some who have read a number of trout diet analyses. You rarely see the name "aphids" in stomach samples, but check the fine text. Like other "minor" categories of trout prey, Aphids are grouped together with other bugs in their order, in the aphids' case that would be Homoptera. Most of the time, trout consuming Homoptera, especially on streams, are eating aphids. Aphids have been noted to provide up to 5-15% of the terrestrial diet on some trout streams, though usually much less. The opportunistic angler should at least consider them a possibility on those days where nothing else seems to work.

Aphids are most common in small streams bordering gardens or cultivated lands, as well as in areas of clear cuts. Aphids are great indicators of ant populations, and vice versa; when you find large colonies of both coinciding, they can both be significant terrestrial forage for trout. As you may know, ants, even the most aggressive and predatory species, will gently milk aphids for their honeydew, and then defend the aphids against some of their insect predators.

There is a very significant correlation between aphids and plants and trees, so much so that two massive texts were written

The dainty frame of an aphid makes it susceptible to even modest breezes.

When aphids are common, bright green "clump" imitations—such as this green X-Caddis—can work well.

to analyze it: *Aphids on the World's Crops* (466 pages) and *Aphids on the World's Trees* (929 pages). Unfortunately they simply list which kinds of plants support various kinds of aphids, not what are the best plants for boom populations of aphids.

Aphids are go through a unique life cycle where an egg hatches on one tree or plant (say spruce) in the autumn, the larvae overwinter on that tree, then adults emerge in the spring, migrate to another tree (say larch). Those lay eggs on the larch, then in the fall another brood migrates back to spruce trees for the winter. This makes for two major migrations, and a summer abundance of winged adults constantly moving about to find more food resources. At all these times, they have the potential of become a noteworthy trout food.

The small size of aphids (1-5mm) renders them almost invisible in flight, but it doesn't mean they are not there. According to Blackman and Eastop, there are "astronomical numbers of aphids in the air" most of the time. Once airborne, aphids are generally at the mercy of the wind currents, as their feeble flying skills are adapt for moving from leaf to leaf, not mile to mile. Like other wind-blown insects, aphids can become concentrated along fences, bridge abutments, high banks, cliffs, or other areas that interrupt wind flow.

As any gardener knows, aphids can be extremely gregarious (where you find one, you find 800!). At least one species has a defense behavior that should be quite interesting to fly anglers. *Acyrhosiphon pisum*...as soon as they land" changes to "When they detect a threat, *Acyrhosiphon pisum* jump off a leaf simultaneously, like a flock of pigeons. Of course, when they land on the water, they face immediate danger.

In a 1984 study, aphids were heavily preyed upon by trout, which turned to feed on them instead of the more common *Gammarus* scuds! The reason for this preference was assumed to be the bright coloration of the aphids. For this reason, on my little aphid pattern I seek bright green dubbing, often the brightest "insect green" (though not a chartreuse) hue I can find.

Pattern

Thoughts on Imitation
A combination of unique color, small size, sporadic availability, and lack of angler imitation makes a simple pattern the perfect choice for aphid imitation. The two keys are size and color. The fly must be tiny (22-28, with 24-26 ideal) and bright green. The wings of aphids are so thin and transparent that they needn't be fancy. I like a simple dubbed body and sparse CDC hackle, which can represent legs or wings and float the tiny hook.

Alphonsus Rex Aphidiorum

Hook: Dai Riki 310, #22
Body: Bright green dubbing
Wing: Chartreuse raffia, coated in Flexament
Hackle: Lime green CDC fibers, short

One pattern should cover the few occasions that demand an aphid pattern. Don't forget to try this as a tiny attractor for picky fish that have seen it all. It may also represent a tiny immature grasshopper or leaf hopper, as well as an array of terrestrial midges or gnats. The same pattern tied in black can function superbly as a tiny beetle imitation.

Baitfish

The Fish—General

As the name of our sport makes evident, fly fishers have long been obsessed with insects. We have, as they say, "put the Plecoptera on a pedestal." We recreate the delicate frame of natural insects with an equally delicate imitation. This infatuation with insects resulted in the inevitable neglect, and often contempt, for non-insect forms of trout prey.

While we marginalize many trout foods because of this obsession with delicacy, the devaluation of forage fish seems particularly audacious. The ignorance of baitfish in stillwaters is glaring, though not altogether unexpected. Of the four most important stillwater trout foods in North America (chironomids, baitfish, *Daphnia*, terrestrials) we only invest a great deal of attention on chironomids. To truly master stillwaters, especially large fish in stillwaters, one must master the imitation of forage fish.

Big fish grow big by eating smaller fish, much like the finalists at the World Series of Poker amass their cache of chips by consuming weaker players. Yet, not all baitfish make equally likely targets. Smaller forage fish tend to swim slower than larger ones, and younger ones may also lack defensive behaviors needed to avoid predators. For this reason, trout usually feed on smaller baitfish than they can ideally consume and they particularly relish young-of-the-year forage fish.

While trout more successfully consume smaller baitfish, when given a choice, they often attack the largest ones they can easily capture, handle, and consume. This often occurs at prime ambush points—near boulders, snags, or cliffs—where even larger baitfish have little "running" room to take advantage of their speed. Brown trout can handle big prey; one study had them consuming forage fish at an average size of 1/3 their body length! That makes a six-inch fly suitable for an eighteen-inch fish! Bull trout and lake trout can top that, consuming fish up to 50% of their body length. Now, you're talking eight to nine-inch flies for eighteen-inch trout. Much bigger than the normal size 6 Zonker that we think of when imitating forage fish!

Anglers often assume that only big trout consume baitfish, but this is not always the case. Smaller trout will readily consume small baitfish when they are abundant and available. In a Scandinavian study, brown trout that reached 13-15 cm in length started feeding primarily on minnows, and Arctic char began once they reached 16 cm. The vast majority of stillwater studies focusing on piscivorous trout reflect a similar theme: on waters where trout feed heavily on baitfish, trout begin the feeding behavior at a young age.

Mudlines concentrate insects, baitfish, and the trout that prey upon them.

Jeff Morgan photo

When is the best time of the year to imitate baitfish? Undoubtedly, it would be from mid-summer through fall. At this time, young-of-the-year fish abound, and many suffer from warm-water infections that make them more vulnerable to predatory trout, and normal aquatic insect activity rapidly slows down. One study of "large" brown trout showed that 30% of the trout had fish in their stomachs during May and June, yet 100% of the trout had baitfish in their stomachs during October and November.

How do trout pursue baitfish? Not surprisingly, it depends. Many of us have seen trout raiding shallows with fingerlings flickering into the air in vain attempts to elude the maw of a determined trout. Surely this active predatory patrolling is common, but it isn't the only way that trout feed on baitfish. In one study, brook trout used a "wait-and-pounce" foraging behavior to pursue northern red-belly dace when there was an abundance of cover, yet they preferred an active cruising strategy when there was little cover.

We often think the best way to imitate baitfish is to locate schools, then proffer imitations in that general area. In many situations, individual baitfish participate in what is known as "predator inspection behavior," where they actually slowly swim towards predators alone or in pairs in order to check them out. This behavior is not unrelated from a squirrel crawling down a tree in order to inspect a dog barking at its base. While this behavior seems as bright as jawing at Mike Tyson outside of a nightclub, it actually benefits the forage fish. Observing predators at close range allows baitfish to figure out trout "tells" that may precipitate an attack. When those fish return to the school, they have a behavioral advantage over their peers.

Anglers should notice that these "inspecting fish" behave just like that curious squirrel in the tree—the same hesitant, cautious movements interspersed with numerous pauses. If a trout takes notice and attacks, the baitfish quickly flees. This array of movements is essential for the angler to match. It also means that the angler needs to master a variety of retrieve and trolling techniques to cover the various resting, inspecting, feeding, and fleeing behaviors of baitfish.

Trolling is perhaps the most underused technique in fly angling. Some say it elicits nightmarish flashbacks of pre-fly fishing experiences trolling Ford Fenders and Wedding Ring spinners. However, trolling provides the ideal imitation of baitfish, keeping the imitation in the strike zone much longer than casting and retrieving. Much to the dismay of some stillwater purists, I regularly troll with an outboard motor. The added speed helps me cover water quickly and allows me to fish in storms or heavy weather that blows all the other fly anglers off the lake. Most importantly, when trout are hyper-aggressive and only enticed by fleeing baitfish, the added speed of the outboard is irreplaceable.

Finally, not all baitfish are the same and a Muddler Minnow, while a superb pattern, is not sufficient to imitate the varied behaviors of all baitfish. Properly understanding the prey species targeted by trout—especially trout fry, sticklebacks, and sculpins—will help anyone become a more well-rounded stillwater angler.

BAITFISH: TROUT AND SALMON FRY

Trout and salmon fry likely serve as the most important fish prey for trout throughout North America. While cannibalism may slightly offend our elevated estimation of trout, ignoring it altogether does us little good in arriving at a better understanding of their lifestyle. In America, where the extent of fry fishing is limited to the "Little Rainbow/Brook/Brown Trout Bucktail" series from the 1950's and a handful of curio patterns, fry imitation remains a relatively unexplored angling frontier. In Britain, however, fry fishing—imitating both trout and coarse fish fry—has evolved into a highly refined science.

The importance of trout fry should not be restricted only to lakes and large trout. Brook trout in a small Californian river consumed 13.5% of their calories in the form of fry. Fry were the second most prevalent food—in terms of calories—for the brook trout in that study. Similar results are found on the trout streams of the Northwest and Great Lakes region, where large invasions of salmon return to sire a whole new crop of alevin and fry for trout to dine on.

Despite their relevance in streams, lakes provide the best opportunities to dupe trout with fry imitations. These patterns work exceptionally well on mountain lakes with few other baitfish for trout to prey upon. Lowland reservoirs with high levels of natural reproduction of trout also produce bumper crops of juvenile trout for adults to gorge themselves with. Fry naturally congregate in areas where the risk of attack is low. During the day, they prefer weedy areas of shallow littoral zones, which offers them fair protection. As dusk falls, larger fish move in closer and fry either pack up in dense schools on barren bottoms or scatter throughout protective cover. The most dangerous place for fry—day, dusk or night—is often right where the thermocline intersects the lake bottom. Depending on the time of the year, this point could be anywhere from 10 to 30 feet deep. Locating this junction is critical to consistent success for larger, fry feeding trout.

While fry exist on most waters where trout naturally reproduce, hatchery plantings of fingerlings create spectacular opportunities for the angler. When fish and game departments plant fish in lakes (and some rivers), it is often cheaper for them to dump a load of two to four-inch fingerlings in the fall rather than stock a much smaller number of "catchable" trout the following spring. While hatchery fish may be kryptonite to some anglers, these little fish are a blessing in disguise.

When a truck or helicopter dumps fingerlings into a lake, most of the little ones swim off in small schools near the surface. However, a number of dead or frail fingerlings feebly move about stunned and easily assailable. Many of these small fingerlings die during transport or from the thermo-chemical shock of entering a foreign body of water. A conservative estimate would assume five to eight-percent mortality, but when you are talking about even just 50,000 fingerlings, between 2,500 and 4,000 dead or injured

Trout fry are subtly colored, except their bold parr marks along their lateral lines.

fish end up in the lake. It doesn't take long for large, piscivorous trout to take notice and mop up the infirm and dopey fingerlings.

While this virtual feeding frenzy does not last long, it focuses intense feeding for 48 to 72 hours in the vicinity of the stocking. It then offers sporadic residual feeding for a week or more after the initial planting. On a lake in British Columbia where sockeye salmon fry are stocked, nearly all fry consumption by cutthroat took place in the first week following stocking. Only 17% of the fry were still alive after a month in the lake! This kind of feeding is something you need to research and exploit on your own. By the time a fly shop or newspaper reports it, the feeding frenzy has likely fizzled out.

The alevin stage is another important stage for trout predation. The alevin stage commences immediately after the baby fish hatches from the egg through when the yolk sac is still attached to the body. During this period, alevins cannot yet move about, so they hang out in or just under the interstitial spaces in the gravel. When wading anglers, rafters, or normal water hydraulics disturb this gravel, the alevins get kicked up into the drift. Lacking any practical swimming ability, these tiny fry are left to the mercy of the current, just like any caddis larvae or stonefly nymph. However, alevins may even be more conspicuous to visual predators like trout, due to their relatively large orangish or pinkish egg yolks sacs. However, when constructing imitations, it is critical to keep in mind just how small these fry are. Salmon fry may only be the length of a size 14 hook and trout fry may even be the size of a #16-18, 2XL nymph hook!

Trout may also consume baby salmonids during the spring migrations of anadromous salmon and steelhead smolts to the ocean. While this migration should interest Alaskan and Canadian anglers, it can also be sporadically important to fish in other regions. Pacific Northwest and the Great Lakes anglers often overlook smolts. However, the smallmouth bass anglers in those regions, used to seeing the darting smolts shooting out of the water with a smallie fast on their tails, don't make the same mistake.

Fry are not important everywhere. On streams where trout and salmon spawn in upper tributary or outlet streams, most fry and juvenile development takes place in the absence of predatory trout. In these small nursery streams, the young fish are relatively safe from trout predators. By the time they return to the main lake, only a fraction of the largest fish are a predatory threat.

On other lakes, adult trout take over the shoal areas and force young trout into open water. The classic example of this behavior occurs in Yellowstone Lake. Here, the biggest cutthroat trout consistently dominate lake margins within fifty feet of the shore, where almost all the food is concentrated. The young-of-the-year and second-year fish thus must roam the relatively sterile open waters of the main lake. Under segregated conditions such as this, trout may rarely, if ever, feed on fry.

Some studies even question how often trout cannibalize, as young trout are more difficult to capture than equivalent-sized forage fish. One research project on Oregon's Lake Billy Chinook revealed that in the 3713kg of forage consumed by 1000 bull trout, only 85kg were either young bull trout or young rainbow trout. Part of the reason for the lack of cannibalism, is that large, piscivorous lake-dwelling fish inhabited deep structure, where young bull trout remain in the relatively safety of the shallow spawning tributaries. The chubs, shad, and shiners that spawn and mature in open water provide a far easier and abundant food resource.

While we are on the topic of Lake Billy Chinook, of all trout predators accessible with a fly rod, the bull trout stands tall and proud above others. These char easily exceed standard angler definitions of "big fish:" whether they are "twenty pounds" or "thirty inches." Bull char thrive in large lakes with good spawning tributaries, such as Flathead Lake in Montana. While other trout exploit their young brethren, bull trout easily devour *adult* salmonids! Capable of consuming prey up to 50% of their body length, bull trout look at a size 4 Muddler like a cocktail weenie. Kokanee in the four to ten-inch range are their preferred food source, though when available, bull trout happily consume stocked "catchable" rainbow in the six to ten-inch range. Kokanee dwell in cool depths, and though they make up a major part of the bull trout diet, fly anglers have difficulty matching them at depths of forty feet. Fortunately, the dumb stocked rainbows hover within a few feet of the surface allowing the angler to troll large streamers (1/0-3/0 4XL hooks, or long, sailfish-style patterns) on a sinking line within fifteen feet of the surface.

For eastern anglers, the term "Kokanee" may not ring a bell unless you like to tip back Canadian lagers. Kokanee are landlocked sockeye salmon, like "landlocked salmon" are essentially Atlantic salmon that do not go to the ocean. Kokanee are only native to a handful of large western lakes, though they have been stocked extensively throughout the region. Kokanee trend small, most range from 6-10 inches, though they can reach a maximum length of about twenty inches. They are a rather popular species for gear anglers, who can reach mid-lake schools holding at depths of twenty to eighty feet. Fly anglers occasionally catch them by accident, though some anglers like to pursue Kokanee during their migrations into spawning streams.

The importance of Kokanee to the angler is not related to their affinity for flies, but rather what they do for large fish. A variety of trout (most notably lake and bull trout, and to a lesser extent, large brown and rainbow trout) follow schools of Kokanee around, picking the off strays and mongo weaklings that venture perilously far from the safety of the pack. The problem for the angler is locating schools of Kokanee—not just any schools, but the shallow (<25 feet) ones that fly equipment can effectively reach. Kokanee imitation requires five things: depth finder (essential), a substantial boat to haul the depth finder and battery, lead core line (or at least full sink type VI and some weights), big white or silvery flies, and lots of patience. This is slow, trophy fishing that rewards those willing to invest the hours.

The relative importance of baitfish to trout on any given water is not a simple two-way street. Much depends on the other creatures that rely on baitfish for food. In particular, it involves large fish, to which even adult trout are just another baitfish like hefty largemouth bass and the soulless killer—northern pike. These two game fish often compete with trout for baitfish, and where they do, trout feed significantly less on baitfish lest they get eaten themselves. A 1997 study of the one-time world-class trout fishery ruined by inept public management, Oregon's Crane Prairie Reservoir, showed that the presence of bass forced trout out of areas where they can feed on chub and stickleback, since the trout perceived a predation risk. Subsequently, bass grew large, and trout did not.

While this may seem like a lot of information, it only scratches the surface of the complex relationship between adult trout and their juvenile cohort. It is easy to lobby fly anglers to invest more time imitating them, but exactly *how* to go about it requires more demanding angler-based research than exists today.

Thoughts on Imitation

We should not restrict the use of fry imitations to big lakes or big fish. Trout and salmon fry contribute as much to the diet of average-sized trout as other stillwater foods and should be afforded the same attention by anglers. Also, before you start out to explore fry fishing, be sure to read the excellent accounts of fry-fishing in Bob Church's *Fly Fishing For Trout* or Charles Jardine's *The Classic Guide to Fly Fishing For Trout*, as these will doubtless make your fry experiments more productive and enjoyable.

Every stillwater angler, especially on stillwaters stocked with fingerling trout, should carry a cadre of fry imitations. The light-wire, 4XL to XL hook is the backbone of all floating fry patterns. From there it is up to your imagination. Mylar tubing over foam makes a serviceable body that will both float and sparkle. Some like to paint the mylar directly, others pull foam or Krystal-flash over the top to create a color contrast. Some people really like to spin, trim, and intricately paint deer hair on floating fry patterns, yet I have a hard time justifying 25 minutes of tying for a fly which will be shredded into an abstract sculpture after only a fish or two. They sure look great in the box though!

Floating fry patterns, while important, should be used only under the right conditions. The day or two following a fingerling planting is the obvious choice, but calm evenings or mornings following an exceptionally windy day can also be productive. Points, shoreline drop-offs, and weedbeds—all places preferred by juvenile fish—are prime locations to try floating fry imitations. The patterns require a fairly substantial tippet, as trout often

Alevins have weak fins and rarely venture away from cracks in rocks.

Brown trout are among the most voracious piscivores and make likely targets for baitfish imitations.

Jeff Morgan photo

smash the frauds with vigor seemingly unworthy of such hapless prey. Finally, fish fry imitations static, with only the occasional twitch every few minutes. Dead and dying fish do not move much. For most anglers, including myself, refraining from swimming or retrieving fish imitations is quite difficult. It takes a lot of patience to watch a fly bob at the surface for five or ten minutes. But most people who use this technique agree that the slower you fish floating fry patterns, the more productive you will be. After resting the pattern for five to ten minutes (or whenever you wake up) you can retrieve the pattern and throw it to another spot. This kind of fishing rewards the laggard. The strikes are few, but memorable. The rise may come in a variety of ways: an erupting shower of water, a retort befitting a angry beaver tail-slap, a porpoiseing head-back-tail inhalation, or a churning, restless swirl leaving a only a whirlpool in its wake. All you can hope for is that your fly is still attached to the line after the strike!

Imitations of alevins, the other "overlooked" baitfish stage, should also be constructed sparingly. Keep their imitations small, no larger than size 12-14, and avoid the tendency to stray towards larger, seemingly more detailed and "realistic" imitations. For my alevin pattern, I use small bead chain eyes and a tiny "yolk sac" of glo-bug foam. I prefer a simple, opaque body on the pattern, since the bodies of the naturals have not yet fully developed and the circulatory system dominates the color feature. A reddish or orangish-gray dubbed body covered with a clear plastic strip creates a nice effect blending opacity and faint color.

Alevin imitations should be fished below riffles and other spawning habitat. A good rule of thumb is to fish alevin patterns in your favorite egg riffle for a month after egg-laying has concluded. Simply fishing alevin imitations dead-drift under an indicator works best, as alevins have no swimming capability in the presence of even a whiff of current. Any "swinging" or stripping these flies in is as unnatural an emerging stonefly nymph.

Fry patterns, like all other baitfish patterns, should be constructed for durability. When you finally find the "hot" baitfish pattern, all too often, a large fish will chew it to a Pollackesque mosaic of marabou, tinsel, and Flashabou. If you're like me, you only carry two to four samples of each large baitfish pattern, which means that you could run out of flies in an hour of hot fishing unless the flies are constructed well. Tight wraps, super glue under the body to prevent spinning on the hook, several whip-finishes, and liberal head cement or epoxy are critical to constructing a fly that can withstand a tussle with a trout wielding the bite-and-chew mentality of Mike Tyson.

"Vibration patterns," similar to the Tullis Bug in America and a variety of billed patterns from England, are a growing trend in trout fishing. Creatively these patterns are really cool—the trout fly-anglers answer to the bass angler's crankbait. But, biologically, it is difficult to understand why they would work better than a more anatomically correct pattern. It has been repeatedly established that trout are visual feeders, not vibration feeders (like bass) or olfactory feeders (like catfish), though trout may react powerfully towards prey that creates surface displacement. I have tried "billed" patterns on many occasions, and only under unusually turbid conditions have they significantly outperformed standard streamers. They may produce reasonably better under the cover of darkness, though that discovery hinges on the exact legality of pursuing trout at night in a particular State.

Patterns

Keys to Match
1. **Dark Back/Light Belly:** All fish have this coloration, if you don't match this you're not fishing an imitation, you're fishing a lure.
2. **Alevins:** Carry a few, keep them small, and fish them like an egg pattern.
3. **Floaters:** Trout like food that has little chance of escape.

Keys to Avoid
1. **Exact Coloration:** At two inches, most trout fingerlings look remarkably similar.
2. **Shoddy Construction:** Fry patterns should be among your most durable.
3. **Vibration Patterns:** Trout are mostly visual feeders, so worry about color, size, and speed first.

Alevin

Hook: Dai Riki 075, #10-14
Tail: Pearl sparkle material and white marabou
Body: White antron, wrapped with clear plastic, colored with waterproof marker on the back
Ribbing: Pearl or Root Beer Krystal flash
Egg Sac: Orange glo-bug yarn
Eyes: Silver bead chain

A good pattern for dead-drifting near spawning areas about a month after spawning. Don't swim this like a standard streamer, as alevins cannot yet swim well and tend to hold in interstitial spaces unless disturbed.

East Lake Fry

Hook: Mustad 9761, #2-4
Under Body: White foam
Over Body: Pearl mylar tubing
Back: Red and Peacock Krystalflash
Eyes: Silver 3D holographic eyes

One of the first floating fry patterns I experimented with and I still have dozens of them in my storage bins. The body can be coated with Soft-ex (a soft epoxy-like material) to make it nearly indestructible. It also gives the fly roughly the action of the Heddon Zara-Spook lure when twitched on the surface.

Dubbed Fry

Hook: Dai Riki 700, #2-10
Tail: Grizzly dyed marabou
Body: Blended hare's ear and pearl Lite Brite dubbing, with back painted dark
Head: Soft-ex
Eyes: 3-d holographic eyes

A simple dubbed fry pattern often works when elaborate marabou patterns fail. The translucent fins of fry create little motion, so "stick" patterns will often fool more trout than patterns that look sinewy and active in the water.

Dinky Deceiver

Hook: Dai Riki 700, #8-12
Body: Silver tinsel chenille
Beard: White kid goat hair
Flanks: Grizzly (dyed blue or green, optional)
Wing: White marabou
Over Wing: Green or Blue Flashabou
Eyes: 3-D molded eye attached to clear plastic and tied along sides of fly

The Deceiver has long been a killer saltwater pattern, but I like a smaller version for stillwater trout. Tie this pattern sparse to match slender salmon and trout smolts, but you can thicken it for juvenile shad or chub.

Alexandra

Hook: Dai Riki 070, #8-14
Tail: Red schlappen
Body: Silver mylar tinsel
Hackle: Black saddle hackle
Cheeks: Red goose biot
Wing: Peacock sword

It is tough to beat this classic British pattern, which has been banned periodically on many English reservoirs due to its lethality. It works as both a fry imitation in larger sizes, and a general attractor when tied on a wet fly hook. In my "first string" of river wet flies, I fish this as the middle dropper between a Royal Coachman Wet and March Brown Flymph. The Alexandra is, unquestionably, the best brook trout fly I have ever fished.

Alaska Smolt

- **Hook:** Mustad 76985, #8-12
- **Body:** Silver mylar tubing
- **Butt:** Hot orange 6/0 Uni-thread
- **Beard Hackle:** Red schlappen
- **Under Wing:** Unravelled silver tinsel
- **Wing:** White Polar Aire and white marabou
- **Cheeks:** Olive or blue dyed grizzly hackle
- **Over Wing:** Peacock herl

One of the most popular smolt patterns in Natnuk, Alaska, I tied this for years for several lodges up there. Took a half-dozen out and lost all of them in the process of duping two nice brown trout targeting juveniles in a rocky lake inlet.

Karen Carpenter's Zonker

- **Hook:** Dai Riki 700, #2-6
- **Body:** Hackle Flash to match body
- **Wing:** Zonker rabbit strip
- **Cheeks:** Red schlappen
- **Collar:** Grizzly hackle

The Zonker has long been a killer smolt pattern, but the rigid mylar-covered body can prove a tad too lifeless when fished quickly. While the fishy-looking mylar body sells the fly to anglers, I have always believed the pattern works because of the movement of the rabbit wing. This version of the Zonker replaces the rigidity of the mylar with the fluidity of Hackle Flash, which blends pieces of tinsel and dyed cotton into a loose, long chenille that pulses just like the rabbit wing. When trout are aggressively feeding on smolts, this is my first choice.

Vibrofry

- **Hook:** Dai Riki 700, #2-10
- **Tail:** White marabou
- **Flash:** Pearl Flashabou
- **Body:** Pearl crystal chenille
- **Head:** Grey and white deer hair

This is a nice pattern for trout feeding on smolts or fry near the surface. The deer hair offers a bit of water displacement, which can attract predatory fish on calm mornings or evenings. Fish this pattern near weed edges and lake inlets.

Marabou Spider

- **Hook:** Dai Riki 270, #4-10
- **Body:** White, tan, grey, or cream marabou
- **Flash:** Pearl Flashabou
- **Hackle:** Teal, widgeon, or gadwall flank feathers
- **Head:** Brass bead (optional)

Chapter V: The Prey

Baitfish: Sticklebacks

Considering the wide range of baitfish that trout consume, one might be amazed that the wealth of scientific literature on the three-spine stickleback (*Gasterosteus aculeatus*) exceeds that of all others combined. This rich scholarship is not unfounded. The three-spine stickleback has a greater distribution than any other trout prey species, baitfish or otherwise. Their populations literally circle the world; one can find the same species of stickleback in the Balkans, North Africa, Scandinavia, Britain, Canada, Northeastern and Northwestern United States, Alaska, Kamchatka, and Japan. The thought that the three-spine stickleback is the only prey species collectively enjoyed by trout throughout the Northern Hemisphere should elicit awe in even the most jaded trout angler. In addition to this broad distribution, sticklebacks inhabit a variety of ecological habitats. From tiny, intermittent California streams to the St. Lawrence estuary to hidden spring pools in New Mexico to Lake Ontario to even the high seas—researchers collected one specimen 800km from the Alaskan shoreline! Their promiscuous habitat requirements make them perfect for the aquarium, allowing researchers to probe further into their lifestyle. It is safe to say that in terms of research, three-spine sticklebacks are the fruit flies of the baitfish world.

That being said, what they heck do they look like? Three-spine sticklebacks only reach about five to six cm in length and stand out from other baitfish due to the three spines rising from their backs (two in front of the dorsal fin and one at the front of the fin). Generally they are olive-backed, with pale olive to silvery flanks, and a silvery-white belly. Breeding males have a brilliant crimson belly and big, bright blue eyes. Taking these two wardrobes into account during the spring can make for extremely effective imitations.

Many people newly acquainted with sticklebacks think that like a porcupine, their spines protect them from predators. Not so, though the small spines keep smaller trout from nipping at them. Large trout will prey readily on sticklebacks, swallowing them head-first to avoid the spines.

Sticklebacks are most readily available to trout during their afternoon feeding activity. Though "active" is a relative term for this fish. According to Samuel McGinnis in *Freshwater Fishes of California*, the sticklebacks "feed primarily on small invertebrates that they pick off the substrate after a series of jerky advances, between which they hang motionless in the water." This fluttering motion with frequent pauses surely makes sticklebacks conspicuous target for hungry trout. The other motion to imitate is the darting "zig-zag motion" of courting males. When a female approaches the nest, the male will flutter and dart about in a rapid, zig-zag motion. Imitating this frenzied movement for with short strips for about one meter, letting the fly rest, then repeating would likely entice cruising trout to investigate.

Sticklebacks often travel in pairs for protection when they leave the safe weedy shallows. This has been observed in a few studies, and may be common throughout their range. For this reason, I would suggest fishing imitations in tandem (one slightly larger than the other).

Some tests show that trout clearly prefer larger-than-average sticklebacks, when available. Sticklebacks clearly agree. In fact, small sticklebacks will usually forage closer to trout when big sticklebacks are around, because they know trout will go after the larger ones! Therefore, I always tie and fish my flies one hook size larger than the average size of the naturals *and* give the fish plenty of second chances if the fish doesn't hook itself on the initial attack. Remember that trout often slam baitfish to stun them, before sweeping around to inhale them headfirst. With the spines on the stickleback, this behavior is even more pronounced. It is essential to pause after a strike before setting the hook.

As mentioned before, during mating, the males take on a crimson hue, with a bright blue eye and red flanks. After mating is finished, the females leave and males guard the nest. Once the eggs hatch and the tiny fry stray too far from the nest, the male will chase them down, suck them into his mouth, then spit the little fry back into the nest. Eventually, the fry are so active that they are too much work for the male to tend to, so he just starts eating them. Typical guy thing. While all this probably means nothing to how trout eat them, I have a soft spot for superfluous biological anecdotes.

After laying eggs, females can form large cannibalistic schools cruising in moderately open water (8-10 feet deep). The voracious pack then descends into the shallows to eat up their former mates guarding the nests as well as the tiny fry. This event is greatly feared by the male sticklebacks—the thought of 400 angry, hungry ex-girlfriends descending on my house would bring more than a little disquietude. However, the trout have the guys' backs, as these open-water schools of Amazonian sticklebacks make easy targets for predatory trout.

Most sticklebacks have a two-year life cycle, though they occasionally survive three years. Age groups of sticklebacks tend to segregate themselves: juvenile, young-of-the-year fish school up near shore, adult females and immature males school up independently in more open water. This suggests that we should use smaller imitations near shore and larger ones in open water.

Sticklebacks make excellent aquarium specimens, due to their interesting mating rituals and tolerance of the low oxygen levels found in small fish tanks. Nothing helps the fly tier more than a living model to observe when constructing imitations, whether it is a stickleback or a sculpin or an aquatic insect.

Anybody wanting to learn more about sticklebacks absolutely must consult *The Evolutionary Biology of the Three-spine Stickleback*, by Michael Bell and Susan Foster. This book contains more information than you could ever use, and will arm you with all the knowledge you need to master this forage fish. Considering the importance of sticklebacks in the trophy lakes of Oregon, British Columbia, and California—not to mention Alaskan lakes and streams, the legendary brook trout waters of Labrador, the lowland reservoirs of Great Britain, and the fjord rivers of Norway—a little extra homework can pay huge dividends.

When swimming, the spines on a stickleback lie down and the defining feature is a sharp body taper.

Other sticklebacks important to fly anglers include:

Brook Stickleback (*Culaea inconstans*): This little critter is easy for trout anglers to recognize because of their similarity in color to brook trout. Brook sticklebacks are prominently olive green, with lighter yellow spots or wavy lines, just like a brook trout. Breeding males can turn nearly totally black. They live in a variety of small streams (in slow, mud-bottomed pools), and vegetated ponds and lakes throughout Canada, and the Northern United States from New York to Montana. They spawn in the spring and summer, and attain a length of about eight centimeters.

Nine-spine Stickleback (*Pungitius pungitius*): The least important of these three sticklebacks to trout due to its more limited range, the nine-spine should be discussed because of its different shape and coloration. This stickleback has a slender body with a number of smaller spines on its back. It also has more of a grayish look to it, with darker mottling on the back and sides. The breeding male coloration is not as pronounced as with other sticklebacks, with black belly and occasionally white fins. Nine-spine sticklebacks can reach nine centimeters in length. It is more of a northerly specie than the three-spine stickleback, though it is found in similar, shallow weedy habitats. Where the nine-spine stickleback exists, it may be a more preferred prey than three-spine sticklebacks.

Thoughts on Imitation

To humans, the spines of the stickleback appear to be its calling card, much like the claws on a crayfish. When sticklebacks swim, however, those spines lie down along the back to reduce water resistance. Spines, if the fish sees them all, only would deter the fish from consuming the stickleback. Thus there is no huge advantage to adding a feature that would most likely reduce your chances of a strike.

On the other hand, do not assume that those spines deter fish altogether. I know many anglers who disregard sticklebacks on the logic that the spines "must tear up the fish." Trout don't chew up a stickleback like we would chew up a fish stick. Like other baitfish and leeches, trout regularly charge sticklebacks hoping to stun them. They then circle around and suck in the stickleback as it freezes in hopes of avoiding detection by the trout. As trout normally swallow fish head first, those spines don't come into play as often as we think. Human reasoning should never overrule trout reasoning when it comes to fooling trout.

If you wish to, several tactical and material options exist to match the spines of the stickleback. An obvious technique would be using goose biots to match the spines. You could also go with deer hair or feathers (like an olive Hungarian partridge feather) lacquered with Flexament and cut to the proper proportions.

Sticklebacks have conspicuously large eyes, which are far more important for imitations than the spines. I like to use big 3-D molded plastic eyes on my imitations, though sometimes painting your own black-on-light blue eyes on clear plastic can be effective. As many scientists assume that large eyes serve as a predatory target throughout the animal world, one would be amiss to omit them from stickleback patterns.

Tiers often overlook the unique body profile of sticklebacks, particularly the thin taper between the body and the tail. This slim rear third of the body distinguishes the stickleback from other baitfish as much as its spines do. I try to match this taper by creating a body out of antron or dubbing, which tapers easily. The front 2/3 of the body is pretty flat and broad. The pectoral fins and tail fins are average-sized, though the tapered body enhances the appearance of the tail motion. To match this motion, construct the tail with a puff of marabou or ostrich herl.

In addition to eyes, spines, and body shape, tiers should pay close attention to the color and size of sticklebacks. You want most of your patterns to have an olive-cream color, though some dingy silver or dingy gold patterns can be surprisingly effective at times. As for size, a size 8 or 10 pattern will be your mainstay, though larger and smaller patterns can also be productive even though they may not accurately imitate a stickleback.

Sticklebacks are best imitated in the shallow margin waters of a lake. As most large trout won't move into extreme shallows to feed except at low light, concentrate your imitation to the first few hours after dawn and the last hours before sundown. Sticklebacks are not built for long-distance movement, so use short fluttering strips interspersed with long five to ten second pauses.

PATTERNS

KEYS TO MATCH

1. **Skinny Taper Near Tail:** Body profile is important.
2. **Olive and Cream/Silver Body:** Worry about the color before the spines.
3. **Notable Eyes:** They always looked surprised.

KEYS TO AVOID

1. **General Attractor Streamers:** The color and profile of this minnow is unique.
2. **Going Overboard on the Spines:** They're there, but not the most important factor.
3. **Not Carrying Any:** These minnows are as widespread as any species on earth

TWURKULATOR

- **Hook:** Dai Riki 700, #8-10
- **Tail:** Light olive marabou
- **Taper:** Olive-cream dubbing
- **Body:** Cream or pearl sparkle chenille
- **Collar:** Cream rabbit
- **Spines:** Three light olive goose biots, secured in place with wraps of chenille
- **Sparkle:** Few strips of Light Olive or Yellow Krystalsplash
- **Back:** Olive synthetic fur
- **Eyes:** 3-D molded eyes

This is a pattern for somebody that just needs those spines on their stickleback imitation. The technique for the spines is to tie them to the hook shank and secure them in place with wraps of the sparkle chenille. The rest of the fly has an expressionistic look to it, with the synthetic fur adding a bit of shimmer and distorting the hard lines of the chenille. Using a collar of rabbit gives the impression of a bulky body and a thin tail taper.

SMOOTH STICKLEBACK

- **Hook:** Dai Riki 700, #6-10
- **Under Body:** Pearl crystal chenille
- **Belly:** Red Fishair
- **Body:** Dingy White Fishair
- **Back:** Olive Fishair
- **Belly:** Orange Fishair
- **Eyes:** 3-D molded eyes, attached to clear plastic and tied in

A fast and easy pattern, the Smooth Stickleback actually fishes as well as any stickleback pattern I have tried. It works especially well when trolled in tandem, with one pattern larger than the other.

BAITFISH: TUI CHUB (*SIPHATELES BICOLOR*)

In the large, trophy trout lakes of the Trans-Cascades/Great Basin country, including Crane Prairie, Diamond, Davis, Wickiup, Klamath, Eagle, Pyramid, and Tahoe, Tui chub are the baitfish of choice for large trout. Thanks to illegal introductions by bait fisherman and the hardiness of the species, you may encounter Tui chub almost anywhere in Oregon, California, Nevada, Utah, or Idaho. Though they quickly overpopulate many of the lakes soon after their introduction, Tui chub can provide a major food resource for trout on waters with middling populations.

The Tui chub is a cigar-shaped fish that ranges in color from dusky olive or brass on the back, and whitish underbelly. The size of adult fish can be as small as ten centimeters in canals or isolated backwaters, or as large as forty centimeters (over fourteen inches) on large lakes. When collecting some samples, I chased them with a fly rod them along the shoals of Oregon's Davis Lake and caught many in the ten to twelve-inch range.

Tui chub prefer shallow lakes with a healthy population of aquatic vegetation. Their daily behavior largely depends on the water you're fishing. On some lakes, they spend their days in deep open water schools, moving to shoals to feed in the evening. On other lakes, they live entirely in smaller schools among the shallows, cruising weedlines of submerged and emergent vegetation. On lakes with exploding populations of chub, the "schools" more resemble one vast Tui Nation, with a constant flow of chub streaming along the weed edge for as long as you care to watch them.

The spawning of Tui chub in late April-early July can be of significant importance to trout anglers. The chub spawn in shallows, one to two meters deep, most often above aquatic vegetation. They tend to congregate into groups with "large, swirling aggregations, apparently with several males attending each female." This can often be observed from a distance—both by you and the fish. If you time things right, you can both arrive at the school at the same time. The swirls and jumps of these spawning schools appear almost indistinguishable from a school being chased by trout. This is just fine. The results of casting imitations all around the area should also be indistinguishable.

The problems that accompany the Tui chub detract from its value as a baitfish. While some accounts claim they feed mostly on detritus, most chub over fifteen centimeters turn to invertebrates and begin to compete with trout. The large size of adult Tui chub (often up to twenty centimeters or eight inches) means that they are just a tad too big for most trout to consume. So chub then eat up all the midges, mayflies, and damselflies, but can't be eaten themselves. The abundance of Tui chub is usually a bad sign for the future of trout fishing, but that does not mean you should not take advantage of them before night falls on the trout population.

On lakes with good chub populations, avoid "rising trout" in extreme shallows. Unless the rise forms are exceptionally large, odds are those rising fish are that eight to ten-inch chubs. Quite the disappointment after you spent several minutes stalking and casting to them!

Creek Chub (*Semotilus atromaculatus*): This common stream-dwelling chub is present throughout the Eastern states, Great Lakes region, and across southern Canada. It can reach 33cm in length, though trout tend to prey only on smaller (three to ten centimeter) chub. Creek chub have an olive back with silvery/white sides, though there can be iridescent purple and green shades on the flanks, while the juveniles have a silver color to them. Breeding occurs in the spring and early summer at around 12C. The breeding usually takes place in riffles, and breeding males often have orange or rosy marks on their head, body, and back, as well as orange pectoral fins. The habitat of this chub overlaps with that of the brook trout over a good part of its range, so it undoubtedly becomes part of the their diet at times.

THOUGHTS ON IMITATION

The chub is a big critter for the tier to imitate, so the tier must consider both size and bulk. For chub imitations I love rabbit strips—lots of motion, a lot of bulk, easy to work with. My ideal pattern for the Tui chub is a variation of the Double Bunny. Instead of gluing the strips together, I use a crosscut rabbit for the body, and then pull over a standard rabbit strip over the back, Zonker-style.

This pattern works best in an olive back/gold body combination, but don't ignore the possibility of a black back/gold body, olive back/white body, or brown back/olive body. Use soft epoxy for the head and place the eyes on while the head hardens up. A couple more layers of epoxy will lock them in place. If tied well, this pattern will last forever.

The other pattern I like utilizes tandem hooks. Growing up on Oregon's Crane Prairie Reservoir, one of the most popular flies was a monstrous tandem pattern called appropriately the "Crane Prairie Special." I rarely fished with it, but loved the thought of a big fish looking at a five-inch tandem pattern like it is an appetizer. When I got older I started experimenting with other tandems. I have found that simple patterns with roughly the same fly tied on both the front and rear hook performs well. This is particularly the case with chunky baitfish like chub, where tandem patterns make the fly wiggle like a jointed Rapala. The two-fly style makes the tandem pattern easy to tie, and if the fish demand a smaller imitation, you can always cut off one of the patterns and you have a wholly functional "mini" pattern.

The key to good tandem patterns is securing the two hooks together. For the rear hook I like a straight-eyed hook connected to the lead hook with 30lb Spiderwire. Super gluing the knots at both ends of the connection will permanently attach the rear hook.

Chub imitations work best around outside weed edges, especially those that border deep drop offs. Unlike sticklebacks, I like to imitate chub with a single imitation. The chub tend to gather in tight, large schools for protection, so a sole chub wandering unnaturally alone in open water appears to be an easy mark for the trout to take down.

Patterns

Keys to Match
1. **Color**: Proper color can range from olive to gold to yellow.
2. **Weed Edges**: Chub cruise tight to weed lines.
3. **Look for Chub Breaking the Surface**: If they are flying, trout can't be too far behind.

Keys to Avoid
1. **Too Small**: Chub can reach ten inches, so scrap the size 8 imitations.
2. **Too Skinny**: They are streamlined, but not skinny.
3. **Too Rare**: If you fish great basin waters, this is an essential food.

Double Bunny Chub

Hook: Dai Riki 700, #2-4
Tail: Pearl Krystalflash
Under Body: Gold variant crosscut rabbit variant strips
Over Body: Olive Variant Hareline Magnum Rabbit Strips
Cheeks: Root beer Krystalflash
Eyes: 3-D Molded Eyes
Head: Softex

This is my best chub pattern, one that works for a variety of species besides trout. It is also a great night pattern because of the bulk of the crosscut rabbit body. One can add dumbbell eyes for extra weight, though because I like to flirt and dance my baitfish imitations, I omit anything that forces a constant retrieve.

Golddigger

Hook: Dai Riki 700 (front), #6 and (rear), #8 (tandem, attached with 30lb Spiderwire)
Tail: Red Schalappen
Body: Gold mylar tinsel
Under Body: Yellow marabou
Over Body: Black marabou
Cheeks: Gold Flashabou
Eye: Yellow 3-D molded eye

Based on the British pattern, the Goldie, this pattern is a bit easier to cast in the wind than the Double Bunny Chub. The two flies should be tied the same, so if the fish want a smaller imitation, you can simply cut one off and fish it as a single.

Baitfish: Sculpins (*Cottus* spp.)

Intuitively, one would think that sculpins get over on trout. With their downward facing mouths, they should be adept at preying on trout eggs, alevins, and fry. Yet over forty studies over the past twenty years looked at how sculpins dine on various stages the trout life cycle. Most concluded that sculpin predation only affects the odd, improperly-covered egg and rarely impacts the overall trout population. It turns out that sculpins rarely eat trout and they are actually one of the more important baitfish types for trout in both streams and lakes.

In Rocky Mountain and Great Basin streams, anglers properly focus on sculpins more than any other baitfish. Sculpins are habitat snobs, shunning all but clear, fast water with an irregular rocky bottom. If this sounds like trout habitat, it is. These fish perfectly overlap in habitat preferences. Moreover, booming sculpin populations correlate with a healthy crop of insects. It has been said that if you can't catch fish on a new stream, look for sculpins. If you don't find them, go home. If you find them, then keep on fishing…preferably with a sculpin pattern. This is not to say that sculpins are only important in the Mountain West, because sculpins can play a role in the trout diet throughout the United States and Canada.

The Latin name *Cottus* derives from the Greek word for "head," which according to Peter Moyle in the *Inland Fishes of California* is, "a good name for a fish that seems to consist mostly of head." It is common to say that sculpins have big heads, but if you look at them from the side, you might not notice. Sculpins have a low, broad head, and their body thickness actually peaks near their "shoulders"—where the pectoral fins connect to the body—then tapers down to a smaller tail. The broad head is the key for imitation, as it can be twice the size of the rest of the body. This radical head-to-tail taper is perfect for holding along the bottom and is essential for any imitation.

The other significant physical features of sculpins are their large pectoral fins, which from the side appear even more prominent than the head. The activity of these large fins likely serves as a visual key for predatory fish. The dorsal and anal fins, while prominent, lack the movement of the pectoral fins and probably aren't as important to fish.

Sculpins range from 6-12 cm in length and remain well camouflaged in their dark, blotchy mottling. When I was younger I used to corral sculpins into the shallows, trying to grab them. As they darted around, all I could see was their movement and I could only grab them when they were slowly hopping around. Once the sculpins settled next to a rock, they became nearly invisible. Mottled dark brown and dark muddy-olive are the most important colors for the tier to match, though all-black patterns work well right at dusk or cloudy/rainy/snowy conditions.

The mottled coloration of sculpins allows them to blend into their cobbly habitats.

It is important to note that during spawning season male sculpin fins develop a distinct orange edge, which makes them more visible to females and hungry trout. This may be a significant trigger for trout, as spawning males and nest-guarding males are notoriously aggressive, chasing off intruders with a narrow-minded fury that causes them to leave the nest and expose themselves. A significant portion of sculpin patterns intended for spring fishing should incorporate this orange signal flare.

The fly angler must pay close attention to both the depth and action of their sculpin imitations. Sculpins live almost exclusively on rocky bottoms, rarely swimming more than an inch or two above the substrate. One look at their body structure and you can tell that they are not built for extended periods of swimming. The swimming motion of a sculpin resembles a "skipping" action—several quick, short darts, and a rest every two meters or so. In lakes (and some rivers) they kick up sand or substrate as they pause between "skips."

Sculpins spawn between late winter and spring—February through May depending on climate. Sculpins lay eggs in a variety of habitats and attach their eggs to the undersides of cobble-sized rocks; thus, there is no spawning migration or egg drift for trout to feed on. The youngest fry live in the substrate until they absorb their egg sac, which usually takes one to two weeks. It should be noted that young sculpins about a month old undergo a "drift" (moving into swift water and passively letting the current sweep them downstream) most likely to disperse the population throughout the stream. On rivers with a large sculpin population, this movement is important to trout just becoming active in the warming waters of springtime. On the upper Colorado, sculpin fry make up 1% of items in the drift, which is more than enough to get the attention of the fish! This 2-3 week event is a good time to dead drift tiny sculpin imitations (about a #16-18 sparse Muddler Minnow works) through riffles and shallow, swift runs. Sculpin usually remain inactive during the day, moving about the bottom a little more in low light and at night to feed on small insects. Mayflies, stoneflies, and caddis larvae compose the majority of the sculpin diet, though they are occasional predators of trout and salmon eggs and alevins in both streams and lakes. While their diet is similar to that of trout, sculpins pick their foods directly off the bottom while trout mostly feed on drifting insects. Therefore there is no true competition for food; they simply utilize different behavioral guilds of insects.

Important Sculpins

Mottled Sculpin (*Cottus bairdi*): The mottled sculpin is the most common sculpin in trout waters throughout the United States and Canada. It can be large (up to 15cm), and is olivaceous in color with dark mottling (black or dark brown) on its back and sides. The male's head often turns dark during spawning. It is most common in bouldery, swift small creeks and rivers, though it can be found in the shallow rocky margins of lakes. Several other common sculpins look nearly exactly like this sculpin, including the Ozark sculpin (*Cottus hypselurus*) and Paiute sculpin (*Cottus beldingi*).

Prickly Sculpin (*Cottus asper*): This sculpin is native to the Pacific Coast from So-Cal up to the Kenai Peninsula in Alaska. It can be an important food resource for rainbow and cutthroat trout, and they are especially important to Dolly Varden where they are found. They are mottled reddish-brown with a light belly, and their coloration is distinctly reddish compared to other trout-stream sculpins. Most of these sculpins are small, 5-8 cm in length.

Thoughts on Imitation

Many anglers don't like to fish sculpin patterns—or other streamer patterns for that matter—in streams. This lack of confidence in sculpin imitations can often be traced to the retrieve techniques used by most anglers. Most anglers cast out streamer patterns, swing them around downstream, then make long and slow pulls to bring the pattern back upstream. While this may be therapeutic casting practice, it will surely reduce the likelihood of a pesky trout interrupting your peaceful experience on the water. Sculpin patterns must be dredged, tickling the bottom constantly throughout the retrieve. It is a frustrating way to fish, because snags and lost flies are common and generally unavoidable. However, if your fly is not in the strike zone (six inches from the bottom) your catch ratio will fall off precipitously. Before you worry about changing patterns, colors, or sizes, consider first where and how you are fishing your sculpin imitation.

Sculpin motion is more of a sharp skipping motion, rather than a fluid swimming motion typical of chub or shiners. This reduces the burden on the tier (as there is little material-imparted motion to include), but increases the pressure on the angler to fish the flies with short, quick darts. I like to keep my "skips" shorter than eight inches. Try to give long pauses between skips, as this matches the natural's need to rest frequently.

Sculpin patterns should be fished on sinking or sink-tip lines, with short stout leaders. The leader material should be an abrasion-resistant brand and it should be checked frequently if you are consistently making contact with the bottom. The hook point should also be checked for damage every fifteen or twenty minutes. A hook sharpener is essential for the avid sculpin fisher.

Many commercially popular sculpin patterns have large eyes on them. If you look at a natural sculpin, you'll notice that their eyes are dark and difficult to spot. I would consider the eyes a luxury feature at best, and very rarely include them on my own patterns.

I tie almost all my sculpins with some blending of color, be it in the body, "wing," or head, matching the mottled camouflage of the natural sculpin. A good way to see if your pattern looks natural is to take them to the relatively quiet rocky margins of a riffle and drop them in (with line attached of course). If you can spot your imitation on the bottom in two feet of slowly moving water, you need to mix the colors more thoroughly. A blotchy effect can be achieved with paints, dubbing blends, deer hair blends, or barred feathers.

Pectoral fins significantly improve the appearance of a sculpin pattern. The large fins can be imitated with hen feathers or partridge feathers. Treating the feathers with Flexament prior to use makes the feathers more durable and helps them retain their shape after a couple of ferocious strikes.

The construction of the head in a sculpin imitation is an important consideration, and there are three common choices for the head: spun and clipped deer hair, bullet-head deer hair, and spun and clipped wool. I am a big fan of spun wool, because it is less buoyant than deer hair and easier to work with. Spun and clipped deer hair works well, but is more buoyant than wool, causing the pattern to occasionally ride too far above the bottom during the retrieve. Bullet-head style flies look sharp, though the material limits the size of the head, making them only applicable on smaller patterns. The taper of a bullet-head also doesn't match the broad, flat proportions of the natural. A cone head can be a fine addition to the front of any of the previously mention head styles.

The orange edge of the front dorsal fin of the male can easily be imitated with a bright orange paint pen (essential for any tier) or standard model paints. A strip of bright orange material (larvae lace, etc) pointed over the front of a Matuka wing works well. This is a significant key for trout, and should be included on springtime sculpin patterns on both lakes and streams.

If your sculpin patterns snag the bottom so frequently that you never want to fish them, you can heavily weight the body and then tie the pattern upside-down. This should reduce some of the snagging, but it won't solve the problem of the fly getting wedged between rocks.

PATTERNS

KEYS TO MATCH
1. **Large Shoulders and Pectoral Fin:** Improves the broadside silhouette.
2. **Mottling:** If the pattern can be seen on the bottom, it isn't mottled enough.
3. **Fish It Deep and Deep Only:** If it is not snagging bottom, it won't catch many fish.

KEYS TO AVOID
Eyes: They are small and dark and hard to see.
Deer Hair: If it takes more time, more effort, and keeps your fly from being where it should, why use it?
Improper Weighting/Fly Orientation: All your great tying goes into the crapper when the fly swims upside down.

ROLAND SCHWINN SPECIAL

MATUKA MONSTER

KIWI MUDDLER

Hook: Dai Riki 700, #2-8
Tail: Black and brown marabou
Body: Black and brown ostrich herl over dark chenille
Wing: Two dark brown variant rabbit strip
Pectoral fins: Short widgeon flank feathers (optional)
Head: Brown and dark olive wool, spun and clipped

A simple wool-head sculpin imitation, but with a twin wing, which adds quite a bit of motion to the pattern. Think of it like a double curly-tail grub lure. This is one of the first patterns I used for sculpin-feeding trout in Montana and it still produces a few fish each season. I tend to tie this one "slender:" it almost looks like a snake or salamander when stripped through the water

Hook: Dai Riki 700, #2-8
Body: Brown sparkle dubbing ribbed with black and brown ostrich herl
Throat: Red marabou, dubbed or wrapped
Wing: Brown dyed grizzly feathers, matuka style
Ribbing: Fine gold wire
Pectoral Fin: Pheasant back feather, partridge, or dyed grizzly.
Head: Olive (30%), dark brown (30%), light brown (30%), black (10%) dubbed deer hair, large

With their broad profile, matuka-style wings help make for great sculpin patterns. The dubbed deer hair head is both shaggy and mottled, and though it looks ragged, it often lasts longer than all but the most well constructed spun and clipped deer hair head.

Hook: Dai Riki 700, #2-8
Body: Sparkle chenille
Wing: Variant magnum rabbit strip, trimmed to a kite shape
Pectoral fins: Olive-brown partridge or widgeon (optional)
Head: Spun and clipped deer hair

The loose-hanging rabbit strip moves freely underwater, making this a great pattern to "hang" near a rock, enticing large fish to strike. The rabbit strip should be trimmed to a "kite" (oblong diamond) shape, with the wing tied down near the fatter end of the kite.

CHAPTER V: THE PREY

Baitfish: Rainbow Smelt (*Osmerus mordax*)

The rainbow smelt, a native to the northeastern United States and much of Labrador and eastern Canada, is an important source of food for a number of species. Most importantly for fly anglers, brook trout, landlocked salmon, Atlantic salmon and lake trout rely heavily on smelt on some waters. Despite its sagging popularity among modern stillwater anglers, this innocuous little fish has nonetheless inspired many of our famous traditional streamer patterns.

Rainbow smelt inhabit both salt and freshwater, though most freshwater species have a more muted color scheme than their saltwater brethren. Landlocked smelt usually appear dark olive (or very dark blue or black) on their backs and exhibit silvery sides with a purple or pink iridescence. They also may have dark or black heads and fins. Smelt have long, skinny bodies, and though they can grow to over 30cm, trout usually target smelt in the range of 5-15cm.

Smelt tend to school up in large, open water schools—only occasionally will one find them in shallow littoral areas. You can find smelt in shallows at night, when they move into shallow water to feed. Smelt can also migrate to significant depths, often following *Daphnia* migrations in the same manner that *Chaoborus* larvae do. Both their open water lifestyle and migrations make them a difficult fish to imitate with a fly rod, though many anglers do it quite successfully.

Spawning usually takes place early in the year as soon as ice breaks up, sometime when the water temperatures hit between four and eleven degrees Celsius. Most smelt spawn near gravel bars and shorelines, while others mate further offshore. Occasionally smelt endure massive die-offs after spawning, and open water lake trout and landlocked salmon move into shoreline areas and feed heavily on the ailing and terminal smelt. As their populations tend to boom and collapse frequently, some people debate the optimality of smelt as forage fish, though salmon tend to grow significantly larger and heavier in their presence.

Don't think that only Eastern anglers pay attention to smelt. On the Pacific Coast, large coastal cutthroat trout have been known to slaughter smelt in coastal lakes. Seattle's Lake Washington is not only known for its proximity to a futile football program, but also for its abundance of anadromous smelt. These are not rainbow smelt, but rather longfin smelt (*Spirinchus thaleichthys*). However, even on Lake Washington, traditional New England smelt techniques can fool many wary cutthroat.

Thoughts on Imitation

Smelt are thin, flashy baitfish that, like sculpins, require more specific and unique imitations that match their body type. Both natural and synthetic materials work well for smelt imitations. For the silver/white body, a combination of Polar Aire, Angel Hair, Krystal Flash, Flashabou, marabou, and kid goat hair suffice. For the back, various colors of Flashabou or peacock herl or duck flank feather (teal, gadwall, or mallard) are suitable. Tying some flashy patterns and some more subdued patterns, will help to match the specific light and water conditions and the mood of the fish. 3-D Holographic eyes and a red throat will complete the fly. There is no need to take the extra time to add fins because of their diminutive size and unimpressive motion.

Traditionally, smelt patterns are tied on long-shank streamer hooks. While this works well, it can't hurt to have a couple tandem patterns. Tandem flies tend to have a little more disjointed movement than the standards. Connect tandem hooks with a stout, abrasion-resistant braided line—like Spiderwire—and reinforce the knots with superglue.

Patterns

Keys to Match
1. **Slender Profile:** Thin, thin, thin.
2. **Blue:** Finally, you can use all that electric blue Flashabou from your fly shop's clearance bin.
3. **Shallow Water in Spring:** The best time to imitate smelt with fly rod is during the spring spawn.

Keys to Avoid
1. **Bulk:** Imitations should have the proportions of a Crayola crayon.
2. **Too Much Silver:** A live smelt looks different than those in the seafood section.
3. **Setting Hook Too Quickly:** Trout smash these fish to stun them, then circle around to eat them. Be patient.

Clender Smelt

Lake Washington Special

Blue Smelt

Hook: Mustad 79580, #2-6
Body*: Small pearl mylar tubing
Wing: White Polar Aire, Pearl Mini-Flash, and Holographic Pearl Flashabou
Over Wing: Black Krystalsplash
Back: Black permanent marker
Eyes: Silver/black 3-D molded eyes
*Whole body and wing coated with Softex or epoxy when finished

More or less a sunken variation of the East Lake Fry, the Clender Smelt is similar to many saltwater baitfish and Northeastern smelt patterns. A great pattern when fish want a slim baitfish imitation. Fish the Clender Smelt in quick strips, since its allure rests in its darting motion and flash.

Hook: Mustad 79580, #2-6
Body: White paint (Testors paint pen, covered with head cement) or white thread, or pearl tinsel
Ribbing: Silver holographic tinsel
Under Wing: White husky back hair, sparse, blended with white antron fiber
Over Wing: Blue Polaraire
Collar: Gadwall flank feathers
Eyes: Small silver/black 3-D molded eyes (optional)
Head: Softex or epoxy

Since the University of Washington Huskies perform their pitiful brand of football on the shores of Lake Washington, this is the perfect pattern to troll around during another one of their embarrassing losses. The husky hair can be replaced with squirrel hair if you lack access to that particular breed of canine.

Hook: Mustad 79580, #2-6
Body: Silver mylar tinsel
Ribbing: Blue Flashabou
Under Wing: Blue Polarflash
Wing: Blue PolarAire
Over Wing: Widgeon or Gadwall flank
Throat: Red Flashabou, trimmed short

A blue-hued fly helps match the iridescent purple and dark blue shades of most smelt. Blue streamers also work well in mornings and evenings, even on lakes that lack smelt. The same fly works superbly in all-silver or all-gold for a shiner imitation.

Chapter V: The Prey

Baitfish: Shad and Alewives

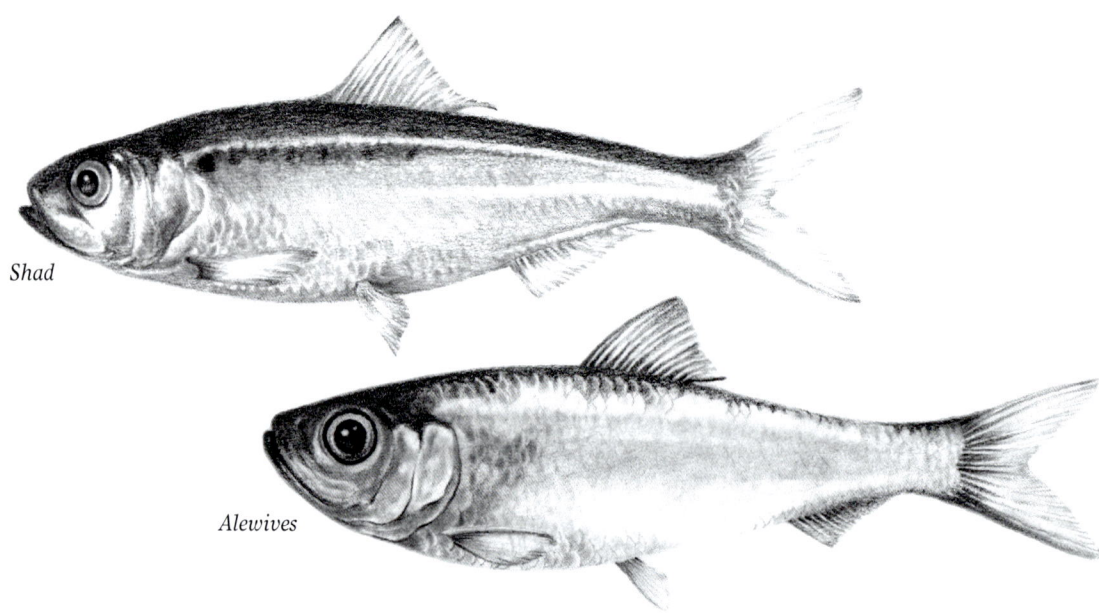

Shad

Alewives

Shad are primarily a food resource for warmwater species like largemouth and smallmouth bass, but on occasion they provide food for trout. In several of the trophy bass lakes of California, shad provide a modest source of food for stocked rainbow trout. However, trout must target lone shad; pursuing the schools can put them fin to fin with 15-pound largemouth bass, which would happily pass up a measly little shad for a tasty rainbow trout!

Shad occur primarily in a handful of trout lakes and reservoirs and can contribute to fast growth and hefty trout. The two shad of significance to trout anglers are the threadfin shad (*Dorosoma petenense*) and gizzard shad (*Dorosoma cepedianum*). Both shad are deep-bodied prey, with the basic outline of a teaspoon. They also share a similar dark blue/black back and silvery white sides, with a pronounced iridescent purple shoulder spot just behind their gills. The shad preferred by most trout and landlocked salmon range from one to three inches in length.

Alewives are an anadromous herring, like shad, and native to the Eastern seaboard. The landlocked form only grows to five inches, and dwell in the Great Lakes, as well as Lake Champlain and the Finger Lakes of New York. They are reportedly quite important to trout in New York and a few other parts of the Northeast.

Alewives are much more specialized *Daphnia* feeders than trout. Where Alewives exist, they dominate the plankton, and larger predatory trout, thankfully, prey on the Alewives. Trout will still follow *Daphnia* movements, but more in order to prey on the Alewives. While trout do feed on Alewives, when other forage fish are available, trout and salmon segregate their diets. Salmon (both landlocked Atlantic salmon and introduced Pacific Chinook and Coho) fed on open water prey like alewives and smelt, while trout fed on near-shore food items (sticklebacks, smelt, killfish, or isopods).

Alewives reach four to five inches in large freshwater lakes like Lake Erie, though I'm not totally sure that Lake Erie is considered "fresh" water. Trout prefer to feed on Alewives between one and two inches long. Only occasionally do trout and landlocked salmon eat larger specimens. Trout prefer the juveniles, not only on account of their size, but that they swim in the same 10-20 foot deep flats and points that trout prefer. Since juveniles are prime targets of trout, they are most important in the summertime when adolescent populations peak. Two summertime samples of landlocked salmon found young-of-the-year alewives in 42% and 75% of the stomachs, respectively.

Alewives have a grayish-green back and silvery sides and share the "teaspoon silhouette" of the shad. These fish also have larger eyes than shad as well as a dark shoulder spot that should be incorporated by any imitations.

Thoughts on Imitation

As deep-bodied baitfish, shad require "fat" patterns usually better suited for bass than trout. Coincidentally, many waters where trout feed heavily on shad, largemouth and smallmouth bass also partake in the feast. Thus shad imitations make an excellent choice to target both species.

Simple silvery-white patterns with dark backs will function as effective shad imitations. Materials with bulk (dense marabou, Polar Aire, kid goat hair) create the best shad bodies. The iridescent dark purple "fake eye" spot is an effective key, though you can fudge it with a simple painted black spot. The faux eye may have taken natural selection centuries to create, but it only takes you and your waterproof pen seconds to replicate. If you cannot apply a spot to the body material, apply it to base of grizzly hackle feather or piece of clear plastic for support material. The eyes can be affixed in a similar manner Some people like to spin white wool for a large, broad head and this can make a good-looking fly.

Trout in shad slaughtering mode are rarely selective. Any close representation will do, as long as you find specific fish that are feeding on shad. On lakes without pike or particularly large bass, look for school of shad breaking the surface, or clumps of small fish on your depth finder. Keep moving until you locate a school with trout nearby, and then pound the water relentlessly until you are confident you have put your fly in front of every trout in the vicinity. On lakes with large predators, utilize shad imitations in shallows; all but the largest trout won't risk becoming a meal themselves in the feeding frenzies surrounding open-water schools of shad. Shallow-water trout may prefer insects, but they certainly won't pass up an opportunity to feast upon a lonely, wayward shad.

As far as alewives go, unless you are from New England, alewives should not top your hit list. Since I am a native Westerner, my experience with alewives is rather limited. However, imitating this open-water fish is almost identical to matching shad. Patterns should maintain a round white/silver profile with a darker gray/olive back. The spot can be imitated with a piece of circular piece of black cellophane glued on, or simply painted on with a plain black permanent marker. For all but the most specialized anglers, shad and alewive patterns are essentially interchangeable.

Pattern

Keys to Match
1. **Bulk:** If a smelt is David Spade, this should be Chris Farley.
2. **Black "Eye" Spot:** One of the defining features of this fish.
3. **Locating Schools:** If the lake lacks big predators, trout will chase the schools.

Keys to Avoid
1. **Too Little Flash:** Few baitfish can match the near luminescence of big shad scales.
2. **Small Eyes:** This fly should look as surprised as a stickleback.
3. **Too Big:** Remember not to make the fly look like those seven-inch long shad crankbaits at the tackle shop.

Umpqua Shad

Hook:	Dai Riki 700, #2-8
Body:	Pearl crystal chenille
Under Wing:	White Polar Aire
Wing:	Silver Flashabou
Over Wing:	Gray Polar Aire
Sides:	Grizzly saddle hackle
Eyes:	3-D molded eyes
Head:	Softex or epoxy
Spot:	Permanent black marker or paint pen

The Umpqua Shad is an tremendously effective pattern for almost every predatory fish that swims. During my Ph.D. research I was "stuck" in central Minnesota during the fall and caught numerous northern pike with this pattern. A bit sleeker than most shad imitations, you can beef up this pattern with the addition of a layer of white marabou in the underwing.

Beetles (Coleoptera)

The Insects

Mid-summer brings many challenges to dry fly anglers across the United States. Hatches start to wane, or at least peak early and late in the day when we are not usually on the water. After getting hooked, caught, and spooked a few times between April and June, trout grow more critical and circumspect of what we lob their way in the late summer. Angling pressure from fly anglers, unfortunately, peaks in July and August, which further educates trout. By mid-August, a trout has advanced far from the freshman days of April.

Many anglers rely on grasshopper imitations to prospect hatchless mid-summer afternoons. However, hoppers, in general, make up a tiny part of the trout diet. Large hoppers (larger than size 8)—the ones that many anglers fish and most shops sell—rarely show up in stomach samples. Even in the legendary "hopper waters" of the northern Rockies, hoppers often make up less than 1-2% of the annual trout diet. Yet, despite this biological reality, anglers continue to bombard the water with hopper imitations when insects of another order are exponentially more important: the beetles.

Why beetles? First of all, in most studies, beetles are three to five times more common in the trout diet than grasshoppers. Secondly, beetle diversity will blow your mind…not to mention a trout's. The 60,000 species in just one beetle family (the weevil family, Curculionidae) alone dwarfs not only the number of mammals (4,500) but also the total number of vertebrates (40,000) in the world. A study on Oregon's marginally productive Lookout Creek found over 850 species of beetles in a one-mile stretch of riparian zone! Finally, anglers rarely imitate beetles, so trout on high-pressure waters feed more confidently on them than on other foods.

Ecologists almost universally consider beetles an important trout food, on par with the more famous aquatic foods. A year-round Vermont study had terrestrial beetles making up 7.26% of the total diet of trout, compared to 5.24% for all stoneflies and 11.82% for all mayflies! Beetles were by far most important terrestrial insect for trout in a study on the North Fork Little Snake River. In another Wyoming study, beetles "only" made up 3.8% of the numbers of items in the annual brook trout diet, but 10% of caloric input. When you consider that, on average, 4-5% of the annual stream trout diet comes from terrestrial beetles, they are a food that should not be mentioned as an aside following laborious tales of specific mayflies that may emerge on a few streams for one week a year.

Beetles undergo a complete metamorphosis, passing through a larva and pupa stage before developing into an adult. Beetle larvae—which look like blown-up maggots or shrunken Twinkies, depending on your point of view—don't matter much to trout, as most spend their time deeply buried in soil or wood. The larvae of aquatic genera (particularly riffle beetle larvae, Elmidae) may show up in bottom samples, but they rarely appear in trout stomach samples. Schwiebert included a whole chapter on the "subaquatic Coleoptera," in *Nymphs*, which was probably overkill. I have yet to meet an angler that successfully imitates beetle larvae regularly; despite my attempts at trying, I haven't either. Beetle pupation often takes place underground, and

Beetles are preferred by trout of all sizes.

Jeff Morgan photo

the adults emerge a few days to weeks later. The adult beetle is the only stage worth the angler's attention.

While we usually consider beetles a late summer trout food, they can be important any time from spring through fall. In a study of an English trout stream, beetles composed about 15% of the drift every month from April through July, but they surprisingly dropped off precipitously after that. Some beetles even are moderately active during the winter months. I would recommend carrying beetle imitations anytime from March through October.

We don't immediately associate beetles with lakes, but lakes can be one of the most important beetle-feeding habitats of all. After finishing a day of fishing on a large, stocked mountain reservoir, I was planning on cooking for several trout for dinner. As I always do when I keep fish, I inspected the stomachs of these fish. To my astonishment, I found almost no aquatic foods and a seemingly endless quantity of beetles. In the end, I pulled out nine different kinds of beetles, ranging in size from size 20 aquatic whirligig beetles to a huge size 8 reddish-brown beetle that I couldn't identify. It took no further prompting to start the next morning with a beetle imitation on my line.

Unlike flying ants, beetles are not designed for sustained flight. Beetles become available to trout when they try to fly across the lake, can't make it, fall to the surface and drown. They then drift to the windward shores of the lakes, where trout feed on dead and dying beetles at their leisure. This is why beetles can make up a big chunk of the summer diet of trout on medium to large stillwaters. Lakes with high winds or lakes with large clear-cuts nearby (clear-cuts = terrestrials!) are choice locales for targeting beetle-feeding stillwater trout. Like with ants, the best beetle lakes have steep shorelines where trout can cruise close to the shore for food without sacrificing the security of deeper water.

Some of you may abhor the following discussion of specific beetles, but the simple biological fact is that trout consume each of these beetle families in greater volumes than *Epeorus*, *Heptagenia*, *Ephoron*, and many other mayfly and caddis genera that angling writers have devoted many pages to over the year. Further research into beetles and trout is inevitable as we continue to learn more about the trout diet.

Important Terrestrial Beetles

Tiger Beetle (Cicindelidae): Tiger beetles become available to

trout thanks to their active, predaceous feeding habits. Their swiftness helps them capture prey and elude predators, though sometimes they run themselves right off leaves and logs into the water. Size can vary greatly from 10-70mm, though their body length usually ranges from 15 to 25mm, or roughly a size 12-16 hook. Long legs and bright colors distinguish tiger beetles from other insects. Their overall body taper resembles a gelatin capsule. Many of these beetles have bright orange, yellow, or white spots on their otherwise metallic green or blue outer wings (or *elytra*).

Ground Beetles: (Carabidae): A diverse family of beetles, ground

beetles are mostly black and have an array of body structures, though most have a reverse-taper body structure. Their legs are not disproportionate to the body (like Tiger Beetles). Since lights attract these beetles, lighted roadside pullouts near trout streams often support good populations of beetles that migrated at night. Two notable beetles from this group are the 10-17mm long, green backed/black bodied green ground beetle (*Chlaenius sericeus*), and the beetles of the genus *Harpus*, which may have black backs, but orangish-brown bellies and legs.

Longhorn Beetles (Cerambycidae): While the larvae of these

5-35mm long beetles bore into wood, the adults feed on bark, leaves, and other external parts of plants. They get their name from their long antennae, which are usually as long as the rest of the body. Their bodies look like elongated cylinders, and they are often brownish-black with lighter spots. The adults fly well but they can get knocked into streams on windy or wet days.

Ladybird Beetle (Coccinellidae): The most commonly recognized

beetle, the Ladybird is popular and welcome even among Coleophobes. Most ladybird beetles are 4-10mm long, with orange or red bodies and black spots. These beetles are most common near gardens and crops infested with their favorite foods: scale insects, mites, and aphids. They occasionally appear in huge aggregations following pest insect outbreaks. I would consider ladybird beetle imitations as important as hopper imitations on many streams in the country.

Metallic Wood-Boring Beetles (Buprestidae): If you see a skinny, hard-looking metallic beetle crawling around the leaves and streams of your favorite trout stream, it is likely one of these wood-boring beetles. Only the larvae bore, so you should find the adults crawling around on flowers, trees, leaves, and dead wood. The adults are most active in the daytime during periods of full sunlight. Their 5-20mm (up to 100mm) long bodies look like thin willow leaves—often appearing like a psychedelic caddis from above. They have a variety of body colors, including metallic blacks, blues, bronze, black-greens, and reds. In my own fishing and sampling, these insects have been the most important kind of beetle for Western trout.

Important Water Beetles

Predaceous Diving Beetle (Dytiscidae): These occasionally massive blackish-brown beetles (5-25mm), thrive in calm, heavily vegetated trout lakes. They are predatory swimmers, constantly probing around shallow margins looking for prey. The hind legs of dytiscids are large enough to imitate, and they kick in unison like that of frogs. With an extremely streamlined body, their body is convex on both sides. These beetles move in short 2-4" movements with each kick. Like backswimmers and waterboatmen, they can fly from water to water, blasting through the surface with a hefty "plop."

Last time I visited the National Museum of Natural History, I watched the diving beetles in a small tank of the insect exhibit for almost an hour. As I scribbled notes into my notepad, I was asked questions every few minutes by visitors who thought I was part of the museum staff! I noticed that these beetles gathered air at the surface, with their rear hanging in the meniscus and their head pointing down at a 45 angle. As they descended, you could see the air trapped under their wings appearing as a thin silvery strip along the sides and rear of the insect. This is the one key I would surely incorporate into imitations.

Whirligig Beetle (Gyrinidae): These 3-13mm long beetles kick around the surface of the shallows margins of stillwaters. They have an oval shape with pronounced forelegs, and appear either black or metallic green. These beetles thrive in the late summer and fall, when new adults emerge. Because the adults almost never dive, imitations must be fished directly in the surface film. They are most heavily preyed on in lakes with steep shores where trout can comfortably cruise the banks.

Water Scavenger Beetles (Hydrophilidae): Big (5-40mm) black beetles common in littoral areas of lakes, these beetles are famously attracted to lights, surprising campers by plopping uninvited onto picnic tables and boat docks. Even though bugs abound in shallow water, I have yet to pump one from a trout. Imitations for the Predaceous Water Beetle will suffice for this beetle.

Predacious diving beetle larva.

The water scavenger beetle retaining its air bubble under its wings.

A predacious diving beetle gathering air at the meniscus.

Riffle Beetles (Elmidae): Thanks to their nomenclature, these aquatic beetles are often the ones most associated with trout. The small, 1-8mm long, black (often with yellow or whitish spots) beetle has the classic elongated beetle shape, along with average-length legs. They are common in "rapid, cool, and highly oxygenated, especially acid, water." Elmids are often found in stomach sample reports, though often in very small numbers. Though the adults are common on many of the small mountain trout streams I fish, I have only caught a handful on a variety of imitations. I would thus advise against investing much time in matching them.

Thoughts on Imitation

Fly shop bins do not reflect the diversity and importance of beetles, making things difficult for the non-fly tier. Most shops carry one or two beetle patterns (often some variation of the Foam Beetle) in size 12-16. As a fly tier, you can exploit this monoculture of imitations by tying both tiny patterns (size 20-24) and excessively large patterns (sizes 4-10), as well as carrying an array of body shapes (narrow, round, etc.) and colors. I carry a full box stocked exclusively with an eclectic selection of beetle imitations, and by the end of the season, that box of 150 beetles is almost empty!

Even among the anglers who fish beetle patterns, most rely on patterns in the size 14-16 range. This is a human choice, not a trout choice. Over the course of your fishing lifetime, you will usually find just as many size 20 beetles as size 14 beetles as size 10 beetles in stomach samples. My very best beetle imitations are at the extreme ends of the entomological spectrum—size 20-24 and size 8-10. These patterns imitate insects that are just as common as the medium-sized beetles, and the trout have never seen an imitation of them.

Of course, tying at these sizes requires creative thinking and problem solving. For tiny beetles, you want to keep things as simple as possible. A tiny foam-backed pattern (a la the Ladybird Beetle) with a sparsely dubbed body and few steps will suffice. Fortunately, tiny patterns don't require much to keep them floating, which expands the tier's options. A small, peacock-bodied beetle like the George Beetle literally takes a minute or two to tie yet floats great and looks just as good.

A jumbo-sized imitation, on the other hand, often needs a lifejacket and half a bottle of Gink to keep it on the surface. A foam underbody and a foam overbody is essential to make these patterns float. A fly like the Coleoptera Colossus requires this kind of therapy to keep the size 8 (or larger) hook afloat. DON'T BE AFRAID OF BIG BEETLES. If you have ever seen a size 8 Foam Beetle you'll realize why nobody would buy one and why they don't appear in fly shops—they're ugly, but effective.

Tiers should also experiment with beetle colors as well. Nearly all beetle patterns in shops or books are either black or peacock. This ignores the tens of thousands of beetle species that have different color schemes. I have found success with black, light brown, dark brown, rusty-brown, dark orange, white with black spots, metallic green, metallic blue, black with yellow back, black with blue back, reddish with black back, and various ladybug color combinations. Sticking only with black is not only unnatural, it also limits your flexibility to offer the fish a counter-culture imitation.

Because of the tendency for beetles to aggregate, selective feeding on beetles can take place and anglers should pack a variety of imitations. On one trout stream, I was faced with a pod of trout intent on feeding exclusively on blue-metallic, skinny wood-borer beetles, ignoring the PMD duns and other "normal" trout foods that were drifting by. Having nothing to match it exactly, I figured regular beetle patterns would work. The only problem was that they didn't. Trout selective to beetles, who'd have thunk it? I ended up cutting the peacock sword off some Alexandra wet flies, then sheathing a stripped-bare size 14 hook with it, securing both ends with some 4X tippet material and a couple half-hitches. While it certainly wouldn't be worthy of a Jim Schollmeyer photo op, it fooled the trout in question on the first pass. Matching the approximate color and shape of the natural worked wonders that day.

Only your imagination will limit beetle tying materials. Even working with the core materials—foam, peacock herl, sparkle

Small streams with mixed canopies make for a prime beetle environment.

dubbing, hackle, and black deer hair—the tier has dozens of options. Adding to this base list, you can add rubber legs, ostrich herl, paints, Krystal Flash, Flashabou, CDC, and even coffee beans (a coffee bean floats and looks almost exactly like a beetle). Because there is no "right" pattern formula, beetles can be some of the most enjoyable flies to tie. Some of the strangest and "ugliest" patterns turn out to be the best!

Of all the flies listed below the one most glaringly "gimmicky" is the ladybug, but this is also the one pattern that is most essential. Ladybug beetles can appear in thick densities in areas of high aphid population, especially clear cuts, gardens, and some farming operations. Here, trout will ignore black beetle imitations of the proper size but freely rise to ladybug imitations. Even on places like Slough Creek, miles from any of those environmental alterations, I have had trout that rejected several beetle imitations, only to succumb to the ladybug. If ever restricted to three beetle patterns, the ladybug would undoubtedly make the cut.

Many anglers complain that they cannot see their beetle patterns on the water. The common solution for this is to add a tuft of orange yarn to the back of the fly. Unfortunately, especially if the tuft is too long, the fish can see it as well. As the fly approaches the viewing window of the trout, this orange mohawk is obviously visible to the fish, just like the wing on a parachute pattern. Instead of this red flag, simply put a dab of orange or chartreuse paint or fingernail polish on the back of the fly. It makes the fly just as visible, and you can add it to your patterns at any time that you have trouble spotting it.

Patterns

What to Avoid
1. **Orange Mohawk:** Your fly shouldn't look like a member of the Sex Pistols.
2. **Beetle Larvae:** They might live in the stream, but like a tomato on my salad, they are discretely passed over.
3. **Beetle Apathy:** Pump a few August stomachs and you'll change your tune.

What to Match
1. **Variety:** There are many beetles, so don't get to addicted to one pattern.
2. **Variety:** Color, shape, size, profile, everything.
3. **Variety:** If you don't have more than four beetle patterns in your box, hit your vise and give me 20.

Diving Beetle

- *Hook:* Dai Riki 300, #10
- *Air Bubble:* clear glass bead
- *Body:* Black soft open cell foam trimmed to cockroach shape
- *Sides:* Silver flash material (Flashabou or mylar material)
- *Head:* Black sparkle dubbing, small or small black bead
- *Legs:* Black dyed pheasant tail

Coleoptera Colossus

- *Hook:* Dai Riki 270, #6-12
- *Body:* Black Flashabou over black dubbing
- *Ribbing:* Black ostrich herl
- *Back:* Black foam, painted with glossy black paint
- *Thorax:* Black foam, painted yellow (optional)
- *Legs:* Black knotted rubber material
- *Head:* Black foam, painted glossy black (optional)

John

- *Hook:* Dai Riki 305, #10-18
- *Body:* Golden Arizona Synthetic Peacock dubbing
- *Back:* Brown craft foam
- *Legs:* Grizzly Spirit River sparkle legs, or brown Flexi-floss legs

Paul

- *Hook:* Dai Riki 300, #10-18
- *Body:* Peacock Ice Dub
- *Hackle:* Black hackle trimmed flat on the bottom
- *Back:* Black foam
- *Spot:* Orange puff paint (optional)

The classic beetle pattern, this works everywhere for all types of trout. On Henry's Fork, a Cascade lake, the River Test, or a stocked lowland reservoir, this fly has caught as many trout for me as any dry fly in my repertoire. The orange spot can help the angler locate the fly in rough water, though because the fly is so big, bulky, and dark it can often be seen without the spot.

Ringo

- *Hook:* Dai Riki 300, #10-14
- *Body:* Dubbed deer hair, brown (20%) and black (80%)
- *Shell:* Brown Body Stretch
- *Head:* Peacock Ice Dub

Ladybird Beetle

- *Hook:* Dai Riki 310, #18-22
- *Body:* Black Haretron dubbing
- *Back:* Red closed cell foam (orange is optional)
- *Legs:* 3 black deer hairs or 3 pieces of Black Krystalflash, tied across and cut short
- *Head:* One or two turns of Black Haretron dubbing
- *Spots:* Black ultra-fine point permanent marker

Pistol Pete

- *Hook:* Dai Riki 300, #12-18
- *Under Body:* Black foam (thin) Over
- *Body:* Metallic blue Flashabou
- *Shellback:* Metallic green Flashabou
- *Legs (optional):* Dark moose

Black Flies (Simuliidae)

The Insect

If Rimbaud or Dylan were fly anglers (and Dylan may be), they surely would have written about black flies, aquatic worms, *Daphnia*, crayfish, alder flies, crane flies, water boatmen, aquatic snails, and the other "grotesque" elements of the trout's diet. These foods teeter on the marginal fringes of angler awareness—outcasts in spite of their standing with fish—for they don't fit into the aesthetic of the angling world, where primacy is begotten to the pretty bugs who sacrificially drift along on smooth currents.

The black fly, or simuliid, is the least known and understood major trout food in North America. D.M. Davies' classic essay "Predators upon Black Flies" cites 71 different studies before 1981 that discuss salmonid predation on black flies. I located nearly twenty other studies where black flies were, at least for a month or two, by far the most important food resource for trout, not to mention dozens more where black flies "only" were more important than every single mayfly species except *Baetis*! In a study by J. David Allan, one of the premier stream ecologists in the country, trout consistently consumed black fly larvae at a much higher rate than their proportion in the drift. While simuliids composed about 10% of the drift, they made up nearly 70% of the trout diets in June and July! If that isn't enough, consider that on the same stream, *Baetis* made up 70% of the drift and yet contributed a mere 20% of the total trout diet, while other common drifters, *Ameletus* (Slate Winged Duns) and *Ephemerella* (PMD) mayflies, went nearly unscathed. What about the importance of black flies in "real" trout streams? Take the McCloud River, for example; simuliid larvae were *the most consumed* summertime prey among large, two-plus year old rainbow trout. Surely, the angling community has long ignored the importance of these insects.

Roger Crosskey's definitive work on the subject, *The Natural History of Blackflies*, leaves little doubt to the relationship between black flies and trout:

"The most important fish predators are the species of Salmonidae with very high commercial and sporting value in Europe and North America, the trout (*Salmo trutta*), the rainbow trout (*Oncorhyncus mykiss*) and the Atlantic Salmon (*Salmo salar*)…all three consume prodigious quantities of immature black flies (the *reed smut* of the fly fisherman), and trout especially also consume many adults. The gut of even a small trout can be packed with hundreds of larvae and pupae."

With a staggering wealth of scientific observation plainly accessible to angling researchers, how could simuliids have been overlooked by experts and recreational anglers alike for so long?

A combination of at least five factors contributes to angler devaluation of black flies.

1. Most anglers probably confuse collected larvae as caddis larvae, particularly "microcaddis" (Hydroptilidae), which look similar to the untrained eye.
2. Simuliids are also part of the order Diptera. Thus, many well-intentioned writers and researchers who take the time to consult professional papers and science books, often see "Diptera" in stomach samples and connect it exclusively with "midges." In the process, they forget that the order Diptera casts a wide shadow: encompassing chironomids, mosquitoes, phantom midges, net-winged midges, crane flies, and of course, our new friend—the simuliid.
3. "Kicking riffles," the preferred sampling technique of most anglers, doesn't knock many of these larvae off the rocks, since simuliids have anchor systems that help them cling to rocks in even the fastest currents.
4. More important than the previous factors, anglers encounter few trout rising to a black fly emergence. This factor should not be underestimated. A quick glance at any pre-1980 fly angling treatise shows the clear bias towards surface "hatches."
5. Finally, black fly activity does not create a concentrated "hatch" like most aquatic insects. Simuliids may endure from four to ten generations each year, with larval growth, emergence, and egg-laying activity all overlapping between generations. This means black flies maintain a modest, but constant, role in the year-round diets of most river-dwelling trout.

These five factors go a long way to explain why anglers have long overlooked simuliids, while trout happily overindulge such an abundant prey.

Black fly larvae are medium-sized insects, reaching 4-15mm in length. The grubs have feathery fan gills and prolegs at the head, and a pronounced anal portion. That Badonkadunk is significant—the rear 1/3 of the simuliid larvae can be almost twice the thickness of the head. Simuliid color can range from smoky gray, dirty yellow, and creamish to black. I have often mistaken the small black larvae for microcaddis larvae, which also have a notably fat butt. The larvae attach themselves to rocks with the hooks on their posterior disc. With their butt firmly planted on the rock, they allow their heads and fans to trail downstream filtering the current for food. To move short distances, black fly larvae excrete a strand of silk and "rappel" downstream, much in the same manner some caddis larvae migrate.

We often associate black flies with stagnant waters, and while some black flies like slower water, they are far more common in swift streams. I have found them in Grayling Creek in Montana, a swift infertile stream, at densities of over 200 on a single softball-sized rock. The stream ecologist Robert Pennak notes their preference for fast-water, where "they may be so abundant that the substrate is obscured." Other scientists verify black fly preference for swift waters, as it provides a higher delivery rate of food particles. I have always had the most success imitating black fly larvae below riffles.

The most important part of the simuliid life cycle is the larvae, especially for trout living in streams with abundant fast riffles. Some fish will graze them off rocks, though this is more a technique of smaller trout and whitefish and almost impossible to imitate with a fly rod. Besides cobbly riffle water, simuliids abound on bedrock slabs, as their silken pad and anal hooks give them excellent holding power against the driving current. Trout also feed on Simuliid larvae at an unusually high rate at night. Some attribute this feeding to the fact that the semi-translucent larvae are easy to detect under the moonlit sky.

After three to ten weeks of larval development, Simuliids pupate for a period of anywhere between two and eight days.

Black flies thrive in nutrient-rich, swift streams.

Barry & Cathy Beck photo

Larvae do not migrate prior to pupation, unlike many other aquatic insects. They usually build their cocoon wherever they happen to be when their biological clock goes off.

Black flies have a unique method of emergence, with important ramifications for the fly angler. Unlike most insects, when black flies burst out of their pupal casing a bubble of air shoots a mature adult directly to the surface. This differs from caddis emergence behavior in two major ways. First, black flies create a far more pronounced shimmering "air bubble" effect than caddis. Secondly, a caddis rides to the surface as a pupa, while the black fly rides to the surface as a fully developed adult. If you take a stomach sample that reveals adult black flies, it is virtually impossible to tell where the trout captured the black fly as a rising adult, a floating adult, or a drowned ovipositing female. Black flies emerge in the morning, from 6:00am and noon; rarely at night or in the evening. This emergence accounts for heavy feeding action throughout the water column, even when no surface action is visible. By the way, black flies offer no visual hint of emergence (i.e. rising trout), since black flies arrive at the surface and fly virtually instantly thanks to the air bubble that kept their body and wings dry. The lack of surface activity to alert anglers to what is going down below the surface is undoubtedly one reason why this insect has been overlooked by so many for so long.

One important exception to the "instant takeoff" emergence is *S. arcticum,* a species common in the northern half of North America. On the Athabasca River in Alberta, the emerging adults were found to drift great distances before emerging: up to 50 flies in one square meter of water. In conditions like this, standard dry fly presentations would perform superbly.

Most anglers are familiar with the adult black fly. Simuliids have (surprise!) black bodies, clear to smoky wings, short dark legs, and (occasionally) red eyes. They can range in size from five to twelve millimeters in length. The adult male black fly, while having a primarily black body, also has subtle silvery marks on the abdomen and front legs, while other legs can have yellow or white markings. However, I have never found many fish selective to black fly imitations. If a fish ignored one pattern, it would not take a different black fly pattern. Despite that, I still carry a range of black fly imitations in sizes 12-18 to cover local variability in black fly size.

The adult black fly is no stranger to the angler or anyone else who spends much time near the water. Adults lounge on riparian plants, and gusty winds can knock them into the water. On waters, with a large number of wading anglers slapping and killing a few dozen flies per hour, it is not unreasonable to expect fish to encounter a disproportionate amount of drifting adults. I have found that an adult black fly pattern can work as superb searching dry flies, especially on heavily fished waters, where fish are more circumspect about the standard line of terrestrial patterns.

Adult female black flies must return to fast riffle water in order to lay eggs. Ovipositing usually occurs at sunset, or within an hour or two of sunset, and all species lay eggs best when the air is still. These females will either lay eggs on rocks or vegetation just above the water line, or deposit them directly on the water's surface like a stonefly. Some species are substrate-specific

A black fly larvae with its fans extended to filter out diatoms.

and will lay eggs on lighter substrates when possible, possibly because the larvae will be better camouflaged amongst the lighter rocks. Female black flies can swarm and concentrate egg laying in a relatively small section of stream. One study found a 10m section of small stream with 3 million eggs, the result of about 3750 females laying eggs synchronously! It is safe to assume that more than a few trout had a hearty dinner that night! While no real black fly "spinner fall" exists—as they don't die within minutes of laying eggs—some females invariably get stuck in the surface film and trout consume them.

After all this on black flies, would I say they are the most critical food source for trout? Probably not, but I would postulate without doubt that simuliids *as a family* are more important than nearly any particular *specie* of insects that we often fuss over. Simuliids are significantly more important to trout, in terms of annual consumption, than salmonflies, hoppers, and even the much-lauded pale morning dun. Salmonflies, even where they are extremely abundant (Deschutes, Madison, and a handful of other waters), compose only about 4% of the annual diet of trout, whereas simuliids rarely contribute less than 6% and often

Clamped to rocks with only anal hooks, black fly larvae often end up in the drift.

more than 10%. It would be safe to say that simuliids, on average throughout the United States, contribute more to a stream trout's diet than any single genera of insect, except *Baetis*. When you consider that large simuliids exist in a stream for the entire year, while most mayflies and caddis remain too small to feed respectable trout for half the year, this leap of faith towards simuliids may not seem so ridiculous.

Thoughts on Imitation

A simple black grub with silver wire ribbing has been the best larvae imitation I have found. No legs, no tails, no hackle—nothing fancy, just a grub. Fortunately, Simuliidae larvae live in swift water and nobody imitates them, a combination that allows for a low-brow imitation. Most of the time, a simple grub-style pattern with a black, smoky-gray, or dirty yellow dubbed body and brown dubbed head will suffice.

On larger Simuliid larvae imitations, I like to imitate the gills with a small tuft of black or gray CDC. Is this necessary? I'm not sure, but it takes only a few seconds longer per fly and it gives me more confidence when fishing them. I also like to include the bulge on the rear 1/3 of the larva's abdomen. Again, it probably makes no difference, but it does not take any more time, effort, or money to imitate a black fly larvae properly. Anglers who are not familiar with simuliids will think your fat assed flies look like chironomids tied by a blind man. Take their jeers in stride and stick to these flies and soon your buddies will be asking to borrow a few of those ugly flies.

As far as "pupae" go, I have tried to imitate them for a few summers with absolutely no notable success. Besides the stray fish that probably would have smashed a Chernobyl Hopper if I had the gall to drift one over its head, none seem to touch dozen different pupae styles I had tried. It was only during my research for this book that I learned that the pupae were not really available at all, since the adults rode to the surface totally enclosed in a bubble of air.

To match the flashy rising Simuliid adult, I prefer flashy materials. Not the subtle "flash" of a caddis pupae pattern, I am talking flash sufficient to sear the eye looking directly at it.

You are shooting for the basic representation of a black body surrounded by a silvery halo. That is where the CDC bubble comes into play. It provides a silvery/clear halo while still keeping the internal black color of the actual body. When tied properly, this fly will retain the air bubble throughout the cast and retrieve, though the fly should be dried or treated with desiccant after a few casts. If this sounds laborious, a simple oblong shiny black bead with red eyes painted on can suffice. Whatever you tie, make sure it is flashy or else you might as well fish a Zug Bug.

The rising adults shoot towards the surface, often drifting less than two or three meters before making it to the surface. This means fish must react quickly to them. While I often fish pupae imitations on a dead drift, I prefer a tight-line technique with a series of one to two foot lifts of the rod to imitate this swift upward motion towards the surface. At other times, I use a downstream presentation with a strike indicator, raising the rod tip intermittently to get the adult to shoot up towards the surface. While the "rise" imparted by the rod tip can be done from any direction, downstream more is desirable, more natural, and more effective. By doing it this way, the fly stays in the same current lane and doesn't accelerate when it rises, which it would do if you were making an upstream presentation.

For black fly adults, many would say, "use a Black Humpy." I do not have any problem with the Black Humpy when searching new water, but if you are targeting black flies specifically, why use that if you could make a more realistic, easier, and faster-to-tie imitation? I like the CDC Sleepy John Estes pattern, which floats well, looks buggy, and nobody else uses it. The combination of the dubbed CDC thorax and CDC wing makes for a fine, "buzzy" surface imprint. One look at the fly from underneath and you—and the trout—will be sold.

I have done best with adult black fly imitations where riffle water starts to slow at the head of a shallow run. I think this is because ovipositing females and rising imagoes are present in the riffle area and the current washes them down to trout. One should also try to use these imitations in bank water, as some females crawl to the waterline and lay eggs on logs, rocks, and vegetation.

Patterns

What to Match

Simple Structure: If no one else imitates them, the fish are more forgiving.

Flashy Rising Adults: Simuliids make rising caddis pupae look like an accountant meeting.

Fish All Stages In Swift Waters: Don't fall into the black flies=stagnant waters mentality.

What to Avoid

Ignorance: Just because you don't know about them, doesn't mean the trout don't either!

Pupae: They emerge as adults, so swinging pupa will work as well as swinging a Royal Coachman.

Poor Sampling: Better sampling techniques will show you just how common these insects are.

Mini Black Fly Larvae

Hook: Dai Riki 135, #18-22
Body: Black sparkle dubbing
Ribbing: Gold or silver fine wire

This is a fine small imitation that works for small black fly larvae as well as some microcaddis. It seems to work regardless of the populations of either insect, most likely because it is small and few people fish small nymphs. I almost always use this as a dropper off another imitation of a fast water insect (*Rithrogena* mayfly, *Rhyacophila* caddis, *Calineuria* stonefly, etc).

Clear Simuliid Larvae

Hook: Dai Riki 135, #12-20
Body: Cream, white, or dirty yellow rabbit/antron dubbing
Ribbing: Clear Larva Lace
Head: Dark brown sparkle dubbing
Fan: White CDC (optional)

This is an amalgamation of a few standard patterns from the east coast, where some anglers (especially on the Jackson River in Virginia) are much more in tune with the bug than we are out West. It was the first Simuliid pattern I had success with, so it holds a special place in my box, though it tends to be a little bulkier than the naturals and seems to get a few less strikes than the bead head pattern.

BH Simuliid (The Insipid Simuliid)

Hook: Dai Riki 135, #12-16
Dubbing: Cream, white, or dirty yellow rabbit/antron dubbing
Ribbing: Fine silver oval tinsel
Head: Small black bead (ideally one size smaller than normal)
Fan: White CDC

The bead head helps this fly stay deep, vital considering the fast-water habitats where the imitations are fished. I've landed fish throughout the United States on this pattern, and it excels in tailwaters and medium-sized montane rivers.

Rising Black Fly Adult

Hook: Dai Riki 305 or 310, #12-16
Under Body: 7 wraps of lead wire (.010)
Body: Black rabbit blended with peacock Ice Dub or black CDC bubble
Wing: Tan lacquered raffia or opalescent sheet (optional)
Hackle: Black CDC
Head: Peacock Ice Dub

Trout that take rising black flies do so in fast water, plus they have no time to inspect the bug as it rockets to the surface, lest they miss the opportunity altogether. This critter is tied soft-hackle style, but should be fished in a Czech-nymph manner in riffle and pocket water. If tied unweighted, the Rising Black fly can double as a general terrestrial attractor.

CDC Sleepy John Estes

Hook: Dai Riki 300, #12-16
Body: Black sparkle dubbing over black foam
Ribbing: Fine silver wire
Wings: Gray CDC
Hackle: Two wraps black CDC
Head: Black deer hair, dubbed

This pattern is growing into one of my favorite calm-water searching patterns. It is surprisingly visible thanks to the gray-on-black wing construction. It also is an excellent floater in slow or fast water. It would logically be a good pattern for wary fish on spring creeks: it is buggy, yet imitates a common food that isn't imitated by everyone and their mother and their cousin Ernie.

Centipedes (Chilopoda) and Millipedes (Diplopoda)

The Insect

For some reason, these critters showed up in amazing abundance in trout stomach samples back in the 1920's and 1930's, though few recent studies have documented them in such numbers. They were especially common in stream samples done in New York State by Paul Needham and Wilbert Clemens. I have occasionally found centipedes and millipedes in stomach samples, but with such irregularity that most imitations would be for novelty purposes only.

These critters likely end up in the water via the same rainy conditions that introduce other ground-bound terrestrials to the water, when rising water sweeps them up from their hiding places under rocks and logs. Of course under these conditions, the current sweeps up other foods, including crane fly larvae, eggs, cased caddis larvae, and aquatic worms. A centipede imitation should not be your first choice, but can work under post-storm conditions.

The centipede is mostly legs.

Thoughts on Imitation

Since the first thing that trout look for after a storm is not a centipede, a centipede imitation should be an easy, fun pattern to close out a tying session with. Since the naturals have a shiny exoskeleton, use a brown sparkle dubbing with a plastic shellback and clear ribbing. For legs, nothing beats a dense, palmered, and undersized brown hackle, trimmed on the bottom. A small head of dark brown dubbing should round out this pattern.

The few times I have played around with this pattern following storms, most trout held tight to slow, flooded riparian zones. Often, trout will hold directly in the flooded "angler trails" that parallel many streams. This slower water makes the trout's breathing easier (due to reduced volumes of sediment) and it offers much in the way of drowned terrestrial food sources. Under these conditions, it helps to give this fly several wraps of lead wire under the body so that the fly can be "high-stick nymphed" through the channels. A heavy fly acts like a plumb weight below the rod tip, which allows better strike detection and fly control.

I am not naïve enough to think that trout may mistake centipede patterns for more common crane fly larvae following storms. But regardless, never underestimate the power of a big, random fly to catch fish. Those same trout that will hit a Panther Martin spinner usually will smack a fat, large fly.

Pattern

Keys to Match
1. **Legs:** Lots of them.
2. **Shine:** These insects have a strong exoskeleton so make the imitation sparkle.
3. **Weight:** This fly needs to sink fast in high-water conditions.

Keys to Avoid
1. **Nice Weather:** On bluebird days, these patterns should stay in your box.
2. **Too Big:** This shouldn't look like something on display at the Smithsonian.
3. **Too Elaborate:** High-water trout don't count legs.

Sonoran Hope

Hook: Dai Riki 270, #10-12
Under Body: 15 wraps .015 lead wire
Body: Tan/brown sparkle dubbing
Legs: Undersized brown hackle
Shellback: Clear or brown Body Stretch
Ribbing: Clear 4X monofilament
Head: Dark brown sparkle dubbing

Chironomids

The Insect

The universal importance of chironomids to trout is rooted in their cosmopolitan choice of habitats. Chironomids live everywhere throughout the world and they emerge nearly every day that ice does not cover the surface. In many British and American stillwaters, chironomids provide the greatest quantity of trout food over the course of the season. Thanks to authors and speakers like Brian Chan, Randall Kaufmann, and Phil Rowley, the fly fishing community is discovering that mastering chironomids is a cornerstone of effective stillwater fly fishing in any environment.

While angling texts popularized the stillwater chironomid among the fly fishing community, the importance of stream-dwelling chironomids continues to languish under the collective angling radar. Stream midges provide some of the most infuriating angling challenges due to their small size and sporadic emergences. Since most scientific studies lump all Diptera (including the more important black fly and less important crane fly) together, it is difficult to ascertain the specific importance of chironomids to trout. However, we may safely assume that chironomids make up at least 5% of the annual trout diet in streams, even more on silty or weedy streams.

Chironomids undergo a complete metamorphosis, passing through an egg, larvae, pupae, and adult stage. Chironomids usually endure a one-year life cycle, though some species have two broods a year (spring and early fall), while some cold-water species may go two to three years before emergence. Multi-voltine species tend to be smaller in size (size 20-24), while those that emerge every other year grow much larger (size 10).

An insect's common name has never done as much to influence angler perception as the name "midge." Even experienced anglers associate midges only with size—usually, size 16 and smaller. This is with good reason; trout waters support hordes of tiny chironomids. However, in the Pacific Northwest, British Columbia, Quebec, Alaska, and northern Europe, midge larvae and pupae often grow larger than 30mm (size 10, 3XL) in lakes and reservoirs. This eclectic size variation alone calls for a variety of imitations, because the necessary anatomical detail of a 30mm chironomid far exceeds that of a 3mm chironomid. Compound this size range with the Crayola Box-like color spectrum of chironomids—from the common browns, blacks, olives, and reds, to the more obscure ambers, clarets, rusty browns, not to mention the transparent hue of the closely related *Chaoborus* larvae—and the chironomid angler faces a range of imitation unmatched by any other insect. The color of midges can even vary in a single lake, depending on the substrate type of particular bays! For this reason, serious stillwater trout, panfish, and bass anglers need to be prepared with a wide variety of chironomid imitations.

While chironomid variability can be overwhelming, practical imitation is more important that taxonomical imitation. On swift rivers and alpine lakes the Chrionomid diversity is often poor and fish accept rough approximations, since hunger tends to override concern for anatomical perfection. Large shallow lakes may sustain a diverse array of chironomids, but various species segregate themselves among different substrates (mud, sand, rock, wood, weeds, etc) and sections of the lake (depending on amount of wind, etc). Patterns that are effective certain kind of substrate often will work on similar substrate types throughout a lake.

Chironomid larvae have a thin, wormy appearance with no significant appendages. The only anatomical feature of

An adult midge is a frail creature...far more svelte than most imitations.

even minor interest to the angler is the small (occasionally) darker head. This is rarely critical, and tiers face the miniscule challenge of imitating a small, limp stick.

Chironomid larvae appeal little to born trout and anglers. Most live in tube-like subterranean caves, while others crawl and squirm under leaves or other pieces of large debris. In these habitats, trout rarely encounter midge larvae. Midge larvae don't migrate in open water, because they cannot really swim worth a damn. They propel themselves—if you pardon the expression "propel"—by thrashing their bodies in no particular direction. The few larvae foolish enough to attempt a foray into open water find themselves targeted and easily overtaken by young trout, baitfish, and damselfly nymphs.

The importance of chironomid larvae usually increases when some outside factor disturbs the substrate, dislodging the larvae. In stillwaters, this occurs most often during and after storms, when heavy wave action churns up the bottom, evicting midge larvae by the millions. These squirming larvae have no direction home and trout simply pick them off like candy. The phenomenon attracts fingerlings and forage fish, which in turn attract hungry large fish that have not the slightest interest in the midge larvae. These ecological relationships make fishing windward banks during stormy weather one of the most successful fly fishing strategies.

In rivers and creeks, midge larvae are most important when one fishes downsteam of other anglers who kick up larvae—in addition to crane fly larvae, sow bugs, and other substrate-dwelling critters—while wading. The term "San Juan Shuffle," used to describe this manmade ecological disaster, was named after anglers on the San Juan River in New Mexico. On this extraordinarily rich and heavily fished tailwater, one angler kicks up the bottom twenty yards ahead of a trout, causing a mini-feeding frenzy downstream. At the

Even on large, rough rivers midges can be an important food resource for trout.

Midge larvae look like nothing more than thin sticks with a darker head.

same time, another angler tosses a small midge larvae (or scud) imitation in the hazy cloud, hoping that a trout mistakes the fraud for one of hundreds of naturals drifting by.

On the rare occasion that trout do feed on chironomid larvae in lakes or rivers, they tend to feed on smaller chironomid larvae. This may be because as chironomids grow larger, they construct deeper and stronger burrows and are less susceptible to disruption.

While chironomid larvae contribute little to the trout diet, phantom midge larvae—a close relative of the chironomid—can be extremely important. The clear or opaque *Chaoborus* larvae look similar to chironomids, save the fact they are predatory and hunt throughout the water column. The importance of the larvae and pupae of this Dipteran exceeds that of chironomids on many waters. They will be discussed at length later in this book.

The most important chironomid stage in both rivers and stillwaters is the pupae. Sure, a couple trout will dredge a few larvae out of the mucky bottom, but most larvae remain well hidden in detritus or in their tunnels during daylight hours. The adults can be seen skimming the surface on calm mornings, but why would any sane trout try to chase down those tiny track stars? The vast majority of stillwater trout (and panfish) consume ten times more pupae than larvae and adults combined.

As we mentioned before, chironomids emerge throughout the season. In lakes, the majority of chironomids tend to pupate and emerge early in the season, often within a few weeks of ice-out. Some species will emerge before all the ice has cleared, crawling and migrating to the exposed edge where they can emerge. Trout, under these conditions, will cruise along an ice edge, feeding like Pac-Men on the concentrated trail of chironomids. I have pursued fish feeding in this manner several times. Fooling these trout is easy. Retrieving and releasing them over a thirty foot wide sheet of ice is not!

In addition to mere availability, the importance of chironomid pupae is also rooted in their conspicuous appearance. Chironomid pupae rise to the surface with the aid of gasses trapped between their pupal skin and the skin of the adult insect. There is no swimming motion to imitate with materials or techniques—just the slow, steady rise that one would expect from an insect filled with CO_2. These gases give pupae a flashy, silvery glint that the tier should strive to imitate.

That chironomids accelerate as they ascend should not surprise the angler. Near the bottom, where water pressure compresses these gasses, the pupae ascend slowly. But, as the insect nears the surface, water pressure decreases and the trapped gasses expand, increasing the buoyancy of the pupae and increasing the rate of ascension.

Aside from the silvery flash of trapped gasses, many chironomid pupae have a natural "hot spot." As they near the surface, the pupae start to pump blood (*haemolymph*) into the wings and thorax of the unborn adult, and this accounts for the swift emergence of the adult. As the pupa pumps haemolymph, a distinct orange/yellow coloration develops at the rear of the thorax. I have pumped the esophagi of trout loaded with chironomids where all of the consumed pupae exhibited the orange-hued wing pads. While this can be a strong visual key for feeding trout, it should be noted that the orange color is not present on all pupae all the time, but only as they approach the surface to emerge.

As they near the surface, chironomid pupae take on one of two body positions: slightly curved and fully erect. Pupae routinely rise with a slight curve to their body, wiggle to loosen their skin just below the surface, and then horizontally straighten out one to three inches below the surface. Occasionally pupae will ascend straight as soldiers, but this is the exception. Carrying imitations of both body positions can prove surprisingly effective, especially in lakes where trout have a long time to inspect and select their targets.

Small chironomids (size 14 and smaller) may enmesh themselves in or below the meniscus when trying to emerge, especially in calm water. Trout consuming trapped pupae at the surface account for 90% of observed surface feeding on midges. Smaller midges often can only emerge effectively when wind disturbs the surface film, while larger midges have enough mass to push through the surface film and emerge regardless of the water conditions. This is why size 8-12 pupae imitations sometimes slaughter trout on a particular water, while smaller imitations fail.

Adult midges, unlike mayflies and like caddis, remain on the water's surface for an extremely brief interval. Usually, midges emerge and take to the air within five to ten seconds of reaching the surface. This emergence time can be significantly increased in cold and wet weather. These are the rare occasions to break out adult midge imitations! Normally, adult midge activity is a poor gamble for the angler. Midge adults waste no time on the surface. Most of the time we see them near the surface, they are flying just above the water, leaving a tiny "v" wake behind them as they buzz along. It is rare to find a midge adult loitering on the surface. This industrious behavior is the primary reason that they are of minimal importance to trout in most circumstances. Occasionally, clusters of midges appear in full orgy-mode riding down the surface of a stream in a whirring, buzzing, mating mass. This is one of the rare occasions where adult midge clusters can prove particularly effective, since the large mass of insects is easier to imitate and more realistic than a solitary midge floating down the water.

Adult female midges lay their eggs by crawling down rocks or logs, or by laying eggs directly on the substrate. The same egg-laying behavior in caddis and *Baetis* mayflies can result in heavy, selective feeding by trout. Yet, paradoxically, this behavior in midges seems relatively ignored by trout. In my experience and in browsing hundreds of professional stomach sample reports, adult midges compose a tiny proportion of the average stream trout's diet. This egg-laying behavior is something you should keep in the deep, dark recesses of your angling mind. Someday on some river, it may just prove useful.

Thoughts on Imitation

Larvae: Imitating chironomid larvae is so quick and easy, that it is tempting to sit and churn out dozens of them per hour. Yet, their relative ineffectiveness on the water (compared to the pupae) should curb your enthusiasm. Even the patient angler who can handle their slow, steady productivity can grow frustrated with the phlegmatic, dawdling retrieves necessary for constant success with chironomid larvae imitations.

Since midge larvae are basically tiny worms—with no significant head, thorax, tail, or legs to complicate tying—they are pleasingly simple to whip out. The best midge larvae imitations use simple bodies made out of fur, biots, synthetic ribbings, or even thread. A ribbing of fine gold or fine silver tinsel should reinforce the body, not to mention give the fly a realistic segmentation. I like my flies to have a little shininess to them to imitate the exoskeleton of the larvae and I am partial to Body Stretch or Flexi Floss for most larvae imitations. But without a skin separation to collect gasses (like midge pupae), midge larvae imitations don't require extremely flashy materials. In fact, too much flash will sometimes render midge larvae patterns worthless. Keep the Krystalflash in the chamber for pupae patterns.

Movement in midge larvae patterns, particularly stillwater midge larvae patterns, is greatly underrated. If you have ever seen a small earthworm squirm in a puddle after a recent storm, you have a good idea what an errant midge larva squirming just above the bottom looks like. Midges don't so much move rapidly in a particular direction than they move rapidly in one place. When midge larvae are separated from the substrate, they squirm and flagellate in a vain attempt to reach solid ground again. Extended bodies of rubber, latex, or extremely sparse marabou (only one or two twisted fibers) can all effectively imitate this motion. Motion imitation is most successful on larger midge larvae (size 14 and up), in smaller sizes, it is difficult to acquire or construct materials that achieve a good wiggling performance. Fish these patterns no more than six to ten inches off the bottom—any higher and you will get few looks from the trout. The most effective time to use these patterns is on the windward shore following a period of heavy wind and wake. The crashing waves will stir up the first few inches of substrate, evicting these larvae from their burrows, leaving them to squirm around until they can settle and start constructing a new burrow.

Thanks to the broad variability among colors in naturals, the color of your chironomid larvae imitations should not keep you up at night. Most people feel that red is most effective and I have seen similar results in my own fishing. Other good colors include black, brown, smoke-gray, olive, and tan. If you aren't getting strikes with these colors, the odds are that imitating another insect would probably work better.

With such a simple pattern, one would think that beginning fly crafters would be able to whip out serviceable imitations of midge larvae in no time at all. Not true. The most important key to these patterns is to keep them thin. If your imitation is noticeably thicker than the hook shank, it is probably too thick! Obese patterns are likely the reason midge larvae patterns have never paid off for anglers in the past. Some people counter "If the body is so thin, can't the fish see the hook?" My answer is "Yes, that is exactly what we want." I try to tie my patterns (save the extended body ones) so they use as much of the shank as possible, utilizing the curve of the hook to mimic the curved body of the larvae.

Pupae: As spring rolls around, the focus of stillwater anglers around the country turns to the glorious chironomid. When cold waters restrict most aquatic life to a Homer Simpson-esque sedation, chironomids frolic and emerge in the warming shallows, providing trout with a consistent source of food. Knowing how to effectively fish chironomids can provide some of the hottest angling of the season. The great thing about chironomids is that they are everywhere, so if you have a well-stocked box of imitations and know

On fluctuating reservoirs with little weed growth, midges prove central to the trout diet.

how to use them, you can see success anywhere, anytime, on a variety of fish species.

Now that we know that trout focus on the pupae, all we have to do is whip up a couple pupae patterns and we are in business, right? Like a Rubik's Cube, chironomid pupae are deceptively complex. For such a simple-looking insect, few insects require as the attention at the vise and skill in presentation than chironomids do.

Looking at many standard patterns today, you would think all you need is a fur body, wire ribbing, peacock thorax, and white head and, shazzam, you've got yourself a chironomid pupae. This couldn't be further from reality. First, look at how trout strike chironomid pupae. Trout take chironomids leisurely and patiently; far different than the reactive, opportunistic strikes that what we're accustomed to with damselfly and dragonfly nymphs. Trout have plenty of time to examine pupae, since they cannot propel themselves quickly to escape. Thick midge hatches also create an abundance of natural chironomid to choose from. If this is starting to sound like how trout react to a Trico spinner fall on a spring creek, it should. Just like Tricos, the good chironomid imitator pays careful attention to pattern, approach, and presentation.

Unlike many other kinds of aquatic life, chironomid pupae have limited body movement. Their locomotion to the surface comes courtesy of the gassed trapped between their unborn adult body and their pupal shuck. Only for a brief moment near the surface will the pupae thrash about to loosen their pupal skins. So unlike damsels, dragons, and other active forage, the tier cannot rely on materials to provide motion and suggest life. This is why exact imitation of appearance is much more important with chironomids than with most other insects.

Yet by focusing on a few specific characteristics, the complexity of imitating the chironomid pupae can be alleviated. The four major factors to consider are shape, thickness, flash, and color. By adjusting these four factors, you can match any species of chironomid anywhere in the world.

Shape: Chironomids usually take on one of two body positions: erect and curled. Like scuds, many people think that chironomid pupae always have a curled body. Also, like scuds, diligent anglers who take bottom samples find tightly curled pupae when they remove the pupae from the water.

When chironomids pupate and rise—the time when they are most vulnerable to trout—their bodies may be either straight or curled, though most are slightly curled. As they move to within an inch of the surface, their body straightens up parallel to the surface in preparation of emergence. Here, straight-shanked imitations excel. However, it is quite difficult to tie realistic patterns (without CDC, hackles, foam posts or balls, etc.) that lie flat in the surface. Here is where creative tying can pay big dividends on the water. A foam-backed fly like Maggie's Midge is one of many creative ways to approach this problem, not to mention UK classics like the a CDC Shipman's or a Goddard's Buzzer.

The standard rule for tying nymphs is to make the abdomen 50% of the body length, while the thorax should be about 40% of the body length, with the head composing the last 10%. On chironomid pupae imitations it is important to remember that the thorax and head combined are at most 20% of the total body length. The thorax is also not much thicker than the rest of the body. Too many standard patterns make the mistake of making the thorax much too thick and much too long.

Thickness: Until recently, most commercially available chironomid imitations were far too thick. If you have ever recovered some naturals from a trout gullet, the bloating of commercial patterns is unmistakable. This self-reinforcing conundrum—novice anglers won't buy overly-sparse flies, but bulky flies catch fewer fish, so beginning anglers learn to avoid chironomids.

However, you're reading this book because you want to break this cycle. Guessing the diameter of chironomid pupae is relatively simple, as most chironomids have the length-to-width ratio of most hook gauges. On a given size dry-fly hook (1X fine), the body diameter should be a shade under twice the gauge of the wire. Easier said than done, but critical to keep your chironomids from looking like bloated summer sausages amongst a bevy of naturals.

Many people have trouble dubbing thin bodies, but with the advent of new synthetic materials, this shouldn't be a deterrent from tying accurate chironomid patterns. Traditional materials like V-rib or Larva Lace can be used to give thin, segmented bodies. Newer materials, like Frostbite, Superfloss, Krystalflash, Flashabou, Lurex, Nymphskin, Thinskin, and

Bloodworms thrive in muddy substrates.

dozens of other domestic and foreign materials, can give your pupae patterns both flash and a slender profile.

Flash: All chironomid pupae gather gasses under their pupal skin, which helps them rise to the surface. Therefore, if you seek to imitate emerging/pre-emergence chironomids, it is essential to incorporate flash in your pattern. I have experimented with traditional patterns fished on the same line within eight inches of each other and found that the ones with a Flashabou ribbing instead of gold wire ribbing caught four times as many fish. If you choose to use standard wire or tinsel ribs, use a silver color, for it better imitates the shade of trapped gasses. These gasses can also be imitated by using a loop of CDC on your pupae imitations, as the CDC will trap a bubble of air next to your fly. A fly tied with a CDC "bubble" is by far the best technique to imitate an air bubble, since a CDC bubble actually gathers and maintains an air bubble. The bubbles can also be imitated by soaking a dubbed pattern in a liquid or paste floatant, which tends to gather air bubbles in the spaces between the fibers.

Color: Midges come in more colors than Crayola crayons, so to break it down, we'll initially assume that they only come in black, olive, and red. My rule for picking colors is: muddy bottoms-red, sandy/rocky bottoms-black, and weedy bottoms-olive. These are the colors I start with, but the great thing about chironomids is that they are most effective when fished in tandems, so experiment with various colors. When these three won't produce, I turn to maroon, claret, or an orangish-brown. About 80% of your flies should be red, black or olive hues, but keep a collection of extras in unusual colors for times that fish won't fall for the old standards.

Because of the gasses trapped under the pupal skin, many chironomids appear to be banded in color, such as alternating red and black. I always carry some banded patterns, because I have a little more confidence with them when fish refuse standard patterns.

All chironomid pupae have a tuft of white gills near their head, and years of chironomid fishing by anglers all over the world has proven the importance of including some white at the head of the fly. I am partial to using a short tuft of white CDC to imitate the gills. In addition to matching the natural color and texture, CDC can trap gasses and add a bit of flash to the pattern. If you don't want to waste spendy CDC on the gills, then try some white antron fibers. White foam adds buoyancy and color, but it doesn't give the "fluffy" look that CDC and antron offer.

As you do more aquatic sampling, you will notice that quite a few of the black chironomid larvae you come across will have red butts. This coloration occurs among certain species of "bloodworm" midges. A butt of red Flashabou or dubbing can be easily incorporated into any standard chironomid pupa pattern without adding much to the tying time.

Another thing ignored by American tiers (but not the English) are the "wingpads" on the thorax of emerging chironomid larvae. These features often turn an orangish hue prior to emergence. Matching this orange wingpad can often make huge difference, and other times the fish could give a rat's ass. So I always tie up some of my standard pupae imitations with an orange Raffia or orange antron wingpad near the thorax. Stocked trout, whether they appreciate the added realism or simply that they inhabit waters rich in chironomids, seem particularly vulnerable to the orange-enhanced patterns.

ADULT

The adult midge is probably the least important stage of the midges, but paradoxically, it is also the most imitated stage by the majority of the angler population. Yet, because the adult midge can offer some dry fly opportunities to alleviate the monotony of January nymphing, their importance to the angler is understandably significant.

The trademark of an adult midge is movement, either positional or locational. You want a fly that looks busy. Palmered hackles and CDC can both create this illusion. These materials also conveniently keep the fly on top of the surface, rather than mired in the meniscus. We often hear about how important it is to be "in the film," but if we specifically want to imitate an adult midge, that fly needs to ride high. An adult midge, if it pauses long enough for you to check it out, has long, skinny legs that allow it to rest well above the surface film. The imprint the trout sees, therefore, is that of only a few dents on the surface of the water. Since trout tend to feed on adult midges primarily under cold, calm conditions where the adults are not active, this delicate imprint is of extreme importance.

Though I always fish midge emerger imitations absolutely static, I like to impart occasional motion to my adult midge patterns. An 8" to 18" slow strip will cause your fly to glide across the surface. This reinforces the importance of a high riding pattern—lest your fly drag through the water or, even worse, dive under the surface when you strip it in. To make sure midge patterns ride high, use a 3X fine wire hook to reduce the pattern's weight.

Patterns
Larvae

Keys to Match
Sparsity: Use as little material you need to achieve the desired effect. Remember you're tying to impress fish not anglers.

Ribbing: Gives segmentation, adds durability, and keeps your fly thin and tight.

Get Low: Lil' Jon says keep it moving and close to the bottom.

Keys to Avoid
Thickness: Keep your fly away from the buffet line in order to keep it in it.

Flash: Save it for the pupae.

Impatient Fishing: If tough conditions warrant the imitation of midge larvae, you are condemned to Dante's 6th Circle of Angling Hell: fishing your fly extremely slowly. Accept your fate, or catch nothing.

Fur Larvae

Hook: Dai Riki 135, #12-22
Thread: 14/0 to match body color
Body: Thin dubbing of rabbit/antron blend, color to match natural
Ribbing: Fine silver or gold wire

The fur larvae is a standard pattern and one that I use sparingly. I never thought plain rabbit had the glint of a natural larvae and found patterns dubbed with the rabbit/antron blend much more successful. Make sure to trim all the guard hairs and stray antron fibers, so that the fly has the neat, simple appearance of a natural larvae.

Biot Larvae

Hook: Dai Riki 135, #14-22
Thread: 14/0 to match body
Body: Turkey biot to match natural (tan, olive, black, or red)
Head (optional): One turn of sparkle dubbing to match body

This is a more aesthetic imitation of a midge larvae and if this helps you gain confidence in such a small pattern, by all means do it. Wrapping the biot body doesn't take any more time than dubbing and ribbing a thin fur body, so I have always considered this pattern interchangeable with the fur larvae. A small layer of super glue under the biot will make the fly nearly indestructible.

True Larvae

Hook: Dai Riki 135, #10-22
Thread: 8/0 to match body
Body: Strip of Body Stretch or Flexi Floss to match natural
Ribbing: Fine silver or gold wire
Head (optional): One turn of dubbing to match body

This is my favorite imitation of most midge larvae. It is simple like the others, but looks more realistic when paired up with the natural. I trim long strips of the Body Stretch with an Exact-o Knife, enough for at least two dozen patterns, before starting.

Three Fingers of Cutty

Hook: Dai Riki 135, #16.
Body: Red marabou, twisted
Collar: One wrap of sparkle dubbing
Head: Black bead, 5/64

If you want a squirming larva, this is the fly for you. The bead head and extended body of marabou, this one will move all over the place. It's main problem is durability—the marabou body is fragile.

Red Diddy

Hook: Dai Riki 135, #14-20
Thread: Red
Body: Red rubber (Flexifloss or red rubber band material), tied extended
Thorax: Few wraps of Red SLF dubbing, or red foam wrapped around the hook
Head: One wrap of black sparkle dubbing

This pattern is a simple, quick-to-tie imitation of a bloodworm larva. This fly is best fished deep, near the bottom, like a wriggling larvae dislodged from the substrate. I like to fish it as a trailer below a booby nymph or floating dragon nymph. That way, I can fish it extremely slowly without hanging up on the bottom.

Pupae

Banded Midge

Hook: Dai Riki 135, #10-14
Body: Pearl or Red Krystal Flash
Ribbing: Fine black vinyl ribbing material (V-rib or Larva Lace)
Wing: Gray CDC
Thorax: Black Haretron dubbing
Gills: White craft foam

This fly started as a killer panfish pattern, but its effectiveness quickly promoted the pattern into my trout fly boxes. The banding effect this fly has is quite unique and can attract fish that have seen it all. But the real jewel of the pattern is the short CDC wing. This grabs a bubble of air and holds it, glimmering, along the body of the fly. While this fake wing is totally out of position compared to the wingpads of the natural, the effect of the bubble seems to remove all doubt from fish. As you probably know, a fish or two can soak the CDC and eliminate the bubble. For this reason, I always carry a tube of CDC-safe desiccant with me, then I can rinse and treat the fly after each fish. The combination of the CDC and foam on this pattern can give it a near neutral buoyancy, which is excellent for fish feeding on chironomid pupae in shallow water.

The Queen Jane

Hook: Dai Riki 135, #10-14
Body: Black 6/0 thread
Ribbing: Fine silver wire
Back: Single strand of Pearl Flashabou
Thorax: Peacock herl
Cheeks: Bright orange antron or Orange Flexifloss

Maggie's Midge

Hook: 3X fine dry fly hook, #10-16
Tail: A few strands of white antron yarn.
Body: Very sparse sparkle dubbing (black, red, or olive) or Flashabou to match foam
Ribbing: Pearl mylar tinsel, fine
Back: Foam strip, colored to match fly
Thorax: Peacock Ice Dub
Head: White CDC, clipped short

When chironomids are just about to emerge, they lie perfectly parallel to the surface film, a position tough to maintain with the emaciated patterns needed to consistently fool picky fish targeting emergers. This pattern achieves what is needed, a flush-floating pattern without the hackle or excessive CDC that would identify it as a fraud. This fly floats best with the addition of some sort of floatant (but not on the CDC), but with the foam and CDC it can usually last a couple fish before sinking. On this, and any other emerging chironomid, you can go crazy with flash, for the naturals are often glistening like the Hope Diamond. You may find it helpful to first rib this fly with fine silver wire, then go over the ribbing with the pearl mylar. This will add to the durability of the foam back.

This pattern is derived from a number of British techniques—from the thread body to the Flashabou strip on the back to the all-thread body. The most striking feature of this pattern is its extremely thin body, which closely resembles the natural. The flash on the back (rather than using it as a rib) may seem unusual, until you look at the fly from the sides. As the fish approaches a chironomid from below, then closes in at the side of the pattern, this tying style provides a tiny bit of flash right when the fish is at the fly and debating whether to strike. This can cause reactionary strikes in fish that would otherwise reject the pattern. Using flash as ribbing can often give too much flash for some fish, and it can desensitize the fish so that the "last-second flash" is meaningless.

CDC BH Brass

Hook: Dai Riki 125, #12-20
Body: Copper Wire
Thorax: Peacock Ice Dub or peacock herl
Wing: Gray CDC
Head: Brass Bead

One of my favorite multi-purpose fast water nymphs, the CDC BH Brass can match a variety of insects, from midge larvae to caddis larvae and pupae. The slim, but dense, profile allows the fly to punch through the water and reach depth without dragging down a dry fly indicator. Probably the best fly I use in shallow, fast riffles where both midge larvae and predatory caddis larvae abound.

Rainy Day Midge

Hook: Dai Riki 135, #8-14
Butt: Red Flashabou
Body: Black thread
Ribbing: Pearl Flashabou or fine silver mylar tinsel
Wingpads: Two wraps of Orange Ice Dubbing
Thorax: Dubbed deer hair, 30% black, 30% brown, 10% olive, 10% orange

This simple pattern incorporates the Austrian technique of dubbing with deer hair to create a buggy, active thorax. Greasing the deer hair and tying the pattern on a lighter-wire hook will allow you to fish it directly in the surface film.

Emergers

Keys to Match
Sparsity: Penny-pinch with your materials for maximum success.
Flash: If the gas is trapped, let it show.
Color Changes: While the body is important, so are the butts and cheeks.

Keys to Avoid
Thickness. Like a Sports Illustrated Swimsuit Calendar, trout will shun the obese.
Bloated Thorax: A chronic problem for many, but must be remedied. If you look at naturals the thorax is rarely more than 2X the diameter of abdomen.
Too Wide of Banding: Thick ribbing can give an imitation too much flash or unnatural proportions.

Raccoon

Hook: Dai Riki 305, #12-16
Tail: Grizzly hackle fibers
Butt: White ostrich herl
Body: Sparkle dubbing, black or dark olive
Shellback: Natural deer hair
Head: Deer hair butts

This simple looking fly is a superbly realistic imitation of a emerging midge, because the shuck (the grizzly hackle fibers) lies parallel with the surface while the adult slides out. While it is not a great floating pattern, you probably won't be fishing emerging midges in anything but flat and calm conditions, so floatation really doesn't matter. With the light deer hair wing and flash of white ostrich, this fly is surprisingly easy to spot on the water. This gem is the paragon of a super-fishing fly that has never sold well. While rarely found in fly shops, it is essential for any stillwater angler.

Escaping Othello

Hook: Dai Riki 305 or 125, #12-18
Butt: Red Flashabou
Body: Sparkle dubbing, sparse
Ribbing: Pearl Flashabou or fine silver mylar tinsel
Thorax: Black dubbing with copper/orange sparkle material added
Wing case and Wing: Black or dun CDC

This fly tied in the European "shuttlecock" style with the CDC wing extending forward. With the CDC doubling as a wing case, the fly tends to hang more parallel to the surface film than other emerger styles. A fine pattern for emerging chironomids of any size.

Adults

Keys to Match
Visibility: It is easier to catch fish with a fly that you can see.
Business: Midges are industrious; give your fly the impression of motion.
Slim Down: Use light-wire hooks to keep your fly riding high.

Keys to Avoid
Up-winged Patterns: Caddis are not up-winged, mayflies are not down-winged, so why is this rule thrown out the window when it comes to midge patterns?
Traditional Midge Patterns: These both have upwings and tails, two things that natural midges lack.
Bulky: A bulky fly will absorb more water and ride lower in the water.

CDC Griffith's Gnat

Hook: Dai Riki 310, #14-22
Thorax: Pearl flash
Abdomen: Peacock Herl or Arizona Peacock Dubbing
Hackle: Grizzly palmered
Wing: White CDC

A classic pattern that still is effective today. The addition of the CDC wing greatly enhances the visibility of this tiny pattern on the water. I love this during the smutting rises at sunset—regardless of what they are feeding on, this unobtrusive pattern never fails to fool a few trout.

Dust Mop

Hook: Dai Riki 305, #12-22
Body: Dubbed dun CDC
Collar: White CDC

A simple, fluffy imitation of a clump of midges, the Dust Mop works because it can float through a hurricane while suspending a team of pupae or larvae imitations. While the fly skitters well, it leaves a big wake. I prefer it on a downstream dead-drift to consistently rising trout.

Shuttlecock Emerger

Hook: Dai Riki 135, #12-18
Body: Lacquered peccary hair
Thorax: Peacock Ice Dub
Wing case: Natural CDC
Wing: Natural CDC

It took years for me to overcome Anglophobia. Since about 1993, the "shuttlecock" midge style has exploded in popularity over in England and I couldn't figure out why they worked, so I never tried them.

However, for emerging midges—and it turns out, nearly any surface-emerging insect—the shuttlecock style is deadly. I love the classic look of the peccary hair, but any sort of sparkle dubbing body with a pearl mylar tinsel rib can work excellently. A small size 16 rusty-brown seal-fur Shuttlecock is one of the most effective patterns that I have used on stream trout that snub everything else.

Walter Bellhaven's VP

Hook: Dai Riki 305, #14-22
Tail: Widgeon flank
Body: Dubbing to match the natural
Wings: CDC to match natural
Back and head: Foam to match natural

A nice emerger pattern to match stillborn midges. The spinner-style CDC wing along with the foam back helps the fly float regardless of the wind or current conditions. This is by far my preferred pattern for smutting trout in rivers.

Simple Buzzer

Hook: Dai Riki #125, 12-18
Body: Pearl Flashabou
Thorax: Peacock Ice Dub or SLF dubbing
Hackle: To match natural, parachute style
Wing: White antron and pearl Lite-Brite, blended

This is an easy parachute pattern that works well on trout feeding on midge emergers in slightly choppy water that may sink sparser patterns. I like it as a lead fly when fishing emergers and pupae in shallow water or fishing tiny midge patterns on streams. It works best in shades of black, olive, and rusty-brown.

Grievous Angel

Hook: Dai Riki 310, #12-22
Body: Stripped peacock quill
Thorax: Black dyed peacock
Hackle: Grizzly, trimmed with a "v" in the bottom
Wing: Dun CDC

This pattern works superbly as an imitation for a variety of midge species. I like it in the smallest sizes, and fortunately it is becoming easier to locate grizzly saddle hackles in tiny sizes. The hanging abdomen suggests both a stillborn emerger and a drowned adult, making it an effective pattern despite the hatch conditions.

Bibio

Hook: Dai Riki 305, #8-18
Body: Black, red, and black dubbing
Hackle: Black, palmered
Ribbing: Pearl Flashabou
Legs: Black or natural knotted pheasant tail

Crayfish (Decapoda)

The Amphipod

Like grasshoppers in the terrestrial environment, crayfish have long warranted a great deal of attention from anglers familiar with the creature from their pre-angling past. Anybody who has spent any time around water remembers seeing—and likely attempting to catch—crayfish while wading through rocky shallows. It is easy to remember these large, lobster-like shellfish with formidable pincers of sufficient gape to snap a toe. While crayfish are not as important as most beginning anglers think, they are not as irrelevant as some experts treat them.

Crayfish and trout go together like cheese and mice, but all trout do not consume the same numbers of crayfish. In a study of Michigan streams, crayfish contributed about 12% of the diets of trout smaller than 16 inches, but made up 43% of the diets of trout larger than 17 inches. Small trout have great difficulty eating 'dads. Unlike bass, which can often just snap, toss up, and inhale a small crayfish, a trout must pick at and position the crayfish so it can be consumed. If a small trout attacks a crayfish, the trout often only plucks off a couple legs before the crayfish safely escapes. The larger mouth of a big trout requires less preparation time, making them more efficient predators.

Crayfish have an incredible size range, with mature specimens varying from just under 10mm to 150mm. Trout anglers, however, should concentrate on imitating those in the 25-70mm range. Very small crayfish (immature forms as well as mature forms under about 20mm) are also quite important to bluegill, warmouth, and other panfish.

Most anglers recognize the basic anatomy of crayfish, so there is no need to go into copious detail here. For the unfamiliar, a crayfish looks like a miniature lobster. It has five pairs of legs (hence the name "*Deca-poda*"), with the front pair greatly enlarged into a pronounced "pincer." Crayfish also have long antennae and glaring black eyes that are stalked and movable. The last feature important to anglers is the fan-like tail (or *telson*), which can be twice the size of the abdomen.

Colors of crayfish, like many other aquatic critters, can vary widely. Browns, olives, reds, and blacks are most common, while oranges (and the rare blue) are less common. These colors usually more or less match the color of the substrate, which also leads to a degree of mottling to help provide camouflage. The tips of crayfish legs and claws can occasionally be much lighter and brighter than the body, something that may possibly be a strike trigger for trout. Bright, rusty orange is far and away the most often imitated color by anglers, which is grounded in biological reality only in the fact that cooked crayfish appear reddish or orange when served on the plate of a fishless angler. Since trout do not really

Crayfish prefer rocky and woody habitat in the shallows of lakes and reservoirs.

prefer poached crayfish, do not let orange patterns overwhelm your fly box.

When moving around, crayfish can crawl slowly in a forward, reverse, or side-to-side motion. [When alerted or endangered, the crayfish will violently swing its tail under its abdomen, and shoot backwards a foot or more with each thrust.] While a crayfish may use this escape mechanism to escape a fish, the motion can only be sustained for a short distance (less than 30 feet) before the crayfish must rest and take up a defensive position under or near a rock or stump. For this reason, trout, which can easily swim long distances without tiring, will show great persistence when they "run down" crayfish and consume them.

Crayfish are nocturnal, spending their days tucked cozily into niches of flooded or fallen timber, rocks, even burrows that they build on shore. Crayfish survival hinges on these shelters and burrows: without them, the crayfish cannot rest, they become more susceptible to predation, and populations collapse. The essential role of structure makes stump fields, boulder fields, and riprap the best places to imitate crayfish. At nightfall, crayfish move out to feed under the cover of darkness, and anglers should be out to imitate them within two hours of sunrise or sunset. When crayfish finally move around, they can cover quite a bit of ground. In some radio tracking studies, sampled crayfish travelled between .41km to 16.99km in only 4 days! This restlessness puts them in the crosshairs of many a hungry trout.

Crayfish are omnivorous scavengers, so they can thrive anywhere there is aquatic vegetation, dead animals, or insects. In fact, one species of crayfish, *Orconectes causeyi*, is so adept at consuming vegetation it has been used to thin out weed-choked trout lakes, making for better trout habitat. While some crayfish prefer natural foods, human-planted baits can attract crayfish. On a high mountain lake in Oregon whose dense crayfish populations supports a commercial fishery, anglers often fish crayfish patterns in the vicinity of buoys marking baited crayfish traps. Another less scrupulous angler has been known to throw a nasty gruel of dog food, fish entrails, and other organic niceties into marked spots on this lake. He then returns to fish the area thoroughly with crayfish patterns both early and late in the day to great success… but I don't know him or anything.

The life cycle of crayfish can have a decided influence on when trout feed on them. Most young crayfish emerge from their mother's burrow (or detach from their mother's exoskeleton) in the spring. They then molt several times into the autumn, when molting ceases. It is in the early molt stages (spring through mid-summer) when the smaller, softer-shelled crayfish are most desirable and consumed by trout. In autumn, copulation occurs, and the cycle begins anew. While some crayfish survive more than one winter, it is rare, and these old, large crayfish are minimally important to trout that exist outside the realm of angler's tall tales. That large crayfish can boldly cross sandy lake bottoms without fear of predation shows how rarely trout try to attack them.

Like all the foods discussed here, trout and crayfish do not exist in a binary, predator-prey relationship. They both share an ecological context. For one, crayfish make small fish (particularly sculpins) more susceptible to trout predation because the crayfish dominate the shelter habitats required sculpins. Fortunately for the angler, the presence of crayfish affects more than just sculpins. Trout also feed on tadpoles when the conditions are right. Like all effective predators, trout tend to feed on injured tadpoles that are less likely to escape. Crayfish tend to injure tadpoles during attacks, though many tadpoles survive; in one study, injured tadpoles were *twenty* times more common in the presence of crayfish than in the absence of them. Crayfish, in streams, can also greatly reduce active predator insect populations (like Rhyacophila caddis or Perlid stoneflies) that live in rock crevices, while ignoring grazers and filter feeding insects that live on the tops of the rocks. This means that even when large populations of predatory insects appear in samples of crayfish-dwelling streams, they spend a lot of time hiding and are not readily available to trout. These are things to keep in mind on crayfish waters, and an important reminder of the interconnection of all aspects of the aquatic world.

The crayfish population in the United States is divided by the Rocky Mountains with the family Cambaridae dominating the eastern half, and the Astacidae exclusively in the West. The only genus of crayfish in western waters is *Pacifastacus*, common in the Snake, Columbia, Klamath, and Sacramento-San Joaquin systems. In the east, a much wider abundance and variety of crayfish exists, particularly the genera *Cambarus, Procambarus, Distocambarus*. The Rocky Mountain is a veritable wasteland of decapods, so enjoy the hoppers and forget about crayfish.

The importance of crayfish depends primarily on their availability and abundance. On some waters, larger trout turn to crayfish as their primary source of food. In other waters, large trout may never encounter a natural crayfish and any strikes you receive are strictly from hunger. Pumping stomachs is usually an ineffective way of discovering crayfish predation, because the pump seldom can pull out an intact crayfish or even pieces of a crayfish. For this reason, the best way to see if trout in a particular lake feed on crayfish is the infuriating process of playing guess-and-check with crayfish patterns on the bottom. If you get nothing, it is only an evening or two wasted, but if you do locate a population of crayfish-feeders, you may have discovered the home of your next trophy trout.

Thoughts on Imitation

An impressive variety of freshwater gamefish feed on crayfish—from trout to bass to warmouth and other panfish. Regardless of species, fish prefer the smallest available crayfish, as they are more easily attacked and consumed. This means the tier should focus on smaller patterns than the big bass-sized crayfish imitations available in many shops. Most patterns should range from size 8 to size 6, with a smattering of larger and smaller patterns rounding out the selection. While "size 8" may seem diminutive compared to the average observed crayfish, it closely approximates the size of most naturals recovered in trout stomach samples.

Since crayfish patterns must be fished directly on the bottom, prudence should inform pattern construction. Who wants to tie an intricate, twenty-minute fly, only to lose a dozen every time you go out? On the other hand, overly simple patterns usually produce few fish. One time, I received a commercial order for "Crayfish Orange" Rabbit Leeches. They were touted as crayfish patterns; according to the person who ordered the flies: "it is a great crayfish pattern for trout." Nothing was further from the truth. I couldn't even catch a smallmouth bass with them on the crayfish-choked Mecca of Minnesota's upper Mississippi. Crayfish-pattern-wary trout proved even less convinced. While these patterns were easy to tie, they bore no resemblance to a natural crayfish in color, silhouette, or even motion.

When imitating crayfish, concentrate on body position, color, and claws. Eyes and antennae are of secondary importance. I usually throw them on because they don't take much time to add (about 25-30 seconds per fly) and they help the flies sell to my customers, but their significance as a trigger is minimal. Perfect leg imitations will rarely "seal the deal" with trout; I have done equally well with patterns with or without legs. The fact that crayfish often lose one or more legs during combat or predator attacks, may make fish less picky about counting the legs of their prey. Adding them should be matter of personal aesthetics. A simple palmered hackle can create the illusion of sufficient leg activity.

As we mentioned above, crayfish can crawl in any direction but they must dart backwards to quickly escape a potential threat. Sure, you could tie a crayfish pattern with a forward or sideways body position, but as soon as you make a quick strip, a wise trout will recognize your pattern as an obvious fraud. For this reason, tie 90% of your patterns with a reversed body position.

When tying crayfish, experiment with a variety of colors. Browns and olives are the base colors I start with, then a few black, red, and orange to round it out. Besides concentrating on the body color, think about the "brighter" colors to line the legs and claws. Adding some bright paint to the fringes of claws and legs can really make a fly stand out to the trout.

Claws distinguish a crayfish pattern from all others. One can create claws from a wide variety of materials: pheasant tail clumps, marabou tufts, cemented and trimmed deer hair, lacquered hen feathers, plastic sheeting, suede. Creative anglers can even take claws off soft plastic baits and mount them by various means to their fly. While you want to include small claws on your imitations, overly large claws may prove counter-productive, scaring off fish that have painful memories of a previous pinching.

One of the hardest things to imitate is the curling of the body when the crayfish makes a quick dart to escape. I can't say for sure whether this is an important feature or not. Part of me says that since this is the "trigger" action that draws the trout in. However, without more research and experimentation I can't take a firm position either way.

A small "bill" of plastic or foam will add some action to your pattern, much like a crankbait. A stiff foam bill (like Scintilla Fly Buoy Foam) that closely resembles the color of the body can be an excellent choice to imitate a wide tail and impart movement to the fly. Make sure any bill is super-glued in place so it doesn't spin around the hook shank during the retrieve. If your fly is tied upside-down, this bill should reduce hangups by "bumping" the fly off debris that otherwise would have consumed your fly.

Speaking of avoiding the bottom, make sure to tie all of your crayfish imitations to ride upside-down. Since crayfish patterns should be fished in the roughest habitat, a up-hook feature will significantly reduce snags and lost flies. At first you may find it awkward to tie flies upside down, but these trifles seem minor compared to not losing a fly every tenth cast.

If all else fails, a brown or dark olive woolly bugger can suffice as a "survival kit" crayfish imitation. If you find yourself in a pond or lake teeming with crayfish, but are unprepared, these patterns will suffice. Woolly Buggers are not a first-line imitation; if you plan to encounter crayfish in any abundance, specific patterns will produce far more and larger trout.

Present crayfish imitations slowly along the bottom with a hand-twist retrieve. Occasionally, give the pattern a strong tug to pop it off the bottom like a fleeing crayfish; return to the hand-twist retrieve. Cruising trout otherwise oblivious to a creature crawling along the bottom should notice this flight behavior, and it often triggers an aggressive feeding response.

When setting the hook to crayfish strikes, remember that while bass inhale crayfish imitations, trout often "toy" with crayfish before consuming them. If you miss a hook set, don't get frustrated and quickly strip in your fly. Missing a hook set perfectly imitates the behavior of an escaping crayfish! If you compose yourself, let the fly settle and restart the slow retrieve—the trout almost unfailingly return to finish the job. On one occasion, I must have missed the hookset 12 or 13 times over the course of a fifty-foot retrieve. The trout still followed the fly to within about 10 feet of the bank where I stood pulling my hair out. While I never actually landed that fish, let it be a lesson of the determined attitude of a trout tuned in to a crayfish.

Patterns

Keys to Match
Color: Don't think orange is the only or best color.
Claws: They define a crayfish—a pattern without claws just looks like a leech
Upside Down: This is for your benefit, not the trout's.

Keys to Avoid
Tying the Fly Forward: When crayfish evolve to dart away head-first, this may just work
Overly Simple: An orange blob of fur only elicits sympathy strikes.
Fishing the Fly too Fast/Not on the Bottom: When crayfish evolve to swim like minnows, that may just work.

Power Craw

![Power Craw]

Hook: Dai Riki 700, #2-8
Head and Claws: Front portion of a Berkeley Power-craw
Body: Crosscut rabbit trimmed on top
Shell: Olive raffia, lacquered (optional)
Ribbing: Brown 3X mono (optional)
Butt: Black bead

This pattern makes for a simple crayfish pattern that incorporates the essentials—it rides upside-down, has prominent claws, and is quick enough to tie so that you don't feel too guilty for losing a half dozen in an evening. This is the first pattern I choose for crayfish-feeding trout because it boldly attracts aggressive crayfish feeding trout, but it is easy to tie and relies on motion to fool trout.

Hungarian Craw

Hook: Dai Riki 700, #2-8
Claws: Lacquered dyed brown Hungarian partridge (or other dyed game-bird) feather, clipped to shape
Eyes: Black mono
Antannae: Stripped brown or black hackle quills
Body: Olive brown or rusty brown dubbing
Legs: Soft brown hackle
Shellback: Brown Body Stretch or raffia, mottled with water proof pen
Ribbing: Brown 3X mono or fine copper wire

This is a more imitative crayfish pattern for clear waters, slower fishing, or selective fish. Like other craws, you should tie it upside down.

Vibro-craw

Hook: Dai Riki 270, #2-10
Claws: Marabou clumps to match natural
Eyes: Black mono
Under Body: 10 wraps .020 lead wire
Body: Dubbed fur to match natural
Legs: Soft saddle hackle to match natural
Shell: Foam to match natural
Tail: Foam to match natural

The Vibro-Craw is the fly version of the crankbait. It works well in murky water, as well as in streams, but it is almost always more effective for bass than trout. Tie the fly upside down, because the weighted body will make the fly roll over when retrieved. Pre-cutting all bodies in advance ensures that the larger tail is trimmed to the proper proportions. The foam bill on this pattern should keep the fly from hanging up too frequently. If you tie the pattern "right-side-up" and without weight, the fly will float up between strips, further reducing hang-ups. Mottling the foam back and tail with a waterproof pen better imitates the blotchy color of natural crayfish.

Crane Flies (Tipulidae)

The Insect

Commonly called "Daddy-Long Legs," "Mosquito Eaters," or "Mosquito Killers" few of us have given much thought to the importance of crane flies. Only a few species of truly aquatic tipulids exist, though most terrestrial larvae prefer the moist soil near streams—making nearly all species potential trout prey. The damp loam coating the floors of my native Western Cascade rainforests is perfect habitat for crane flies. The riparian zones of this region teem with crane fly larvae, until one of the common Northwest rainstorms flushes them out to hungry, waiting trout. Despite their abundance in the damp Pacific coastline, these insects are quite versatile and have adapted to live in the harsher conditions that exist in the Great Basin and Rocky Mountains. Excellent populations also exist in portions of the Midwest and Eastern seaboard. Any environment that supports trout, pretty much supports crane fly larvae, either under or very near the water's edge. Most angling texts have only given nominal consideration to crane flies, contributing to the culture of neglect that has befallen many trout foods. Despite the lack of angler fanfare, crane fly larvae and adults are a familiar food to most North American small stream trout.

[The family Tipulidae—at 14,000 species…and counting—is the largest family in the Diptera order, a surprise to those who are indoctrinated to worship the chironomid as the only significant member of the Diptera order.] The size of individuals in this order is about as varied as any aquatic insect. Crane flies wing lengths range from 2 millimeters (*Dasymolophilus*) up to 40 mm (*Holorusia*)!

Most people can recognize the adult crane fly with its skinny body, long wings, and even longer (and frailer) legs. However, the crane fly are probably foreign to anyone who has not actively looked for them. Crane fly larvae resemble thick worms: with an usually cylindrical, occasionally flattened, body that is somewhat blunt at the head and slightly tapered at the rear. Crane flies have a lusterless color palette, with grays, light olives, and light tan specimens commonly found. A retractable head easily distinguish crane flies from other large, grubby-looking larvae. Usually herbivorous in nature, some crane flies aggressively prey upon midge larvae. Most stream ecologists categorize crane fly larvae as "shredders," which is a reminder of their prevalence in and around small, forested streams.

Nearly all species of crane flies spend their larval stage underground. Therefore they become available to trout only when flooded out by a spate storm, and not because of their particular feeding habits. When washed into a stream, trout eagerly seek out

The adult crane fly has a solid body, but spindly legs

drifting crane fly larvae. These larvae have no swimming ability whatsoever. Once caught up in the drift, they are mere pawns in the trout's game. Since crane fly larvae commonly reach one to two inches in length—some exceptional specimens push three inches—you can be sure that trout never ignore such a large morsel.

Most tipulid larvae dwell in the subterranean realm, thriving in the moist soil near, but not in, streams. There are some fully aquatic crane fly larvae, which prefer mossy substrates or areas where the riparian soil is too dry or rocky to support stable burrows, such as in the Great Basin or the Southwest. Fully aquatic tipulid larvae thrive in areas of thick moss or rooted aquatic vegetation. They often burrow around in the soil-water interface zone. A quick check only requires grabbing a wad of plants and ripping them out by the roots, and then dabbing the root-wads in your hand or in a collection container. When searching for either of these insects, it is important to remember to stir up the first several inches of substrate. Many anglers never find crane flies in their bottom samples because they neglect to do more than kick their feet through a riffle. On many streams, especially small streams that you suspect of harboring good crane fly populations, it is wise to carry a small hand trowel. You can use this to dig down in search of terrestrial tipulids. Concentrate your search to only the top six inches of soil and within ten feet of the bank, for this is where terrestrial tipulids are most vulnerable to spate flooding.

Consistent light rain is perfect for terrestrial crane fly larvae and pupae, as the moistened soil aids their burrowing activity. However, heavy rainfall has the potential of drowning the larvae and a sustained (5-7 day) period of heavy rains can drown or wash away pupae, ruining a generation of adults.

The pupa stage of crane flies holds little significance to anglers. Almost all tipulid larvae—terrestrial and aquatic—migrate to stable and dry riparian ground prior to pupation. Tipulids pupate under the soil (or leaves or logs if the soil is unsuitable) for one to two months Since crane fly emergences extend throughout the spring, summer, and early fall, and since pupation takes place on land, the exact emergence period matters little to the angler.

Adult crane flies start to emerge during March at lower elevations and late May at higher elevations. They continue to emerge throughout the summertime in a variety of habitats throughout North America. Crane fly larvae "seasons", like many other insects, coincide with the most favorable environmental conditions. In Michigan, Tipulid populations exploded in mid-May when "favorable water, temperature, and food conditions of floodplain pools are available for the soon-to-be-produced larvae." In the Far West, adult populations often boom in September, when hatching larvae find an unlimited banquet of leaf litter, with a light dressing of October rainfall to aid digestion.

Mature crane flies prefer shady and cool riparian zones during the summer, and can be found hanging around ferns or rootwads of fallen trees, as well as streamside rocks and brush. If you enter a stream corridor that is twenty degrees cooler than the surrounding countryside, you are in perfect adult crane fly habitat! These cool, humid habitats are not just preferred, they are required; adult crane flies can desiccate quickly thanks to their large surface area. Hafele and Hughes note that adult crane flies take flight after summer rains moisten their habitat and raise the humidity level, making post-storm hours crucial times for cranefly imitation.

Adult craneflies range in color from brown and gray to cream, yellow, and tan. The adults also can vary in size from 2mm to nearly 35mm, though their gangly legs and wings provide a larger profile. Most anglers only imitate the smaller ones (10mm in length), but trout will feed on the larger ones readily if they are available.

Adult crane flies are clumsy fliers and long-lived. With a life-span of between two weeks to two months, adult crane flies can maintain a relatively long existence in the presence of cool and moist niches where they can conserve body moisture. Crane fly mating swarms rarely occur, as mating happens almost immediately after emerging, and emergence is a summer-long endeavor. The desire to mate is so urgent that one author notes, "males have been observed to grasp females as the latter are extracting themselves from their pupal skins." Some females will lay their eggs by dropping on the water, dragging their abdomens in the water as they fly along. If this egg laying behavior is observed, break out imitations and hang on!

We see few imitations of crane fly larvae or adults in our local fly shops. Perhaps dense hatches of other insects on many of our "glamour" streams overshadow them. Perhaps anglers just do not know, do not show, or just do not care about what is going down in the riparian zone. Rivers like the Deschutes, Yellowstone, and Henry's Fork have moderate populations of tipulids, but they also have enormous hatches of PMD's, stoneflies, and spotted sedge, so crane flies fall by the wayside. Regardless of how you rank them on large streams, the value of crane flies to the small stream aficionado cannot be disputed. Like with terrestrial insects, the smaller the stream, the greater the shoreline to surface area ratio. The greater the ratio, the more crane flies wind up in the stream.

Thoughts on Imitation

Imitating crane fly larvae is a relatively simple endeavor. Most of the time, crane fly larvae safely reside under several inches of soil, however, spate flooding can cause many to be washed into the flow. Most fly anglers avoid streams the day or two after a heavy rain, preferring to tie flies or count their stock options. Crafty anglers will not be so easily dissuaded, dredging those roily creeks with big crane fly larva imitations. Maybe those imitations float under a strike indicator; maybe they float under the deft rod tip of a Czech nympher. Either way, those anglers put the fly in the right place at the right time. If you can get on the water in the days following a heavy rain, fishing crane fly larvae can be extremely productive.

Patterns

Keys to Match:
Chunky Larvae: This is one imitation where thicker is better.
Skinny Legs on the Adult: Make it look like Kate Moss and Shawn Bradley playing Twister.
Light, Airy Adult: It should be easy to skate on the surface.

Keys to Avoid:
Barr's Crane fly Larvae:
Dear Barr,
Gold bead, big peacock head, tail...what the Hell is that?
Sincerely,
Trout
Big-Head Larvae: No matter how much we want them to, trout don't understand elephantitis.
Erring Small: Don't be afraid to give the trout the big one.

Crane Fly Larvae #23 and #35

Hook: Dai Riki 270, #4-12
Under Body: .025" lead wire
Body: "*Gray Crane Fly Mix*"—50% olive/gray Hare's Club, 20% dark olive Scintilla, 20% gray Scintilla, 10% olive Scintilla "*Brown Crane Fly Mix*"—50% Brown and Copper Caddis Emerger, 35% Chocolate Brown Caddis Emerger, 15% black and copper Caddis Emerger dubbing
Ribbing: Fine silver oval tinsel
Head: 80% black Haretron, 20% peacock Arizona Synthetic peacock dubbing

Fly tying experts always advocate erring on the sparse side when tying flies. Forget that with crane fly larvae. If you find a natural, you will see that is a chunky-looking grub, and segmented bulk is a trigger for trout. Another common problem shared by most crane fly larvae imitations, is that they make the head far too large. If you find a natural, you can see how the head is very small and can retract into the body. When tying this fly make the head tiny: less than 10% of the length of the body.

The Subterranean Greek

Hook: Dai Riki 700, #4-12
Weighting: .025" lead wire
Under Body: Light-colored small chenille or ultra-chenille
Over Body: Olive, Gray or Brown Body Stretch
Ribbing: Fine mono
Head: Black Peacock Ice Dub

This is an extremely simple pattern to tie, and surprisingly effective for feeding-feeding trout. With this pattern you don't have to get mired in dubbing ratios, just whip them out. If properly weighted, neither this pattern nor Crane fly Larvae #23 and #35 need additional weight to get to the bottom. Lots of weight is important, because these crane fly larvae patterns are most effective during high, swift flows. You may even need an extra-large strike indicator just to keep the fly from dredging the bottom!

Z-lon Daddy

Hook: Dai Riki 270, #8-12
Body: Z-lon tied extended-body style
Legs: Six knotted pheasant tail fibers; four behind hackle, two tied at the head.
Wings: Grizzly hackle tips
Hackle: Grizzly, brown, or brown-dyed grizzly

The Z-lon Daddy is my basic adult crane fly pattern, tied with an extended body of twisted Z-lon. It can be tied in any shade of brown or gray, and looks very much like a natural crane fly. This fly should be fished dead drift near overhanging trees and brush, where the naturals reside. It can also be effective greased and skittered erratically on the surface. I will eagerly use this fly where "dapping" is the only feasible presentation style. Dapping is perfect for this pattern because dancing just over the water's surface is exactly what the natural does.

Experimenting with crane fly larvae also proves deadly when you find yourself hemmed in below other anglers. One of the best experiences I ever had with crane fly imitations was downstream of an aggregation of nearly twenty anglers at Buffalo Ford on the Yellowstone River. The inept and incessant wading of the anglers on this section of river evicts thousands of larvae into the drift every hour. I watched four happy trout devour dozens of larvae while finishing the last chapters of Eric Alterman's excellent work, *Ain't No Sin to be Glad You're Alive*. Five steps into the cobbled head of the lead island at Buffalo Ford, I sight-nymphed a crane fly imitation straight into the mouth of a nineteen inch Yellowstone cutthroat.

One should fish crane fly imitations dead-drift near the bottom. Natural cranefly larvae swim like a quadriplegic frog. Keep your imitations near shore, where the larvae originate, as trout holding close to the bank are more conditioned to seeing the naturals. Of course, imitating crane flies on small streams, where the shoreline is in perpetual proximity is usually more productive than on large streams.

Imitations of crane fly larvae should be simple. These critters look more or less the same as a worm or grub. Since many of the larvae are translucent, a thin dubbed body of pale-olive, gray-olive, or dark gray dubbing, brushed out and clipped short, with a small head of black ostrich herl or dubbing, can slaughter crane fly feeding trout.

Fly tiers often go overboard imitating the head of crane flies, creating massive Dom Delouisian heads at the front of their patterns. The natural crane fly cranium is almost indistinguishable from the tail end, so keep the head restrained. We don't put big mono eyes on an adult mayfly, and make the equivalent mistake with this important peer. A small 1/8" black nickel beadhead is appropriate for large larvae imitations. A small ball of black sparkle dubbing works perfect on smaller patterns. Also, avoid bright gold or copper beads. Through several

Starkville City Jail Crane Fly

Hook: Dai Riki 305, #8-12
Body: Brown sparkle dubbing (or cream, gray, orange, red, or dark olive dubbing)
Ribbing: Pearl Krystalflash
Legs: 4-6 knotted pheasant tail fibers
Hackle: Brown or brown/grizzly mixed

This is my small stream "daddy" pattern, where fish aren't as picky and a slightly smaller fly is preferable. It is a little less bulky and quicker to tie than the Z-lon version. This fly also works well for early season panfish and bass, especially when skated over nesting sites.

Mack Pappy

Hook: Dai Riki 270, #8-12
Body: Tan, cream, or gray vernille, with the butt-tip burned
Legs: Six knotted pheasant tail fibers, two tied in front of hackle
Wings: Gray or cream raffia strips, trimmed to wing shape
Hackle: CDC to match body
Head: Brown squirrel blend

A CDC version of one of my favorite bugs, this is a superb pattern for spring creeks or skating on stillwaters. A dense CDC hackle, while usually a no-no, enhances this pattern, especially when skated. The wings can be swapped out for any synthetic wing material.

Who's Your Daddy?

Hook: Dai Riki 270, #8-12
Body: Tan, cream, or gray vernille, with the butt-tip burned
Legs: Six knotted pheasant tail fibers
Wings: Gray or cream raffia strips, trimmed to wing shape
Hackle: Brown, sparse and tied back
Head: Black, copper, or gold bead

Proudly featured in *Playboy* because of its salacious title, Who's Your Daddy imitates the unfortunate naturals who get enmeshed in the surface film and drown. The crane fly's gangly body is doomed once part of it is trapped in the surface film. In rough, broken water, a crane fly is almost instantly consumed by the water and drifts underwater until finally consumed by the trout. This fly should be fished dead drift under an indicator, though it can be easily sight fished because of its large size. On this pattern, I only tie four legs and use Raffia for the wings, which is very realistic when wet. The main benefit is its large size, which keeps small fish off the hook, thus making this a much more desirable nymph than a simple Hare's Ear.

Crane fly imitations can be effectively skated across shallow riffles.

controlled experiments on rivers with infestations of crane fly larvae, I found that crane fly imitations with gold bead heads catch significantly fewer trout than the same pattern tied without the bead. Tails, legs, shellbacks, and other "improvements" really are not improvements, because the natural lacks these ornamental features.

Another good pattern for crane flies only requires a strip of Body Stretch (or any synthetic plastic sheet) wrapped up over a length of a hook coated with vernille. The resulting is a segmented body, tapered at the head and tail, a very good imitation of the natural. You should weight all crane fly larvae imitations, because they need to drift right along bottom. Extra bulk seems to only improve the success of the pattern. Do not fear maximizing the size of these nymphs. I have tied cranefly imitations imitations on size 4, 4XL streamer hooks and still hooked plenty of trout. However, size 6 through size 12 imitations will generally produce well in most situations.

Since the "emerger" stage of crane flies is totally unavailable to trout, don't waste time or materials on it.

Most American adult crane fly "imitations" are embarrassingly amateur. When flipping through the entire encyclopedia of American fly tying in 2000, the only thing that approximated crane flies were spider patterns or simple, super-sized midge imitations. To look for good imitations one must investigate the innovations of European fly tying. One of my favorite crane fly imitations was adapted from a Davey Wotton pattern designed for large Anglian reservoirs. Extended deer hair imitates the body, while knotted pheasant tail fibers simulates the legs, and the wings are matched by pre-cut Spirit River wing material. The resulting pattern is sparse, quick-to-dry, highly visible, and a near-exact imitation of the natural. One of the greatest benefits of this pattern is its bulk—small trout inches simply cannot get it in their mouth, keeping your catch limit to larger trout. This is a virtue on small streams. The key to any adult crane fly pattern is to make it gangly and gaudy, just like the natural.

Adult crane fly imitations excel in two particular ecosystems: small streams with dense overhead canopies that provide near-constant shade, and meadow streams. In both these locations, adult activity peaks during calm, warm evenings. I rarely pull out crane fly adult patterns in the heat of the day—wait until the shadows hit the water. When fishing adult imitations, keep them near shore, where fish are likely to have encountered the natural before. It can be effective to skate these patterns by applying ample floatant and skittering them across the surface. Despite the aggressive strikes this technique can produce, it rarely produces more fish, day-in-day-out, than a simple dead drift.

While one can easily construct larvae patterns, tying any effective adult crane fly pattern is a lesson in division of labor. Constructing these patterns individually restricts your output to three to five flies per hour, not exactly an Olympic pace. Tying the flies in steps will save a lot of time in the long run. First, construct the legs, which are the most distinguishable feature of these insects. A simple overhand knot in a pheasant tail fiber makes a great leg, though "classic" Irish and British crane fly imitations have two knots per leg. Granted, two joints are biologically correct, but making two-jointed legs can take a lot of time. I usually attempt 200-300 legs per sitting, and you consider that six legs go into each fly, 300 legs is only good for a shade over four dozen, one knot per leg seems quite sufficient! After you knot the legs, cut the wing material into strips. Finally, cut out foam or chenille bodies, and prepare the hackles. Doing this kind of step-by-step prefabrications during the course of watching a football or basketball game makes "lazy time" seem more productive, and will also make the actual process of creating adult crane fly imitations seem far more productive.

Damselflies (Zygoptera)

The Insect

All fly anglers, at some point in their angling careers, seem to get attached to a few insects, focusing their efforts on imitating these select critters above all others. The insects that they exalt, in turn, reflect what the particular angler enjoys about fly fishing. For some, the early season resurrection of rising trout makes March Browns a highly valued insect. Others enjoy reaping the rewards of patience, a patience incumbent to imitating chironomid pupae. For many stillwater devotees, the bestial, blood-thirsty strikes elicited by damselfly nymphs makes imitating any other insect as tedious as watching C-SPAN on a Friday night.

As active predators, damselfly nymphs prefer the insect-rich weedy shallows of lakes and reservoirs. Damselflies almost universally inhabit stillwaters throughout the United States, Canada, and the rest of the world. Like the dragonfly, even the non-angler has little difficulty in identifying the adult damsel. Also like dragonflies, the average nature watcher praises damselfly adults both for their aesthetics and their utility.

While most people recognize and study the adults, trout and other fish focus on the nymphs. Damselfly nymphs are long, thin creatures ranging from 15-30mm in length at maturity. Along with their sparse profile, damselfly larvae have long legs, and pronounced "buggy" eyes set wide apart. Their colors are highly variable and range from pale olive to tan, and many species are noted for their ability to adapt their coloration to the substrate or weed pattern. Some damselfly nymphs have a pronounced mottling to their bodies, though this is not a consistent trait among all nymphs.

Under normal conditions, damselflies spend most of their time clinging to or phlegmatically crawling along stalks of aquatic vegetation. They lie patiently in wait for wayward insects (especially *Callibaetis* or chironomid pupae) to wander into range before pouncing on the hapless prey. If you ever examine a damsel nymph clinging to an aquatic plant, you'll notice that the larvae are inconspicuous, looking like stems or leaves. Only when prey or danger approaches will they move. Damselflies escape their pursuers with a rapid swimming motion that can elude many aquatic predators. However a false confidence in their escape speed often entices them into losing duels with hunger-motivated trout. Smart anglers know it is in their interest to devote their attention to matching this escape behavior.

Damselfly tails (their caudal *lamella*) are flattened side-to-side and look like little olive alder leaves. This physiological adaptation tells us how they swim: a side-to-side wiggle like a snake. The side-to-side disjointed swimming movement of damsel nymphs is a key factor in constructing proper imitations. The tails, however, are not. Many damselfly nymphs lose their tails, and in turn, they swim slower. At this slow clip, trout can easily overtake them. Compared to the dawdling swimming rates of most aquatic insects, damselflies are veritable speed demons, though determined trout have almost no problem consuming them.

While damsel nymphs normally use their long legs for clinging and crawling on plant stems, they tuck their legs along their body to reduce drag when swimming. But, if attacked, damselflies often arch their backs and extend their legs in a slowly sinking "parachute" position. It takes creative tying to match this tuck and flare of the prominent legs of the damselfly.

Damselflies tend to inhabit shallows (<4 feet deep) where small prey abound, so when they decide to emerge it is a less momentus event than with dragonfly nymphs, which may migrate many hundreds of feet to emerge. Damselflies often swim towards shore only a few minutes prior to emergence (usually midmorning). Some species, like *P. nymphula*, will swim near the surface, perhaps to orientate themselves towards the shore by swimming through various temperature gradients. Many anglers have experienced good success fishing with damsel nymphs just under the surface during the peak of emergence activity.

The front portion of a damselfly nymph is a collage of a large head, long legs, and a developing wing pad.

Chapter V: The Prey

Adult damselflies are some of the most beautiful insects in the world, with a color spectrum spanning an array of blues, greens, tans, and reds.

Once a damselfly reaches a suitable log, rock, or piece of emergent vegetation, the nymph crawls onto it and, within a few minutes, the adult damselfly emerges. The process can span nearly three hours, as it takes a while for the wings to fold out and dry. Emergences take place at night or the early morning, during breaks from windy conditions that could blow the adults from their perches. It has been reported that some trout will cruise along reedy vegetation, bumping stalks to knock emerging nymphs and drying adults back into the water in order to eat them. This ecological inference stems from trout that smack juvenile damsel imitations within seconds of touchdown near reeds and other prime emerging vegetation.

While that explanation is highly unlikely—does a trout spot emerging nymphs 20-100 cm above the surface, then pick out what reed they are on, or do they waste time and energy bumping every reed stalk they encounter?—another interpretation seems to better explain what is going on.

Adult damselflies, like adult dragonflies, are aggressive predators.

Sometimes, nymphs will back down or jump back into the water to seek a more suitable emerging habitat. A nymph rapidly appearing and then darting to another reed surely alerts trout, which often cruise the same reed lines.

Once metamorphosed into an adult, damselflies become relatively unimportant to trout. While some anglers report excellent success with adult damsel imitations, many more anglers have yet to catch a trout with them. It is safe to say, considering the lack of real evidence for it, that an angler can ignore adult damselflies without sacrificing too many fish. Despite my general pessimism towards the damselfly adult as a legitimate trout food, an imitation in your box can't hurt, even if it is just to hedge your bets!

Damselflies in streams are not as important as in lakes, since damsels prefer slow, weedy water where they can find refuge and abundant prey. Slow, weedy water is not exactly typical of most trout streams, though a few exceptional streams (tailwaters and spring creeks) can support good populations and trout will feed on them. Damsels in streams aggregate in shallow margin water (often called "frog-water" because of its slow, weedy appearance), as they can find refuge from trout there. In contrast, they are rarely found in deep pools, where hungry trout willingly gobble them up. Imitation of damsels should focus on the seams between the frog-water and swift water.

As stream habitats are more severe than that of stillwaters, damselflies often may overwinter as eggs, in streams, hatch in April or May, then grow and emerge by mid-summer. This may be an evolutionary response of Pacific Coast damselflies, which seek to avoid the dangers of spate flooding during winter and spring, not to mention the low water and predation risk that comes with fall. Though this behavioral pattern is certainly not universal for all stream damselflies, I have only seen success with damsel imitations on rivers during the early summer months (May-early July).

Anyone seeking to do further research on damselflies or dragonflies, must reference *Dragonflies: Behavior and Ecology of Odonata*, by Philip S. Corbet. This excellent book has nearly 700 pages on everything you ever would need to know about the behavior of damselflies.

THOUGHTS ON IMITATION

Anglers often imitate damsels on faulty principles. There are two traditional schools of fly tying: impressionists and imitators. The problem with impressionistic patterns is that they are too bulky for a wise trout to confuse them with the emaciated proportions of a natural damsel. On the other hand, the "imitators" are tremendously realistic patterns with extended bodies and tiny plastic legs. If you put one in a vial with alcohol, they could probably fool undergraduate entomologists. Unfortunately, when fished, most these patterns have the action (and appearance) of a Madame Tassaud's wax statue. There must be a happy medium.

Damselfly nymphs have three essential characteristics: sparsity, motion, and eyes, in that order. The damsel nymph is terribly thin, a problem that requires constant attention lest your fly blow up like Marlon Brando, circa *Don Juan DeMarco*. Thicker patterns pick up the occasional opportunistic trout, but when targeting trout feeding selectively on damsel nymphs, sparse patterns will out fish the chunky ones five to one. Seal or seal substitute dubbing is a great material for the body of damsel nymphs. It has a sparkly opacity, and one can dub it very thin and still brush out random fibers that appear like legs. Try to avoid chenille, Estaz, and other bulky materials, as they tend to produce bloated flies. Make sure that the body girth is no more than two and a half times the gauge of the hook you are tying it on.

Motion, while not as important as shape, still matters. The damsel nymph swims with a side-to-side motion of the abdomen, something anglers have tried to imitate for years (with minimal success) by changing materials and retrieves. This is why most of my patterns on short hooks with a long, sparse tail. The long tail combined with a lightly weighted body makes the imitation dance about aggressively. Many tiers dress their damsel nymphs for the full length of the hook shank, with only a small puff of marabou at the end. While this may seem the perfect visual representation of a damsel, it sure doesn't act like one. These patterns, while producing the occasional fish, simply cannot compete with patterns designed in a motion-centric paradigm.

Many people debate the importance of eyes on damselfly nymph imitations. I follow the wisdom of great Cascades Lakes tiers like Jim Cope, who uses eyes on almost all of his damsel nymphs. For eyes, I recommend olive mono eyes, which you can buy pre-formed or make your own. Eyes dominate the front end of damselfly nymph. More importantly, by using mono eyes, you give the nymph a large flat head. The head of a damsel nymph can often be as much as two times the width of the rest of the body. These things add more realism with little added tying effort, so I wholeheartedly endorse them.

Beadheads, in contrast, rarely benefit damsel nymph imitations. They cause imitations to sink head-first, in direct contrast with the naturals, which sink in a more uniform manner. I use

Shallows like this are prime damselfly territory.

beadheads on some of my patterns, particularly those that I plan on using in shallow water with quick retrieves. In this situation the fly does not pause (and reveal its flaw) for long. Positioning a bead in the thorax area is also an option, though it should be kept small and preferably painted.

Another significant factor with damsel nymphs is color. I tie my imitations in a variety of pale olives hue, with a few tan and a few more boldly bright green (for post-molt specimens). Naturals often have an opaque olive or tan color, something tough to imitate with most dubbing materials. Avoid the phosphorescent bight green "damsel" or "insect green" dubbing blends, as well as dark olives and yellow-greens. These are generally unnatural shades, though one wouldn't know it by looking in most fly shop bins.

Stream-dwelling damselflies limit their movement in order to reduce their availability to trout. For this reason, two retrieve techniques imitate them well. First, a rapid swimming motion—akin to how you would fish an emerging damsel imitation in stillwater—is a good bet. Cast a damsel nymph near "frog water" and strip it out towards the current. Few trout hold in frog water (since no current means no food), so you must make your fly skirt the edges with enough current to hold trout. If the swimming motion does not work, try a dead-drift. I love to sight-fish damsel nymphs to river trout. Simply fish it like a regular nymph, but use the occasional twitch of the line or rod tip to make the nymph look like it is trying to escape to shelter. Fishing a damsel nymph deep under a strike indicator may seem sacrilege to purists, but on deep, swift weedy pools, it is deadly. On Yellowstone's Firehole River, just above and below Firehole Falls there are many deep pools perfectly suited for this technique.

All this ento-jibberish about the technical aspects of imitating damsels has no relevance to why anglers actually like to fish the imitations: the strikes. Trout hit damsel patterns like Barry Bonds. There are no light takes or gentle taps; a damsel nymph could escape at any moment, and no right-minded fish will afford the nymph even a second to escape. Always up your tippet at least one X-size from what you normally fish to absorb those thundering hits.

Patterns

Keys to Match
1. **Sparsity:** Thin, thin, thin, thin, thin...thin.
2. **Broad Head:** Fly should strongly taper from head to tail.
3. **Movement:** If you don't got it, you won't get it.

Keys to Avoid
1. **Bright Color**
2. **Stiff Bodies:** Tie your body with stiff materials and the fly will move with the realism of Pam Anderson.
3. **"Hard Colors:"** Shoot for translucent, not transcendent.

Approximate Damsel

Hook: Dai Riki 270, #14-8
Weight: 4 wraps of .010 lead wire
Tail: Marabou, sparse
Body: Light Olive/Brown Hareline Caddis and Emerger Dubbing
Back: Medium pearl tinsel
Ribbing: Fine copper wire
Legs: Olive CDC
Eyes: Olive monofilament

This pattern is on my line 80% of the time when I am damsel fishing. It has plenty of motion and a realistic silhouette in the water (and in my box!). Fish it on an intermediate or sink-tip line near weeds, especially bulrushes and cattails, which the nymphs crawl out on to emerge. Usually short(1-3"), quick strips will produce the action that you are looking for, though long, slow pulls are effective.

Mike Skinner's Dry Your Eyes Special

Hook: Dai Riki 270, #14-8
Tail: Marabou sparse
Body: Dubbed light olive sparkle dubbing
Ribbing: Fine gold wire
Legs: Olive Hungarian partridge, two wraps
Collar: Olive ostrich herl or olive sparkle dubbing
Head: Copper bead, 3/32" or 1/8"

This is a pattern derived from several European patterns, and I like it when I am fishing a damsel pattern at speed just below the surface. It looks good in the box, but doesn't usually fish as well as the other damsel pattern. When fish are aggressive or opportunistic, this fly works well. However, when trout want a slowly presented damselfly one would be wise to choose one of the other patterns.

Keak da Sneak

Hook: Dai Riki 700 or 320, #12
Tail: Olive pheasant tail
Body: Blended olive, yellow, and brown seal fur substitute
Ribbing: Small mylar tinsel
Collar (optional): sparse Olive hackle

This is a variation of the traditional "stick fly"—minimalist patterns with untapered bodies and little adornment. This is certainly a deviation from the other two patterns, but it matches the sparse profile of the natural perfectly. However, when quickly stripped at the surface—where damsel nymph imitations are most effective—this fly looks more natural than a far more elaborate pattern. It doesn't hurt that even a novice tier can whip out a dozen of these in a half hour.

Hal Leveleer's Damsel

Hook: Dai Riki 320, #12-14
Body: Extended braided damsel body
Wings: Blended white and gray antron and pearl Lite Brite
Fore Wing: Grizzly hackle
Post: Blue or tan foam
Eyes: Black or olive mono

The adult damsel is not the most important stage for trout, as adults rarely rest on the surface for extended periods. However, trout will occasionally turn on them near reedy edges.

Daphnia

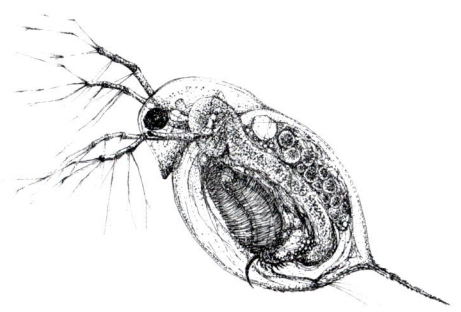

The Crustacean

I know what you're thinking. "Morgan is nuts. I'll put up with mundane talk of alder flies and inchworms, but this is ridiculous. Put the pipe down, son!" Before I spent a year in the library researching this stuff, I would have agreed with you. I'd rather spend a weekend in Cabo than research yet another trout food! If it weren't for dozens of British angling experts lamenting the seasonal importance of *Daphnia* to average and larger trout, I never would have discovered the vast and impressive literature on *Daphnia*. However, investing seven straight days reading over twenty years of professional essays on *Daphnia* and trout predation convinced me that I spent my time well.

Since gaining a vague awareness of their importance from the classic contributions of Charles Jardine fifteen years ago (dreaming I could trade running sprints with my basketball team for hand-twisting wet flies on Esthwaite), I have landed hundreds of trout over sixteen inches with *Daphnia* lining their mouths and esophagi. When these crustaceans undergo their seasonal population explosion, some exceptional waters can see populations from 200 to 500 *Daphnia* specimens per liter. Many lakes have *Daphnia* populations approaching 14,000 per square meter of open water! When prey in the 2-4mm size range abound—the size of smaller *Tricorythodes* mayflies and midges that most anglers respect as viable trout "hatches"—trout take notice. So should you.

"Anecdotes," you say! No American author has promoted the imitation of *Daphnia*, so show me where trout eat them?

Points with deep-water margins are a highway for trout to transition from shallows to the Daphnia*-rich depths.*

Jeff Morgan photo

In addition to the hundreds of lakes where *Daphnia* prove a significant portion of trout stomach samples, anglers should check out professional studies. In a particular Seattle's massive Lake Washington, *Daphnia* composed roughly 30% of the adult cutthroat trout diet throughout the season. Trout just did not feed on any old *Daphnia* there either, they were selective a particular species in a particular size range (1.2-2.0mm in length). In another study, *Daphnia* were the most important component of the trout diet until they reached 35 cm in length, whence they converted to a primarily baitfish diet. On this water, *Daphnia* were only the *second* most important food source for trout larger than 35 cm! On Castle Lake in California, *Daphnia* in the diet composition of brook trout and rainbow trout ranged from 25 and 30% during the autumn. In this small (.21km^2) lake, the trout consumed nearly 6 kg of *Daphnia* per day! A study by Robert Behnke, one of the most distinguished fish ecologists around, revealed that *Daphnia* made up a whopping 68% of the diet of Pike's Peak Cutthroat trout, while contributing "only" 32% and 28% to the diets of rainbow and brook trout from the same waters. The same study said that the Pike's Peak strain fed almost "exclusively" on *Daphnia* in August and September.

There are dozens of studies establishing the importance of *Daphnia* to not only juvenile trout, but also to large, adult trout. Despite the wealth of professional studies on *Daphnia*, the "stillwater trout diet" studies of many angling authorities omit *Daphnia* all together. Regardless of the alleged stillwater trout diets previously put forth by experts, understanding the proper role is essential to becoming a well-rounded lake angler anywhere in the northern hemisphere.

Anyone who recalls their middle school science class recalls looking through a microscope at tiny little reddish critters kicking around in a drop of water. Those were the same *Daphnia* that trout eat. Now, those microscopic specimens probably ran .5-1.5mm in length: too small for heavy trout predation. But, *Daphnia* can reach 4mm (more commonly 1-3mm) in length in certain trout waters. These larger specimens are the trout equivalent of M&M's.

Daphnia maintain a Spartan existence, slowly swimming through open water grazing on microscopic algae. Like we have covered earlier, if you want to find where trout eat a particular bug, you have to first locate where the bugs themselves feed. Like Chewbacca, wild creatures always follow their stomachs. In the case of *Daphnia*, the buffet line of drifting algae hovers nears the surface where sunlight sparks photosynthesis. *Daphnia* dwell at the surface under low light and nighttime conditions, when trout (and other predators) are less likely to gobble them up. They then dive deep when the sun reaches its apex. This keeps *Daphnia* in the 15-35 foot level, exactly where summertime trout seek out cool, well-oxygenated water. When trout dwell in deep and relatively open water they tend to feed on the only available food—*Daphnia*.

Light-induced migration is the critical behavior of *Daphnia* for fly anglers. Color, size, locomotion, and reproduction all are relatively mundane, as understanding daily *Daphnia* migrations keys the angler into trout positions in open water/deep water situations. Even when trout don't cohabitate with *Daphnia*, trout may "dive," plunging to the *Daphnia*-dense depths to graze for a few minutes before ascending to their normal cruising level.

Population fluctuations are another important factor in the importance of *Daphnia* to trout. Calm waters, low-flushing reservoirs, and cool water temperatures all benefit *Daphnia* populations. While *Daphnia* are filter-feeders, their populations collapse in waters with high levels of suspended sediment. Reservoirs that experience large inputs of silt-laden water (for example, below clear-cut forests) may see depressed levels of *Daphnia*, and subsequently, *Daphnia*-related feeding on the part of the trout.

Trout generally feed by swimming through swarms of *Daphnia* with their mouths agape. This feeding is not particularly efficient and trout tend to only ingest the larger individuals. As a general rule, when trout prey on *Daphnia*, they eliminate the largest specimens in a lake first and lower the overall mean size of *Daphnia*. This is not always the case—in one study, trout were actually selective to a specific size range of *Daphnia*, ignoring larger available specimens!

Daphnia are important to anglers because many summertime stillwater trout react directly to the *movement* and *densities* of *Daphnia* populations. A wise stillwater angler will keep these diminutive creatures in mind when normal tactics prove futile, especially in the late summer months. In August, spending time in deep, open water, far from the pontoon-riddled flats can often pay rich rewards for the Western angler.

Thoughts on Imitation

How the Hell do you imitate a 3mm long *Daphnia*? Simple. You don't. The one potential exception—sight-fishing to trout cruising shallow bank waters—is not as productive as it would at first seem, since *Daphnia* prefer deep, open water. I have tried to fish a tiny size 22 pale red or orange imitation in this situation, and found it no more productive than any random pattern.

Medium-sized wet flies with plenty of motion are usually effective for *Daphnia* feeding trout. Color is rarely the deciding factor, though red and orange colors are widely agreed upon for luring *Daphnia* feeding trout. Fish feeding on *Daphnia* are also susceptible to *Chaoborus* (phantom midge) imitations, as these insects shadow *Daphnia* movements throughout the day in order to prey on them.

When imitating *Daphnia*, the controlling factor is the ability to put your imitation where *Daphnia*-feeding trout suspend. The easiest way to locate deep fish in open water is with a depth finder/fish finder. The other, much slower, technique is to locate a likely cove or point, cast your flies, and let them sink to various depths before starting your retrieve. Having two or three other anglers with you can quickly cut down your prospecting time, as everyone can fish different depths at different speeds. Fish can descend extremely deep (20-30 feet) when making daytime feeding runs on *Daphnia*, so do not quit prospecting with *Daphnia* imitations when you get no strikes at 20 feet.

Wind-drifting across broad swaths of open water can be quite effective once the depth of Daphnia *schools is established.*

Once you locate the holding depths of *Daphnia* and trout, note the water temperature and sunlight conditions in your angling log. *Daphnia* on certain bodies of water tend to suspend at consistent depths, depending on the water temperature and amount of sunlight. Also, look in the gullet of the fish you catch at any depth for presence of *Daphnia* –the fish look like they have been eating Denison's Chili. This will quickly tell you if you caught a random fish or the *Daphnia*-feeding fish you were targeting. Good note taking, a good memory, or a good depth finder will reduce future prospecting time when targeting *Daphnia*-feeding trout.

A variety of retrieves work on *Daphnia* feeders, but I think a slower, hand-twist, retrieve is best. Summer trout feeding on *Daphnia* are often lethargic—they seek the cool depths for the oxygen, not the food or scenery. Patient retrieves will usually work best on these stressed trout.

Ever see those "crazy" type VI or VII full sinking lines in a fly shop clearance bin? Get one! They may not seem all that useful when imitating damsels or scuds on shallow flats, but in deep *Daphnia* water, they add a great deal of effective fishing time. They cut your sink-time in half and allow you to spend more time with your fly at the depths that trout are concentrated in. While a type VII sink tip is an excellent line for this kind of fishing, stay away from lighter sink tips—they just don't dive and remain deep enough for effective fishing.

While *Daphnia* prefer open water, trout don't. This leads me (and many others who follow *Daphnia*), to focus effort near points and small bays. In those areas trout can cruise at comfortably shallow depths, then "dive" down to nearby *Daphnia*-rich deep water. I have never had success with *Daphnia* imitation on broad, gently-sloped banks, as trout must wander far from prime feeding zones in order seek out *Daphnia* populations.

Common sense may lead one to assume that wind drives *Daphnia* to windward side of lakes, but this isn't as common as expected. *Daphnia* spend most daylight hours at 15-30 foot depths, where surface wind action has little effect. Even if they do get pushed to the windward shore, the heavy wave action makes them tough for trout to see them among the clouds of stirred-up mud and silt. To be sure, concentrate your efforts along windward banks; but think leeches, snails, and baitfish, not *Daphnia*.

A depth finder can be a useful, if not irreplaceable tool in locating *Daphnia* feeding trout. I like to scan open water, 20-30 feet down, looking for "random" fish during my lunch breaks on the water. If I start to see a trend, odds are that those fish are feeding on suspended *Daphnia*. If you use a larger boat in a larger lake, the depth finder can save hours of random casting to locate *Daphnia*-feeding trout.

Patterns

Keys to Match
Red and Orange Patterns: Trout look for globs of *Daphnia*.
Locate Depth: Find *Daphnia* and you will find summertime trout.
Locate Structure: Points and small coves offer easy access to *Daphnia* depths.

Keys to Avoid
Prospecting with Individual Imitations: Does a #26 pattern in 25 feet of water elicit much confidence? Didn't think so.
Chuck It and Chance It: Open water is not conducive to guess-and-check fishing
Ignoring Them: In the hot late-summer months, *Daphnia* can save the day!

Red Bastard

Hook: Dai Riki 070, #10-16
Tail: Short marabou puff to match body
Collar: Red or orange dubbing, brushed up
Hackle: Soft starling, grouse or partridge

This is my primary *Daphnia* pattern, and I carry about half orange and half red. When trout feed on Daphnia, anglers are not a threat, so pattern choice is should be of lesser consideration than location and depth. I like a light tippet not because of tippet-wary trout, but rather because I like the fly to have as much "jiggling" motion and activity as possible.

The Chuckwall

Hook: Dai Riki 070, #10-16
Tail: Peacock sword
Body: Red dubbing
Ribbing: fine gold tinsel
Thorax: Peacock herl
Hackle: Brown or orange-dyed Hungarian partridge

While this pattern started out as a joke for an Army Ranger friend of mine, it started catching fish in lakes at such a consistent rate I felt I had to classify it somehow. This incarnation has a few changes from the original in order to make it a more effective daphnia pattern. This style adds a red marabou tail and an orange/brown hackle (instead of light partridge). It works well fished extremely slowly in open water.

Daphnia Clump

Hook: Dai Riki 305, #14
Body: Red or copper wire
Dubbing: Red or orange Polar Dub
Globs: Red or range fingernail polish

This is pattern I saw first from Milwaukee, OR fly tying master, Ronn Lucas Jr. The wire body helps the fly stay deep and the fingernail polish globs is a perfect imitation of a glob of *Daphnia*.

Hot Wiggler

Hook: Dai Riki 320, #10-14
Tail: Red, orange, or peach marabou
Body: Same as tail
Ribbing: Pearl Krystalflash
Collar: Red, orange, or peach Estaz

When imitating *Daphnia*, imitation isn't as essential as locating trout in open water. This fly works because trout that cannot see the flash of the Estaz collar can feel the motion of the marabou tail. The Hot Wiggler is an attractor pattern, plain and simple. Can actually double as a sweet spring bluegill pattern as well.

Dragonflies (Anisoptera)

The Insect

Dragonflies, apart from being a beautiful and engaging insect order, are one of the most primitive members of the insect kingdom. Evolving 250-300 million years ago, the wingspans of some ancient dragonflies reached wingspans of nearly seventy centimeters! I would love to see the paleo-trout that gobbled up their larvae. Despite their smaller modern dimensions (or perhaps because of it) dragonfly larvae remain a crucially important food resource for stillwater trout.

Like grasshoppers, even people who have never wet a line can easily recognize and identify adult dragonflies. Thanks to their attractive coloration, dragonflies have been favorites of scientists and nature lovers for centuries. The adults are beautiful, fun to watch, and helpfully prey on mosquitoes and biting flies. Thus, the adults, unsurprisingly, receive a disproportionate amount of attention from entomologists. Dozens of dragonfly monographs abound with details on dragonfly emergence, breeding, flight, and egg laying behaviors. Yet the psychedelically-tinted adults are an afterthought in the minds of trout, which feed almost exclusively on dragonfly larvae. An angler hoping to master the dragonfly must master the behavior and appearance of the larvae.

Where do dragonfly larvae live? Like other aquatic insects, potential food and physical structure play an important role in their distribution. Dragonfly larvae prefer stillwaters and sluggish streams, though on occasion they appear in modest numbers in swifter rivers. Unlike damselfly nymphs, which abound in weedy or reedy lakes, dragonfly nymphs can be common in rocky, silty, and weedy lakes. A lake that incorporates all three of these habitats can have enormous populations of dragonfly nymphs. One oligotrophic lake in the Oregon Cascades abounds with so much dragonfly diversity and density, that its forty-seven species of dragonfly are commercially harvested (illegally, mind you) for trout bait on the dozen more famous lakes in the region. Needless to say, I have spent many solitary evenings dredging dragonfly patterns on the bottom of this lake for its monster brook trout, safely removed from the crowds jostling for position on the more famous waters.

The importance of dragonfly larvae to stillwater trout is analogous to the importance of large stonefly nymphs to river trout. The dragonfly larva is usually the largest invertebrate available to stillwater trout, thus a highly desirable and calorie-rich prey. One dragonfly nymph has the equivalent caloric content of 52 chironomid pupae or 67 cased caddis larvae! However, also like the salmonfly nymph, the dragonfly nymph is a relatively rare delicacy in the trout diet. They are simply difficult to locate. Many dragonflies lie camouflaged in the substrate or clutched to the dark side of a flooded stump, remaining inconspicuous and unavailable to trout. They are mostly available in the short period of migration and emergence, which can last as long as a month (in large waters) or as short as a few days on smaller ponds. Overall, dragonfly nymphs make up 5-7% of the diet of most stillwater trout. Exceptions to this norm are common and significant to anglers. On California's Eagle Lake, dragonfly nymphs contribute nearly 62% of the total energy consumed by brook trout over the course of one season! Like the largely unavailable leech, the high potential energy ensconced in dragon nymphs make them prized targets for hungry trout.

As trout grow progressively larger, dragonfly nymphs form a growing proportion of their diet. When trout feed on dragonfly larvae, they tend to target larger ones and ignore smaller specimens. This is why many of the repulsively large patterns that go unsold at fly shops often prove the best patterns! While dragonflies may be significant to trout throughout the year, their importance peaks during migration and emergence. Some studies show that trout slaughter over 85% of the emerging larva under

Dragonfly larvae exhibit an astounding array of body profiles that require specific imitations.

ideal conditions. Once adults safely emerge and fly away into the atmosphere, their relevance to trout drops enormously.

Dragonfly larvae are not just an important food source for trout; they compose a significant portion of the insect diet of bass, and some large panfish. The once-legendary dragonfly population of Crane Prairie Reservoir in Oregon was an essential factor in the fecundity of its illegally stocked and officially tolerated bass. Since I kill every largemouth on Crane Prairie in a ceremonial ritual I call "'Biologist' Terry Schrader's Bureaucratic Security Memorial Bass Execution," I afterwards dissect the bass stomachs and have discovered upwards of twenty dragons consumed by a single bass. During early summer, when most anglers merrily throw poppers to post-spawn warmwater fish, I love to dredge the bottom with a dragonfly nymph.

Dragonflies live in most of our trout lakes and many of the slower reaches of our trout rivers. Riverine species generally hold tightly to the bottoms of deep pools, hidden in the substrate, only moving to pounce on their prey. Given the negligible currents in these areas, and the acute ability of the nymphs to shoot water out of their ass to propel them back to the substrate, the nymphs rarely are involuntarily caught in the drift. On occasion, stream trout will consume dragonfly larvae at night, when larvae crawl about to locate new ambush sites. Unless your state allows nighttime fishing, these events are of little relevance to the fly angler.

Dragon nymphs prefer weedy, woody, and rocky structure because it conceals them from their prey, which includes just about anything that swims. Mayfly nymphs, water beetles, leeches, tadpoles, smaller dragonfly and damselfly nymphs, and even small fish are not safe from these voracious predators. Dragonflies have a unique method of capturing prey. Shooting out their extendable, spoon-shaped labium (bottom jaw), they grasp their prey and retract it into their mouth. If you have seen Julia Roberts eat anything, you can visualize it. The dragonfly's extendable jaw is an entomological wonder—large dragonfly nymphs can capture prey at a distance of twenty-five millimeters! The reach and speed of this bug grab allows dragonflies to be effective predators whether swimming around or lying stationary.

The nymphs commonly reach twenty to fifty millimeters in length before they emerge, and they live underwater for two to four years before they mature and are able to transform into adults. Over the first year, dragonfly nymphs grow rapidly until the larvae reach their final instar stage during the late summer or early fall of their second year. The larvae then remain approximately the same size until they emerge six to eighteen months later. Dragonfly larvae have a cryptic, mottled coloration, and several genera are capable of changing color to match their substrate. Some smaller larvae often have alternating light and dark stripes. It is also important to consider that as larvae molt, they often take on a radically different shade, usually a bright green or pale tan, which can make them more conspicuous to patrolling trout.

Dragonfly nymphs develop different profiles depending on how they feed: *streamlined* (for active predators) and *flattened* (for ambush predators). The nymphs also have long legs, especially in the case of sprawling-type larvae. Tiers should be prepared to imitate both body types on any stillwater.

While dragonfly larvae usually crawl amongst the substrate, they have a unique movement to capture prey or elude predators. They make use of a mini jet-propulsion system by taking in water and expelling it out their anuses. This shoots the nymphs forward in four to twelve-inch bursts; however, longer bursts help the larvae overtake prey or flee from a threat. For the angler, the latter motivation matters quite a bit. A bug that obese moving that fast certainly catches the eye of nearby fish. Even an uninterested cruising trout will take notice and pounce on such a juicy morsel before it can escape.

The other important defense mechanism of dragonfly larvae is *reflex immobilization* (or death feigning), a behavior documented in all dragonfly families common to trout waters. When contacted by a fish or other predator, the larvae freezes with legs either extended or tucked against the body, depending on the species. If you remember that earlier we discussed how trout sense motion in prey, you'll understand why this is an effective defense mechanism.

Unfortunately for the angler, most of the time dragonfly nymphs lie stationary to ambush their prey, a lifestyle choice that makes them unavailable to fish. Trout find these bugs far more obtainable when they migrate towards the logs, rocks, and reeds near shoreline prior to emergence. The migration takes place usually between March and August, but is concentrated on most trout stillwaters from May-early July. Counter to most angling theory, which alleges that dragonfly and damselfly emergences creates a month or so of trout gluttony, the emergence of dragonflies is very brief on each particular water. Some studies show that 40-60% of larvae in a lake can emerge in a single night, and 85% might emerge in a five-day period. For the stillwater angler, this concentrated emergence resembles the salmonfly emergence in rivers.

The beautiful adult dragonfly certainly serves as a welcome distraction on slow fishing days. But despite their large size and proximity to water, I have never seen a trout eat one of the adults buzzing on the surface. Professional ecologists agree that only under exceptional circumstances will trout prey on adult dragonflies. In a Wyoming study, simply finding two adults in trout stomach samples was worthy of publication in the journal, *Entomology News*. Obviously, the rarity in which trout prey on adult

Log-strewn lake edges abound in dragonfly larvae.

While dragonfly adults have stunning colors, trout rarely prey upon them.

dragonflies means that merely documenting such an ecological aberration is reason enough for publication. The 670-page *Dragonflies: Behavior and Ecology of Odonata*, the primary textbook for dragonfly study, devotes all of three sentences to fish predation (of any type, let alone trout) on dragonfly adults.

For a serious stillwater angler chasing anything from brook trout to bluegill to bass, dragonfly larvae should have serious representation in your fly box. Below are the three most dragonfly families in trout waters, each has a distinct coloration, shape, and behavior specific imitations should incorporate.

Family: Aeshnidae (11 genera, 39 species)

With a streamlined body and active predatory style, aeshnids are the most important family of dragonflies for the angler. Aeschnids are the largest dragonflies in the West, approaching two inches in length as mature nymphs. These nymphs also exhibit a distinct coloration, displaying a darker mottled-olive on their backs than on their bellies. They also have shorter and thicker legs than bottom-sprawling larvae. Aeshnids perpetually hunt aquatic insects, annelids, and small fish, and this exposure makes them prime targets for a cruising trout.

When not pursuing their prey, these dragon nymphs are claspers and climbers—crawling throughout aquatic vegetation and darting between gaps in the vegetation. Aeshnids abound in areas of heavy plant growth, often cohabitating with damselfly nymphs. If you remember anything about their escape methods, remember that they escape by (1) expelling water out their rectum; (2) rowing with their legs; (3) tucking their legs along their body as they expel more water; (4) repeating the process.

Family: Libellulidae (26 genera, 105 species)

This family of dragonflies is more stubby and stout that aeshnids, and they prefer rocks and logs to weedy flats. The nymphs of this family rarely cruise open water looking for active prey. Rather, they partially bury themselves in the mud to camouflage themselves from their prey, which like Aeschnids, consists primarily of small insects and small fish. Anglers should imitate Libellulidae larvae extremely close to the bottom to match this behavior. Though they have a wide distribution and tolerate an array of water conditions, Libellulidae still prefer silty and rocky habitats that facilitate their ambush tactics.

While libellulids range in color from mottled shades of brown to dark olive, they can adapt to the color of their surroundings. These dragonflies usually grow to a smaller size than the aeshnids, ranging from 8 to 30 mm in length when mature. They also take longer—three to five years—to mature. Their smaller size and longer larval stage is most likely due to their sluggish lifestyle, which doesn't account for much caloric consumption.

Family: Cordulegastridae (1 Genera, 8 species), Gomphidae (15 Genera, 97 species)

The two most common deep-burrowing dragonfly families in North America, the dragonflies in two genera will settle into a choice location to ambush prey. They (gomphids especially) can be common in streams, where they bury their abdomens and legs in the substrate, exposing their head and labium for sensing and capturing prey. While these may be common, in bottom samples, their tendency to bury themselves makes them largely unavailable to trout. Even when threatened by fish, many species escape by simply burrowing deeper. Most dragons of this type become available to trout only during the month prior to emergence. Anglers can easily distinguish these larvae from others by their noticeably flattened, almost disk-like 13-35mm long bodies and camouflaged colors. Many in this family also have long legs for sprawling on the bottom.

THOUGHTS ON IMITATION

Dragonflies occupy a unique niche in the tier's repertoire. Despite their diversity in size, behavior, and body structure, most tiers and anglers only imitate them with one or two patterns. However, in one lake, the streamlined Aeshnidae may predominate, and in another lake the elliptically-bodied Libellulidae thrive. Though both fall under the moniker "dragonfly," the differences in body structure, color, and behavior require the angler to arm themselves with a variety of imitations and tactics.

Every stillwater angler, regardless of the fish species they pursue, must pack several distinct unweighted imitations. Floating patterns are preferable to weighted ones for one major reason: they can be fished naturally. Unweighted dragons allow the angler to ply deeper waters with a slow retrieve, keeping the fly in the strike zone without hanging up. An unweighted imitation can also match the "reflex immobilization" defense technique used by many dragonflies to their own peril.

A weighted imitation requires a constant retrieve, just the opposite of the sit-and-pounce behavior preferred by most natural dragons. Weighted patterns, however, do have their uses. Most notably, they are excellent for "mucking:" resting the fly on the bottom before quickly shooting it up in a puff of silt and strip of line.

To create a floating imitation, foam is an excellent choice. I am usually bearish on foam, as its bulk and monochrome spectrum combine to produce rather unanimated and cadaverous patterns. Ribbing foam with a slightly different color of material beaks up the monotony and makes the fly more realistic. Since dragon larvae patterns should be bulky, an underbody of foam and an overbody of Woolly Chenille, dubbing, or ostrich herl will not result in an undesirably chunky imitation. Another option is a fly with spun and clipped deer hair, in the style of the Kaufmann's Floating Dragon. This style of tying creates viable and vibrant patterns, but spinning and clipping deer hair adds quite a bit of tying time.

Legs are essential for the tier to consider. While relatively thick, long, and active when crawling on vegetation or on the substrate, during escape, the dragonfly's legs collapse against the body. The tier should design legs that move when the fly is stripped in. Superfloss, or any variant of it, imitates this leg movement well, as they stick straight out when the fly is still, but sweep back on the body as the angler strips in the fly. Avoid relatively stiff material like stripped hackle stems, moose mane, or molded plastics (ala Stalcup Damsel Legs), as they stick straight out and make your fly look as lifeless as it actually is.

Eyes are another prominent feature on most dragonfly nymphs, as most dragons feed by sight. Simple monofilament eyes work best, though some people like knotted vernille or ultra chenille for eyes. Bead chain eyes will work on some patterns, though not on flies intended to float or hover.

Flat libellulids are challenging to imitate. I found that I needed better imitations after standard imitations did not work, despite the abundance of naturals in subsequent substrate and stomach samples. Once, out of desperation, I tried on a brown crab pattern (sans the claws)—a wayward refugee from a previous bonefish fly order. This pattern had the color, broad profile, and leg motion to fool enough fish to force me to rethink the standard methods of dragonfly nymph imitation.

Remember the front-to-back taper we've applied to nearly every fly pattern to this point? Throw that strategy out the window with dragonfly nymphs. While the exact body proportions should vary between imitations of different species, the rear of the abdomen should be as large as or larger than the head of the nymph. Also, tails should be omitted on most all dragonfly nymph patterns. As the naturals have no tail (which would inhibit the use of their ass-jet), tails only wind up on patterns to fool fishermen and not trout.

I almost always fish my dragon nymphs on a full-sink line, because they should stick close to the bottom. The modern stillwater fetish of intermediate and sink-tip lines has resulted in a decline in the popularity and effectiveness of dragonfly larvae imitations. A heavy sink tip (type V) will get the fly to where it needs to go, but give it some time before starting the retrieve.

Dragonfly nymph retrieves should be composed of cyclic darts and pauses. One of the best retrieves I use is three quick, 6-8" pulls followed by a 15 second pause. Cruising fish will see the movement, and the long pause will sell the fraud, since most fishing flies do not stop and hover, so be ready. Most strikes come on the start of the strip. Also, when retrieving your fly do not set your hook on every bump. Remember that the larvae often will freeze after an initial attack, hoping to slowly sink unmolested into the safety of the substrate. If you pause your retrieve for a few moments, then start your retrieve again instead of stripping quickly to make another cast, you can often coax second or third strikes from trout.

While you still may pick up a few trout trolling dragon nymphs, it is not a preferred technique. These nymphs are not suited to sustained locomotion, which is exactly what trolling imitates. Consider trolling dragonfly nymphs about as often as you would troll snail patterns.

Focus on imitating dragons primarily in the few weeks prior to the major emergence period (May-early July). They also make for excellent choices in the early season, when lethargic trout do not want to chase down fast-moving prey. The floating-style dragon is perfect for these fish. You can tailor your retrieve and depth to match the mood of the trout.

Patterns

What to Match
1. **Floaters:** Floating patterns give the angler far more retrieve options.
2. **Big Butt:** Give it elephantitis of the ass.
3. **Legs:** Rarely is the most ignored feature the most prominent one on the natural.

What to Avoid
1. **Adult Imitations:** Trout don't eat them.
2. **One Kind of Nymph:** There are too many variations to commit to just one.
3. **Retrieving Too Fast:** Dragonflies need lots of rest breaks.

Floater (For Charlie Patton)

Hook: Dai Riki 270, #6-10
Under Body: 2-3, 1/4" wide strips of foam
Body: Dark brown sparkle dubbing or dark olive Woolly Chenille
Back: Brown foam
Ribbing: Brown ostrich herl
Legs: Dark Olive or Brown Superfloss
Wing case: Treated brown raffia
Head: Dark dubbing
Eyes: Black monofilament, medium

Many people recoil at the profile of the Floater, especially in large sizes, but trout don't mind at all. Since the pattern floats, the angler can fish it at a slow crawl near the bottom without snagging. Sometimes the fly works great fished nearly static. As the fly floats and hovers, the legs will jiggle and wave with only the slightest movement of the line. This is often too much for a hungry but lethargic early season trout to stand.

Third World Cantina Dragon

Hook: Dai Riki 070, #8
Body: Brown, tan, or dark olive craft felt
Legs: Olive or Brown Super Floss, mottled with pen
Head: Dark dubbing to match body
Eyes: Black bead-chain or mono eyes

This fly, a variation of Caribbean crab imitations, is most effective when sight fished, where you can let the fly sink down and rest on the bottom and dart away as a trout approaches. The flat profile is critical in the success of the pattern, the same technique with other body styles is not as productive. Conversely, this is not a pattern you want to strip or troll; it must be fished in short bursts off the bottom, and allowed to resettle. Obviously, the precarious nature of the retrieve means it is best used on lakes with a relatively clean sand or silt bottom.

Kern County Dragon

Hook: Dai Riki 270, #8-14
Tail: Filoplume to match body, short
Body: Spun and clipped olive, brown, or black deer hair
Legs: Filoplume to match body, short
Wing case: Treated raffia to match body
Eyes: Black or olive monofilament
Head: Sparkle dubbing to match body

Promoted by both Randall Kaufmann and Skip Morris, deer hair dragon bodies have been popular in the Northwest for decades. It took me years to find success with this pattern, but once I learned how to fish it properly it quickly ascended into my top ten Stillwater patterns. I convince myself that I'll only need twenty of these for a season, and end lamenting my shortage after the first week of stillwater season!

Deschutes Special

Hook: Dai Riki 070, #8-10
Tail: Grizzly hackle tip
Butt: Red thread
Body: Chenille (black, dark olive, brown, light olive, yellow, purple, red, black/yellow)
Hackle: Grizzly, palmered
Tinsel: Gold or silver mylar tinsel, small
Head: Red thread

With all these hundreds of strange patterns, I try to keep looking for new ways to do things. Yet this pattern, an ancient variation of the woolly worm and the first fly I ever tied, is still one of my top ten stillwater flies for trout, bass, panfish, and even chain pickerel. As a kid, I would look at dad's fly boxes filled with dozens of Deschutes Specials tied in various colors, and they all seemed to work! I still consider this as one of my best two or three dragonfly patterns, and still carry dozens with me on most any stillwater I fish.

Grasshoppers

THE INSECT

Next time you walk through a grassy field down to a trout stream, don't look down. Those fateful moments on the walk from the car to the side of the river account for the greatest misallocation of angler effort: the grasshopper. While the mayfly has long ridden the high tide of angler good favor, the tides of experience are shifting to place them in a more realistic, humbled setting. The 1970's and 1980's movement of "sophisticated" fly fishing shifted strongly towards "realistic" terrestrials to fill the intervals between summertime hatches and to break the will of hatch-focused trout. Grasshoppers were the *prima armae* in this new style of warfare. Like trench warfare innovators and automatic weapons during the First World War, sophisticated trout and hopper patterns arrived at a wary stalemate.

New fly anglers undoubtedly embrace hopper patterns because they are something they could relate to in their pre-fishing days. Non-anglers see hoppers jumping through fields and carrying on conversations in children's cartoons—no such propaganda praised the lowly scud or simuliid larvae! Students of history and agriculture learn about the effects of grasshoppers and locusts on farming communities throughout the world. Beginning fly anglers with experience in other angling fields recall that hoppers and crickets are also a preferred bait for gear anglers—because they stay on a hook. Grasshopper-shaped crankbaits, known as the "Crickhoppers," are even sold by Rebel. Grasshoppers, seemingly, with their random, haphazard leaping and plague-like abundance, should be a superb trout food.

Unfortunately, trout simply do not eat hoppers…at least, not in the quantities we think they do. Anglers usually see the trout world through terrestrial eyes. We look at insect colors from the top, we use dry patterns of insects that we see flying about while trout feed on the easier-to-eat pupae, and we choose our terrestrials by what jumps around when we walk from our car to the stream.

Tiny streams lined with grasses and short willows are prime hopper habitat.

Jeff Morgan photo

Grasshopper colors usually match their environment, making a diverse spectrum of imitations important.

After reviewing hundreds of professional trout diet studies, I am convinced that grasshoppers are little more than a novelty item in the diets of most trout. Numerous summer studies have grasshoppers totally absent from trout stomach samples, including some samples conducted on summer fish looking for terrestrial components of the trout diet!

Even when grasshoppers appear in stomach samples, the numbers hardley impress. In a June through September study on a Wyoming creek where 1657 recognizable prey items were recovered from brook trout stomachs, a whopping total of *two* were hoppers. Grasshoppers were least common prey item among twenty-seven foods in that study. In another sample of 143 summer-caught fish, one grasshopper was found: sharing the least important food ranking with other freak show foods like a snipe fly and adult dragonfly (which are notoriously unimportant to trout).

The overestimation of grasshoppers can be partially attributed to trout diet surveys conducted in the ancient past. In *Caddisflies*, LaFontaine describes the inadequacies of the 1939 Paul Needham study that served as the cornerstone of many 1960's and 1970's estimations of the general trout diet. While the Needham study is one of the most famous exaggerations of hopper importance, there are many other samples that have been uncritically embraced by a broad swath of angling writers. A study of the trout streams in upstate New York during 1920 stated that grasshoppers were essential to "large brown trout," contributing a whopping 80% of food volume! Since this study is a inadequate, we should take a closer look. Those "large brown trout" came from a sample size of nine trout (between five and twelve inches in length), and these nine trout were caught in the month of September (if there is a prime hopper month, September is). Hardly a sufficient sample size to warrant any broad conclusion on the importance of hopppers to trout.

In 2000, I had an inkling that grasshoppers weren't as important as everyone says, so I decided to head to the high altar of grasshopper angling: Yellowstone Park. Taking samples of fifty trout caught on dry flies in several different streams (Gibbon River, Slough Creek, Yellowstone River, Madison River, Blacktail Deer Creek, Fan Creek, Glen Creek), even I was surprised how few hoppers were consumed by Yellowstone trout (see table). However, this surprise was amplified by the abundance of their imitations found in local fly shops.

	Number of terrestrial insects/ parts found in trout	Relative Abundance	Number of terrestrial patterns found in Fly Shops	Relative Abundance
Beetles	29	38.1%	13	13.1%
Ants	18	23.7%	13	13.1%
Horseflies	8	10.5%	5	5.1%
Inchworms	7	9.2%	2	2.0%
Crickets	6	7.9%	10	10.1%
Grasshoppers	4	5.3%	52	52.5%
Wasps	4	5.3%	4	4.0%
Total	76	100.00%	99	100.00%

Have you ever noticed how most fish assault a hopper pattern right after it plops on the water? These reflexive strikes occur because trout usually rise to hoppers out of instinct rather than choice. In the summer of 2001, after catching sixty fish on hopper patterns on streams in Yellowstone, I found that over 70% of rises occurred within two seconds of when the fly hit the surface. Ant patterns fished on the same set of rivers caught more fish, but most rises took place long after the fly touched down. The hopper-caught fish did not make circumspect rises typical of selective fish—they attacked it out of instinct. When a big chunk of food hits the water, trout don't think—they eat. This instinctual reaction probably accounts for most fish we catch on hopper and cricket imitations. Why else would the Chernobyl Ant work?

Another problem with hoppers is that anglers adhere to a limited cadre of patterns: Dave's Hopper, Joe's Hopper, Whit's Hopper, Parachute Hopper, and in the West, the Henry's Fork Hopper. The Chernobyl Hopper could be included here, but I am still trying to forget that it exists.

Hoppers elicit an "instinctual" strike, which explains the success of gaudy Chernobyl-type patterns.

On heavily pressured waters, hopper imitations serve the angler best by remaining in the fly box. On Yellowstone's Slough Creek, a stream where hopper imitations are supposedly as essential as polarized sunglasses and bug repellant, many anglers report that large hopper imitations actually spook leisurely-cruising trout. Because most anglers turn to hoppers as their first choice during August and September, most fish on popular waters get stuck once or twice, and trout on heavily pressured streams get caught at least a couple of times on grasshopper imitations. After watching faux hoppers drift overhead for weeks, some fish on the Henry's Fork will swim off into deep water when yet another obvious fraud plops down nearby. Hoppers should only be used as strike indicators for smaller terrestrials and nymphs when fishing most popular streams.

While all the science tells us trout rarely feed on grasshoppers, imitations continue to fool trout. Sometimes, they are the only pattern that works. My father fishes a stretch of a the Yellowstone river, where he never fails to catch fish with grasshopper imitations. The funny is, he does best there in mid-September (when most fish vacate that section of stream), and he catches them early in the morning (7:30-10:00am), often at sub-freezing air temperature. He has even fooled those cutts on hoppers in the middle of a snow flurry! At that time of the year, any grasshoppers surviving the freezing night air certainly are not moving around, let alone taking an early morning swim. Regardless of the lack of rational explanation, hoppers always seem to fool a few fish on this stretch, while even the most thorough nymphing results in only a random strike or two. Cases like this are the anecdotal phenomena that make people fall in love with hopper fishing. It also invests a false hope in the widespread productivity of hoppers.

Since hoppers can occasionally be important, let us consider characteristics of these insects that may help us better imitate them.

One common thread in hopper orthodoxy is that grasshopper imitations fish best during the late season, August-October. Maybe. More hoppers actually appear in the drift in the early season when they are sexually immature and lack wings. Have you ever tried to throw mammoth, two-inch grasshoppers in the water? Wind up and hurl it at the water like a bitter Roger Clemens all day and the hopper will still fly off before touching down on the water thanks to their well-developed wings. By September, when most species have matured, the adult hoppers actually appear less frequently in the trout diet as their wings help prevent them from landing in the water.

For the same reasons outlined above, small hopper patterns (size 10-14) can prove significantly more effective than large ones. Small hoppers are more available to trout, more susceptible to high winds and rains (because they are weak fliers or unable to fly at all), and they are more prone to accidentally leaping into the water. Plus, with everyone else chucking size 4/0 monstrosities, you can still fool seasoned fish.

Immature hoppers, slimmer and lacking effective wings, are far more common in the trout diet than adult hoppers.

Ever thrown a hopper in the water and watched it for more than a few seconds? Usually the hopper kicks in a circle until it locates the bank, then kicks aggressively in that direction. While this is yet another reason why they are not that important to trout, it is also a realistic behavioral pattern that can spark the interest of otherwise lethargic trout. Try casting towards a trout and giving the fly a handful of short two to three-inch twitches while gently pulling the fly towards the bank. This technique is best for targeted, individual trout, as extended drifts are impossible when you twitch the fly.

Thoughts on Imitation

Fly tiers have arrived at a consensus on the significance of matching the hopper's legs, and any hopper pattern should include them in some form. Knotted and trimmed hackle fibers, rubber, knotted pheasant tail fibers, and a variety of other materials can all suffice. Remember to tie up several patterns with red legs to imitate the occasionally common species of red-legged hoppers. On small patterns, like a size 14 Letort Hopper, they are not essential.

While most patterns sport long wings, many natural hopper wings are shorter than their bodies. Imitating the long body and short wing sometimes can create a seductive and unique silhouette on the water.

Like with ants and beetles, be sure to carry a variety of hoppers in shades ranging from bright yellow and light green to tan and dark gray. Try to match the color to the general habitat: using greens and tans in meadows, gray on rocky streams, and brown in sparse vegetation/desert is a good guideline. Most hoppers also have a decidedly mottled appearance to aids in their camouflage, so I like to incorporate variant coloration in my patterns.

Since fishing hopper-dropper rigs is a popular technique, I make sure to tie my hoppers with rather buoyant material. I rarely spin deer hair on my flies—the advent of foam and CDC rendered it an elaborate and often superfluous step. However, A fly such as the Irresistible Hopper, when tied properly, will float forever and it is a worthwhile expenditure of tying time.

Elk hair, foam, CDC, and thick hackle all can help keep your imitation on the surface.

Fight the urge to tie hoppers on heavy-wire hooks. Many large commercial outfits tie their hoppers on streamer hooks more suited to tarpon than trout. A lighter-wire hook should still hold your trout, but will also hold up on the surface. My preferred hook is a Dai Riki 270, but there are many other long-shank normal-wire hooks perfect for hoppers.

Effective hopper patterns must be *different*. Anglers tend to obsessively over-rely on hopper flies, especially on western spring creeks (Silver Creek, Henry's Fork, Rocky Ford, Fall River). A unique pattern must ignite the visual keys that trout use to target hoppers, without reminding the fish of previous harrowing experiences with the creatures.

We often hear about the "plop:" that thin, wild, mercury sound that draws trout to a grasshopper. This is certainly true in many cases, but often you can fool cruising trout by just having your pattern passively drifting with the current. As cruising trout often dwell in places of high angling pressure, they usually see fake flies come into their window with ripples emanating, since some dolt touched the fly down just seconds before the trout arrived at the target. The "dead hopper" technique—casting the fly yards ahead of the cruising trout, allowing it to settle long before a fish comes into range—requires observation and patience, since the angler should approach nearly ten yards ahead of the fish and wait for it to slowly swim up to the fly.

When and where hoppers are used is more important than particular pattern choices. Here is a quick outline about how to maximize the use of grasshopper imitations in your own fishing.

When not to fish hoppers

1. Slow water situations. Fish with plenty of time to inspect a fly often look at a hopper long enough to rekindle bad memories. Additionally, natural hoppers in slow water have more than enough time to kick back to shore, and their drifts are extremely short.

2. During hatches. While tiny beetles and ants draw away fish locked into a particular emergence or spinner fall, hoppers rarely elicit the same reaction from trout.

3. Mornings. When the grass is wet and the air is cool, hoppers lay low. When they are not active, they are not available to fish. Trout rarely rise to an adult Hexagenia imitation at noon, and the same goes for hoppers fished at the improper time.

4. When fishing more than five feet from shore. Spend any amount of time on a western stream and your see several anglers wasting time throwing hoppers in the middle of the stream. These fish see hoppers about as often as OJ looks for the "real killer." These casts may draw the occasional strike, but putting your fly consistently near the shoreline means you present to more receptive trout.

5. Heavy pressure situations. Since most shops carry the same cohort of hopper patterns and anglers cannot resist using them, excellent anglers catch their share of trout with them while poor anglers tend to spook dozens of trout with the same flies. Either way, trout quickly learn to avoid them. Now is the time to experiment with tiny ant and beetle patterns, and to keep the hopper patterns tucked deep in the dark recesses of your fly box.

How to maximize your hopper fishing?

1. Fish Hoppers in deep water. Hoppers are big juicy morsels that have the ability to draw fish to the surface from a significant depth. I really like to fish hoppers in "canyon water," which is the name I use for swift pocket water that runs three to six feet deep. Here, a trout needs a significant reason to expend the energy needed to go to the surface, and a small beetle, ant, or Royal Wulff just won't cut it.

2. Using a Hopper-Dropper combo. In the late fall, as the water cools and terrestrials grow less common, fishing dry flies during a non-hatch period is a sketchy endeavor. However, none of us are quite ready to forgo the elegant dry fly for the cumbersome indicator nymphing setup required during the cold-weather months. The hopper-dropper setup gives the angler a happy medium. Composed simply of a large, buoyant hopper pattern with a small beadhead (or other lightly weighted nymph) connected to the hook bend of the hopper via a two to three-foot length of tippet. This setup excels at searching the water because it allows you to experiment with several types of nymphs without sacrificing the explosive strikes the hopper brings. Of course, if one fly is producing all your fish, you can get rid of the other one.

3. Fish Hoppers on small streams or less-pressured waters. There are two major problems fishing hopper imitations, fish don't eat all that many naturals and anglers tend to regularly use imitations. Though the first is a problem impossible to overcome without tinkering with genetics, by using hoppers on streams that receive little pressure, you can eliminate the latter complication.

4. Fish small hoppers. One of the biggest myths in angling is that hoppers aren't important until late summer/early fall when they grow larger. Hoppers are wingless most of their lives, only growing them during their final instar (their adult stage). The smaller hoppers are much more likely to end up in the water after an errant jump than their winged elders. The ideal hopper size should range between size 10 and 14, though most shops only carry size 10 and larger. It is important that you inspect these smaller hoppers, for they are often different colors than the meaty monsters that are more readily visible.

5. Windy and rainy conditions. Strong winds can blow jumping hoppers into the water, and trout seem much more responsive to the imitations when the water's surface is slightly riffled. Beware though, when hoppers are blown into the water, so are beetles and ants that dwell on the waving riparian grasses and leaves. Imitations of these insects may be just as, if not more, effective. Rainy conditions cause terrestrials to be knocked off their riparian perches as much, if not more, than windy conditions do.

Finally, the Chernobyl Hopper doesn't really exist, does it?

Patterns

WHAT TO MATCH:
1. **Legs:** A defining feature.
2. **Smaller Patterns:** If you have to fish 'em start small and start early.
3. **New:** Don't go to the honey hole with the same #8 Joe's Hopper that has been dragged through the pool every day of summer for the past fifty years.

WHAT TO AVOID:
1. **HUGE Patterns:** Big hoppers don't end up in the water much.
2. **Pressured Fish:** The goal when presenting to tough trout is to give them something they have NOT seen before.
3. **Morning Hoppers:** Give them time to warm up their legs before you imitate them.

Van Smack's Jungle Hopper

Hook: Dai Riki 270 #4-14
Tail: Red hackle fibers
Body: Antron bright green, yellow, or cream
Ribbing: Brown hackle, palmered and clipped
Legs: Knotted dyed grizzly hackles, clipped short
Wing: Lacquered turkey quill
Head: Deer hair, tied bullet style

This is my general grasshopper pattern, which works well in most situations from riffles to flat water. I like to add a bit of superglue at the tie-in point for wing and legs to help keep them in place and to prevent the head from spinning around after a couple fish.

The Sarah X

Hook: Dai Riki 270, #10-14
Tail: Light elk hair
Body: Yellow craft foam
Under Wing: Rootbeer Krystalflash
Wing: Light elk hair
Over Wing: Pink antron
Legs: Spirit River Grizzly Legs or Chartreuse-tipped jig legs
Head: Elk hair, tied bullet-head style

A better pattern for fast, deep water, the Sarah X has enough buoyancy to function as an indicator for a weighted nymph. The muppet-like pink mohawk allows the angler to see it better as it drifts through turbulent water.

Dubbed Deer Hunter

Hook: Dai Riki 270, #10-14
Body: Foam strip to match body
Wing: Mottled precut wing material
Legs: Yellow-dyed grizzly hackle stem, trimmed and knotted
Head: Blended deer hair, dubbed

Another experiment in deer-hair dubbing gone awry, the Deer Hunter works because it breaks up the standard profile of a hopper. The scraggly head helps to imitate the smaller, and rarely imitated, forelegs. Works extremely well on heavily-pressured fish in calm waters.

Rep the Yay Hopper

Hook: Dai Riki 300, #12-14
Body: Pale yellow, tan, olive, or brown dubbing
Legs: Knotted pheasant tail
Over Wing: Turkey tail feather
Head: Dubbed CDC

This simple hopper works best on flat water, as the CDC leaves a "busy" profile at the head of a fly imitating the busy forelegs of the natural.

Letort Hopper

Hook: Dai Riki 270, #10-18
Body: Gray, dark olive, light olive, or yellow dubbing
Wing: Lacquered turkey quill or synthetic
Head: Deer hair, spun and clipped

Horseflies (*Tabanus*) and Deer Flies (*Chrysops*)

Horse fly.

Deer fly.

The Insects

While the gentle pricks of biting mosquitoes over the years inspired anglers to imitate them the muscle-tightening pain of a horsefly bite leaves most anglers praying never to see one again, let alone "match the hatch". Adult horseflies are certainly not absent from trout stomach samples, often conspicuously occurring in the early summer when trout are focused on the other hatches. In my comprehensive stomach sampling of Yellowstone Park 2000-2003, adult biting flies ranked as the fourth most common terrestrials, behind ants, beetles, and leafhoppers (and still twice as common as hoppers).

My first encounter with horseflies came on Yellowstone's Slough Creek. As I kneeled in a cut bank waiting for a large cutthroat to return to its normal crusing pattern, I felt a stabbing pain in my calf. After a reflexive slap (like other Slough

Marshy lake and stream margins can harbor huge horsefly and deer fly populations.

Jeff Morgan photo

PATTERNS

THE HEART ATTACK MACHINE

Hook: Dai Riki 300, #10-14
Body: Black foam
Ribbing: Bronze Arizona Peacock Dubbing
Wings: Tan or gray treated raffia
Legs: Black elk or deer hair or black hackle
Head: Black sparkle dubbing
Eyes: Red monofilament, burned red ultra chenille or painted red spots

BROWN LIGHTNING

Hook: Dai Riki 300, #14
Body: Bronze Arizona Peacock Dubbing
Wings: Golden brown mottled wing material, cut to rough triangle shape
Legs: Golden brown deer hair

Creek addicts, I can now identify bugs by how they bite), and the large black/gray horsefly that I expected tumbled into the water about a foot from my feet. As the cutthroat returned, it vectored left just before reaching my fraudulent beetle to inhale the big horsefly. At first I thought "Hey, maybe that is why the big beetle works!" Then I thought, "why not a specific horsefly imitation?" After doing so, I found them an effective pattern on high recreational-use waters, where many fall dead.

Horseflies and deer flies are actually aquatic insects, though I consider them terrestrials since the larvae aren't readily available to trout. The larvae live in the marshy borders of many trout streams, and many streams that flow through waterlogged meadows are exceedingly rich in these insects. The larvae, however, are safely concealed underground and are rarely available to trout. The larvae resemble creamy maggots and range from 7-14mm in length. The larvae, while rarely as important as the adults, can appear in ridiculous quantities in the diets of some stream trout. In July on one Wyoming stream, nearly 80% of the total diet of trout was composed of Tabanidae larvae! Freak occurrences like this are very random, and I wouldn't recommend wasting time imitating the larvae

The adults emerge following ice-out, and remain common for 1-3 months afterwards. Horseflies range from 10-18mm in length (hopefully you don't encounter any larger!) and are often banded black and gray, with a hefty build and clear wings. Deer flies, conversely, have a mottled dark brown body and the wings provide the insect with a triangular appearance. Deer flies are also notably smaller than horseflies, rarely exceeding 12mm.

The combination of stabilizing riparian zones or improving water quality on many of our streams plus the increasing recreational use of our waters (meaning more bugs getting slapped to death) will likely combine to make imitations of both insects even more useful in the years to come.

THOUGHTS ON IMITATION

While many beetle imitations serve as effective horsefly imitations, my experiences on the flat water of Slough Creek encouraged me to experiment with unique patterns that I could be confident that fish had not seen before.

Because of their size, horsefly imitations need a foam body to ensure floatation. Black foam or dark gray foam w/black stripes are the two best colors to work with. I also add clear Raffia or wings to my horsefly imitations to distinguish them from beetle patterns. I alternate between clipped hackle legs and dubbed deer hair for legs on the Heart Attach Machine, though either works well enough. The red eyes of this pattern are purely to give the fly a menacing look in the fly box.

Don't shy away from these patterns during the early summer "bug" season. Trout will eat them in respectable numbers. If I am targeting a sighted, slow-water trout holding near a bank in June, I am just as likely to try horsefly or deerfly imitations as any other terrestrial. Never underestimate the power of a large, realistic, and most importantly, "different," fly pattern!

Honeybees (*Apis mellifera*)

The abundance of flowering plants near orchards and gardens make honeybees an occasional trout food on streams with cultivated riparian zones.

The Insect

One of the classic anthropocentric fly patterns in fishing history is the McGinty, a wet fly that generally resembles a bumblebee. Other than that, there are some novelty bee patterns out there, but none really popular outside of a shop here or a club there. Is there reason to look closer at honeybees and trout?

Honeybees randomly occur in trout stomach samples, often lumped together with ants in the order Hymenoptera. Rarely does their total exceed 1 or 2% of total terrestrial food. For this reason I would consider honeybees an unlikely trout food.

In a few instances, particularly on small streams bordering gardens, orchards, or agricultural lands where bees are trucked in to pollinate plants, bees may become slightly more available to fish. In natural forest lands, "wild" hives may occur on trees near the water, and evicted bees (some bees are periodically killed and dead bees are unceremoniously evicted from the hive) may end up drifting in the water. The other possibility of a watery grave occurs during the spring swarms, where windy conditions may blow some strays onto the water.

I carry one or two honeybee imitations with me, but outside of a couple incidents near orchards, they seem to work no better than any general attractor. The body of my preffered pattern is made of golden yellow dubbing, ribbed with black sparkle dubbing, the wings of tan treated Raffia, and the head and legs are golden yellow and black (85% and 15%, respectively) deer hair.

Pattern

Honey Nut What

Hook: Dai Riki 305, #14
Body: Golden yellow dubbing
Ribbing: Black sparkle dubbing
Wings: Tan treated Raffia
Thorax: Mixed dubbed deer hair (golden yellow 85%, black 15%) or light brown ostrich herl (if you use herl, add two black Superfloss legs to each side).

Leeches (Hirudinea)

The Worm

Omnipresent, relatively large, and with a seductive locomotive behavior, leeches seem the perfect trout food. Indeed, rarely does the angler have to actually "match" the leeches of a particular water, they just have to make their fake look real when it matters—when a trout is approaching it. But before we get all hot and bothered with how leeches should be imitated by all stillwater anglers all the time, we need to ask a simple question. Do trout eat leeches? The answer is a fascinating one, and rather surprising.

This question was investigated in a 1985 study where over a dozen stomach samples from brown trout in British and Irish lakes were compared. Over the course of sampling these 2000+ trout, leeches showed up in only about 8% of the trout, for a total diet composition of less than 5%. Another study on one of the legendary trout stillwaters of America, Oregon's Crane Prairie Reservoir, revealed that leeches made up, at most, 0.5% of the trout diet! This number was shocking, but confirmed by several other professional stillwater trout diet investigations that also found a very modest representation of leeches in the diets of trout. In fact, I did much of the research on this book before getting to the leeches, and I never noticed the lack of them in the trout diet until I went back and rechecked the stomach samples I used in other sections of this book. Based on all the samples I've located, a liberal estimate for leeches in the diet of the average stillwater trout is a paltry 2-5%.

These numbers are far below what a lot of stillwater books claim—most stillwater experts purport that leeches contribute 15-20% of the total diet—and may not elicit a ton of confidence when fishing leeches. It is also important to consider factors of *availability* (leeches are mostly nocturnal, so trout don't normally encounter them except at dawn and dusk) and *desirability* (one leech equals dozens of chironomids) of leeches to trout. A trout is less likely to pass up a leech meal than say a backswimmer or mayfly nymph. For many anglers, including myself, leeches imitations are perennially some of their most effective stillwater patterns. So regardless of the evidence, we know leech imitations catch fish even though trout do not readily consume the naturals. A variety of leech "imitations" in an array of sizes and colors is essential for anyone planning to fish for trout, bass, and panfish in stillwaters and slow rivers. However, do not fall into the trap of becoming wedded to your leech patterns when they don't seem to produce.

There is no doubt that leeches appear in incredibly dense numbers on some trout waters. Certain lakes can harbor as many as seven hundred leeches per square foot of bottom. Leeches thrive almost anywhere, but they are most common in slow moving rivers, lakes, ponds, and springs. However, leeches inhabit an enormous range of saline, acidic, thermal, and dissolved oxygen conditions. They can be found in sterile mountain lakes, as well in waters with higher salt concentrations than sea-water. Some species can even survive the absence of oxygen for up to sixty days! A few species lurk in swift trout streams, often in the pool sections, but leeches are more common in the slower water downstream of prime trout habitat. Leeches need something to attach themselves to in order to rest, so they are not incredibly abundant on streams with substrates of pure mud, silt, or clay. Regardless of what type of water they inhabit, leeches thrive in waters less than 6-8 feet deep, and rarely venture into open water or the profundal zone.

The physical structure of the leech is pretty basic: imagine a dark earthworm squashed by Mama Cass and you'll get the picture. Leeches have suckers at both the "head" and "tail" end (commonly called the "mouth" and "caudal" suckers, respectively), though these are more often utilized to attach the leech to the substrate than to live up to their dubious reputation of sucking human blood.

Leeches vary significantly in size, anywhere from a few millimeters upwards of six inches. Trout prey mostly on smaller leeches in the 20 to 45 millimeter range. Size variability often depends on how

The same leech can appear svelte when swimming and fat when crawling and searching.

long particular leeches live. In northern waters, some leeches live two years before reproduction and can grow to an extremely large size. In more temperate trout lakes, the average trout-consumed leech is only 25mm (the equivalent of a size 12 4XL hook).

Like Shepard Smith, leeches are hermaphroditic, but they need a partner in order to reproduce. Many leech populations have a staggered reproduction season, with a spring brood and a late-summer brood. For fish this is important, as it means that large leeches are available throughout the angling season (April-September). The relative importance of leeches generally increases from summer through fall, as chironomids, phantom midges, damsels, dragons, *Callibaetis*, and caddis progressively emerge and leave the ecosystem.

Colors of leeches vary greatly. While most anglers presume leeches are dully bedecked black, brown, or olive creatures, many specimens exhibit a brightly mottled, spotted, or longitudinally striped body. Pinks, yellow, and orange spots or lines are not even out of the question! When the leeches are preserved (or dead in a fish gut), they lose most of their ostentatious color, which is why most anglers settle for the standard "red, brown, and black" colors for their leech imitations. Two other factors that tiers should keep in mind: leeches often become paler under the cover of darkness (meaning they are lighter eight feet under the surface than in your hand) and the belly shade of a leech is almost always lighter than their backs.

Matching leech motion is critical for anglers. Leeches move in four primary motions: *crawling, swimming, searching*, and *alert freezing*. *Crawling* takes place along the bottom, and closely resembles the motion of inchworms or caterpillars. *Swimming* leeches swim with either an up and down (dolphin-style) or a side-to-side (trout-style) motion. For the most part, leeches are accomplished swimmers, though some individuals will "tread water" (thrashing madly about with little forward propulsion). These swimming leeches may be the most important for trout, since they draw attention to themselves and rarely can escape quickly. *Searching* is a slower motion than swimming, in which the leech body waves slowly and the head moves about seeking vibrations of potential hosts or prey. *Alert freezing* occurs as a leech locates a predator and ceases its spastic movement in the vain hope that it will remain undetected. Sometimes it works and the leech lives another day. Other times, it makes them an easy target. When a leech freezes, it extends its body and remains motionless for some time, usually slowly sinking in the process. Regardless of how they move, most leeches only move around at night since they are nocturnal.

If you regularly sample stillwater trout you may wonder, "Why do I rarely find leeches if they are so important to fish?" One reason may be that leeches have soft bodies and are quickly digested without any physical trace, undetectable without serology. As most leech predation takes place at dawn and dusk, if you only sample fish caught in the afternoon, you will likely never find a leech in the samples. Yet even professional studies, which take into account these factors, still show a limited importance of leeches to trout. This leech-feeding enigma comes dangerously close to "Hopper Syndrome," where we may imitate something on based on human perceptions, not what the trout are eating.

Yet unlike hoppers, I am tempted to say "to Hell with all this predator-prey stuff," because leech patterns work so well. Will future anglers and researchers make a breakthrough that will show us why these patterns work so well? Perhaps in exploring that question, we will learn that our love affair with leeches has blinded us to the possibilities of imitating more important foods like *Chaoborus*, *Daphnia*, and baitfish. Or, maybe, we will learn just what it is about leech patterns that catch so many trout.

THOUGHTS ON IMITATION

Many materials can imitate the motion of leeches. Let us start with the obvious: marabou. Selecting the right marabou for your leeches is critical for leech patterns. Many tiers use only the spiky barbs at the tips of the feather. I believe the best bards are the supple, light barbs at the rear of the feather stem. Good quality marabou will have enough barbs on each side so that each feather should tie two flies. You don't need many of these soft barbs; 15-25 should give your pattern an adequate tail. Too many and your fly will actually have a reverse taper, which looks ugly to both the angler and the trout.

Leather is another effective leech pattern material. "Ultra-suede," usually available in craft stores, comes in a variety of leechy-looking shades and creates superb patterns. It is significantly thinner and suppler than the thick leather often sold in fly shops for anglers looking to tie Whitlock's Leech. While a properly crafted and weighted ultra-suede leech is almost indistinguishable in the water from a natural leech, Woolly Buggers will often catch far more fish!

For the collar of an ultra-suede leech, wooly chenille, mohair yarn, or loosely dubbed fur or sparkle dubbing can create a slight "halo" effect that can simulate movement. I personally prefer mohair, but it is important not to tease out the mohair so much that you have a blob instead of an elongated swimming leech.

Weighting is a great debate amongst leech imitators. Most all agree that some weighting is necessary to achieve the proper swimming motion. The argument among tiers often centers on where to place the weight: at the head (like a bead head), at the front of the hook, or elsewhere. I fall into the elsewhere camp. Weighting the front of a fly results in a fly rising and falling in a linear manner (regardless of materials), like a popsicle stick on a string. By placing the weight at the rear of the fly, you can get a more disjointed, dysfunctional, and subsequently lifelike motion underwater. Weight-forward flies certainly work well, but by applying alternative weighting to your flies you can actually better imitate leeches and create patterns that at times can radically out fish the standard models.

In another example of things looking different out of the water than in the water, leeches are longer and narrower than we imagine. While they can be rather long (many reach 3-5 inches while swimming), they certainly do not appear obese as they swim through the water. How leeches appear on the bottom, on your skin, or in your hand is not worth a hill of beans when trout only encounter them while they are swimming. For this reason, keep your leech imitations sparse and long. Heavily-hackled patterns or patterns with thick marabou tails deaden movement, making your fly look like Shaq instead of Kobe. While "bunny leeches" certainly have their moments as true leech imitations, they leave much to be desired. Bulky attractor patterns they certainly are, but they do not match the realistic elegance of a sleek leech imitation.

Leeches patterns are also fun because they give the tier a lot of latitude in terms of color. With the recent boom in tying materials, there is virtually an unlimited set of possibilities for the creative tier. I have tried dozens of shades, and amazingly enough, most of them have had a moment when the trout wouldn't touch any other color. Black, brown, maroon, and deep olive are essential colors for leech patterns. Highlights often effectively spice up leech patterns. By imitating the natural spots and lines that decorate many natural leeches. Yellow, orangish, or purple spots and lines can be created with strips of Flashabou or spots of "puff" or fabric paints. Of course, some two-tone patterns (black-olive, black-brown, brown-olive) are totally essential to any lake angler. Krystalflash nearly always makes leech patterns more effective, though there is apparently no biological reason why. White, yellow, chartreuse, bright orange and bright red leech patterns will also surprisingly catch fish. On many lakes, random white and bright orange leeches can be "the" patterns for otherwise picky trout. Yet, they do not truly imitate a leech and should be considered "attractors"…not that there is anything wrong with that.

I like to have flies that I can use to imitate the various movement patterns of leeches (crawling, swimming, searching, freezing). Many "swimming" imitations exist, as any weighted pattern you strip in will reasonably imitate a moving leech, so the challenge to the tier is to imitate the crawling, searching, and freezing leech movements.

Crawling leeches can a headache to imitate. First of all, they move slowly, tight to the bottom, and tend to keep a thicker body profile than leeches found swimming in open waters. For this, a stout, full-bodied BH Mohair Leech with dumbbell eyes is effective, as it is slightly thicker and can be worked and bounced directly off the bottom without snagging.

Searching leeches move with a slow, ambling, and curious motion. This is something that you can imitate with a "floating leech." Constructed with foam and leather, this pattern can be slowly crawled near the bottom on a full sink line and short leader. I like to provide mine with a thin foam under-body: the amount of foam is important, because you don't want your pattern to rise at rest. Also, it should be a long skinny pattern, since the naturals stretch out when falling—possibly to make themselves look larger and less vulnerable to trout. This can be a superb mid-summer and early-season pattern when trout shy away from swiftly retrieved patterns.

A "freezing" leech is something tricky to construct, because it cannot be weighted, otherwise it sinks too quickly. I tend to use the same pattern I do for a searching leech, and just kill my retrieve every couple feet. Let the fly sit at rest for 5-15 seconds before resuming the retrieve. Generally, I imitate both "searching" and "freezing" leeches on the same cast.

How you fish leeches is as, if not more, important than how you tie them. Try utilizing a "killing" technique with missed strikes when fishing leech imitations. As mentioned earlier, when leeches sense danger they freeze. Unfortunately when many of us get strikes with leech patterns, we set the hook and quickly strip the fly in; exactly what the natural **does not** do! What we should do more often is "kill" the fly on any strikes that do not hook themselves. As you slowly strip in the pattern and you get a strike, stop retrieving and drop your rod tip. If you are trolling the fly and feel a strike, drop your rod back as far as you can to let the fly descend as long as possible, then set the hook. This technique, especially when using an unweighted or semi-buoyant pattern mimics the "freeze" perfectly, and can make a huge difference at the end of the day. It is counter-intuitive and takes some restraint, but it does pay off.

Thanks to their variety in coloration, body shapes, and methods of locomotion, leeches allow tiers vast creative freedoms for experimentation and creativity. Leech patterns are critical to fly anglers on stillwaters, regardless of whether they pursue trout, sunfish, perch, or bass, and nobody should hit the water without them.

Patterns

Keys to Match
1. **Movement, Movement, Movement:** It works for Britney and trout!
2. **Movement, Movement, Movement:** How you fish a leech pattern matters more than what it looks like.
3. **No Movement:** Sometimes leeches freeze like a deer in headlights.

Keys to Avoid
1. **Fishing Too Quickly:** Leeches move up and down, not forward.
2. **Thickness:** Leeches may look thick in your hand, but trout only see the skinny swimmers.
3. **Weighting All Patterns:** You want to make some be able to "freeze."

WC Fields Special

Hook: Dai Riki 700 or 270, #8-12
Tail: Black marabou
Butt: One or two, black (or any painted color) brass bead(s)
Body: Black mohair yarn

This pattern works well for a "thick leech"—ideal for murky water or low-light conditions where fish feed by vibration rather than sight. The bead-butt style works well, though you may want to add a bead head or dumbbell eyes to get a stronger "jigging" motion to bounce the fly off the bottom without snagging.

Brakeman Leech

Hook: Dai Riki 270, #6-14
Bead: Black or olive-brown at rear of body
Body: Foam to match leather, sparkle dubbing (optional)
Overbody and Tail: Ultra Suede leather, pulled back over the top
Ribbing: Fine gold or copper wire or 4X monofilament, overlaid with sparkle dubbing to match natural.

A pattern specifically to imitate the "thrashing" motion of a swimming leech, one should fish the Brakeman in rapid, short strips to make the fly wiggle furiously. The foam and bead combination ensure that the fly sinks butt-first, but very slowly, so that the fly still works on a slow retrieve.

Standard Leather Leech

Hook: Dai Riki 270, #6-14
Under Body: Sparkle dubbing to match body, sparse
Body: Ultra-suede strip, 2-3 times the length of the hook
Sparkle: One or two strands of Krystalflash
Collar: One or two wraps of mohair yarn to match leather
Head: Brass bead

This is my best true leech imitation. It has fooled everything from trout and bass to perch to even walleye, sauger, drum, and kelp greenling. The fly works best as a true leech imitation, and rarely catches fish under general conditions as woolly bugger. But when fish do target leeches, this is what to turn to. Make sure the leather strip is roughly ten times long as it is wide to ensure fluid movement when stripped through the water.

Mosquitoes (Culicidae)

The Insect

Few creatures have plagued humanity for as long as the mosquito. Between malaria, yellow fever, and innumerable livestock diseases, mosquitoes have been despised by humans and denigrated in both high literature and folk songs throughout history. For obvious reasons, the mosquito has been the subject of intense scientific research for centuries. These studies have discovered hundreds of fish species that can contribute to mosquito control… and. Unfortunately, trout are not one of them.

"Skeeter" habitat rarely overlaps with trout habitat, as the larvae live in shallow ponds, bogs, and temporary pools where trout are largely absent. The behavior of the larvae makes this choice of habitat essential. Mosquito larvae hang from the surface, breathing through a respiratory tube that extends from their anal area. In this way they can breathe while feeding by filtering algae and tiny bits of organic debris from the water. When disturbed, the larvae wiggle furiously downwards, hoping to reach the bottom to hide in the substrate. This is why they need shallow water: if the water is deeper than a couple feet, those wiggling larvae would be slaughtered. This downward wiggling motion is of extreme importance for the angler, and essential for imitation.

Most larvae are 4-15mm in length, with spiky hairs on the body. They slightly resemble chironomids, but their tail area is significantly larger thanks to the respiratory tube and a pronounced brush on the anal segment. The pupae are similar in size and proportions to chironomid pupae. Despite their visual similarities, the mosquito pupae will hang at the surface for a day or longer, much like *Chaoborus* pupae. Their body often takes on a strikingly curved position, almost resembling a ball. Adults, which we are all familiar with, have a banded body and are 5-14mm in length. If you find any bigger than that you should stop fishing altogether, and go find a body of water that is safer for your circulatory system.

The only place trout anglers should consider imitating mosquitoes is on small alpine lakes, or shallow reservoirs and desert lakes with extended flats between one and three feet deep. Mosquito imitations will also slaughter pre-spawn sunfish holding in ultra-shallow water. Outside these ecosystems, mosquito imitations should not displace *Chaoborus* or chironomid imitations in your fly box.

Thoughts on Imitation

Like many other trout foods, where and how you imitate mosquitoes is more important than exactly what pattern you choose—yet matching where and how to imitate mosquito larvae forces you to fish only a pattern designed specifically for their lifestyle.

You are best off concentrating your mosquito imitations, especially larvae, to shallow margin water only a few feet deep. Most mosquito larvae hang perpendicular to the surface film, and when disturbed, wiggle off towards the bottom. This flies in the face of how we usually imitate them. Most of us use the standard hand-twist, rising chironomid tactics that cause the fly to move either horizontally or towards the surface. The best way to imitate mosquito larvae is with a sinking or sink-tip line with a short leader, just about the depth of the water. Using a floating larvae imitation, you can make a short handtwist retrieve causing the fly to dive *down* like the natural. Almost all strikes occur within a few seconds of starting the retrieve, as the key for trout is the actual dive. Once the fly reaches the bottom (about four to six feet of retrieved line) quickly strip in the fly, dry the fly, and do it again. This technique is a killer on alpine lakes with cruising trout that patrol shallow shorelines.

If this is the best way to fish the imitations, how do you create a floating nymph that: (1) floats, but with its head hanging down so that it can, (2) can swim downwards, while (3) maintaining a skinny profile when underwater? If it seems like

Note that mosquito larvae are comparably thicker than Chironomids and also sport a noticeable anal brush.

Even shallow lakes like this are too deep for most mosquito larvae.

mission impossible, it is—if you stick to the traditional ways of making a mosquito or chironomid larvae.

I tie my larvae pattern with a dense, short butt of CDC. When tried properly, it has enough buoyancy to float the pattern in a perpendicular manner. A parachute hackle would work, in theory, but when stripped underwater the hackle destroys the silhouette and the fly loses any semblance of a mosquito larvae. The CDC usually loses its air bubble quickly, and while the fly has a fat ass it is much more realistic than other potential imitations. Plus with the respiratory tube and ventral brushes, the CDC puff is more realistic than it may at first seem. This fly can either be fished static or swum, thus streamlining your fly box by filling two niches at once.

The biggest downside to this pattern is that if you swim the fly, you must dry the CDC after every cast in order to make it to float. For this reason I like this technique for cruising fish in shallow water, where I target individual fish rather than covering the water blindly. It is amazingly effective on fish without a "readable" cruising pattern, as the motion of the larvae seems to get the attention of fish and draws them off their normal route (something they wouldn't do for just "another chironomid").

Also, the diving mosquito larvae is tied with a spiky dubbing of either light or dark hare's ear dubbing or squirrel dubbing, and then ribbed with Root Beer Krystalflash. The spiky look imitates the hairs on the larvae. The CDC butt is matched as closely to the body color as possible. It is important to keep your head small on these patterns, and I like a two wraps of Black Quick Descent dubbing, for it dubs tightly and I can keep the head size restrained.

The rare occasions when trout feed on mosquitoes is generally fixated on the larvae, so I almost never tie up imitations for pupae and adults. I am including an adult mosquito imitation here, but that is more for fun than for actual fishing success.

Patterns

What to Match
Upside-Down Hang: Must hang eye-down cause real larvae don't "flip turn."
Swimming-Down Motion of Larvae: The naturals go down, the imitations go up, and the fish go away.
Spiky Body: Hare's ear dubbing to match the hairs of the natural.

What to Avoid
Standard "Mosquito Pupae": They match the natural like a Parachute Humpy matches a *Baetis*.
Fishing Larvae Deeper Than 3 Feet: You wouldn't eat a hot dog in a tree would you?
Adult Imitations: They might be all over you but they are not all over the water.

Ma Rainy Larvae

Hook: Dai Riki 305, size 12-14 (310 for size 16 and 18 versions)
Tail: CDC loop or puff (2-4 feathers) short, color to approximate body color
Body: Spiky light or dark hare's ear
Ribbing: Root Beer Krystalflash.
Head: Two turns of black sparkle dubbing

This fly is quick to tie, so it isn't much of a problem to have a couple tucked into the recess of your stillwater boxes. It should be fished on a sinking tip line and a leader just longer than the depth you are fishing. This is also a superb spring bluegill and panfish pattern.

CDC Adult Mosquito

Hook: Dai Riki 300, size 12-14 (310 for size 16 and 18 versions)
Body: Light moose mane wrapped over black thread
Wing: Dun CDC
Thorax: Dubbed black/white mix CDC
Hackle: Two wraps grizzly

Again, this pattern is more for novelty purposes than for serious use as a mosquito imitation. It works well on high alpine lakes when nearly any dry fly would work because alpine trout generally have about as much food as a pre-hurricane Piggly Wigglys. It probably works best as a large midge/terrestrial imitation during the spring.

Moths (Terrestrial Lepidoptera)

The Insect

Rarely do anglers associate inchworms with trout. Though many husky adult moth patterns were constructed over the years as waking attractors for bass, trout anglers rarely paid moths much mind. However, trout rarely ignore the larval stage of some moths, commonly called inchworms. On a relatively open-canopied Colorado stream, they were the second most important terrestrial insect, comprising the fourth largest component of the total trout diet in the month of July. In more arboreal habitats, inchworms can prove far more important. On one British Columbia stream sample, they were twice as important as any mayfly for summer trout!

The adult moth, with all its aberrant spinning and fluttering on the waters surface, is the most visible life stage for Lepidoptera. Yet, trout rarely consume these adults. We must assume that trout do not like their taste; as the activity of helpless, drowning adults agitates the surface of many lakes on summer evenings.

While inchworms spend many months safely grazing on tree and shrub leaves, when they descend, they offer themselves up to predation. Since the larvae cannot see the substrate that they descend into, many just rappel onto the water's surface, where they only thing they pupate into is trout food. The larvae will float for a while, but in rough water, they can quickly drown and trout will feed on them below the surface. It is tough to distinguish where in the water column that trout acquired the larvae you find in stomach samples, so one should carry and use both floating and sinking imitations.

Of course, descending larvae must drop from something, so streams flowing through forested riparian zones provide far more inchworms than meadow streams. On open canopy streams or meadow streams, trout rarely encounter Lepidoptera larvae. Forested streams are a different story, but the exact tree species also play an important factor in the abundance of Lepidoptera larvae. Oak, in particular, can produce boom crops of inchworms. They can also be quite common in old growth Douglas fir and spruce forests where they been shown to contribute almost 17% of the trout diet over the summer, more than any other food source.

For a long time, I considered inchworm patterns a novelty—like the hopper, a conspicuous food source that excites humans far more than trout. One day on a small Pennsylvania stream, I stalked a trout that that rose repeatedly to what I thought were pine needles. Knowing that trout occasionally consume even the least palatable of random flotsam, I thought nothing of it and kept watching the fish. It rose to another pine needle, which was enough of a clue for me to put on an inchworm (something I had previously never used). If the trout enjoyed the taste of pine needles, dammit, I'll give it a pine needle. I hooked the fourteen-incher on the first cast, and upon checking its stomach, those two pine needles turned out to be two of the six inchworms I found in its gullet. Looking up I could see why inchworms proved important. The pool the trout inhabited was downstream of a 50 meter-long riffle, gurgling about four feet below a thick hemlock canopy.

For the small stream angler, especially in thick-canopy streams, inchworms should be as common as hopper patterns. It is essential to carry a half-dozen in tan, bright green (bright "insect"

Trout rarely encounter or target adult moths.

Inchworms are simple creatures with nothing more than a simple wormlike body.

Some moth larvae have hairs that are effectively imitated with wrapped ostrich herl.

green is about the right shade), and chartreuse. These patterns can be constructed out of foam or deer hair, but be sure to test them out in a water dish to make sure they will float without being too bulky.

For sunken larvae, a simple pattern with a tiny gold bead threaded over bright green chenille works well. A handful of imitations in one size and the three aforementioned colors will cover most of the situations you will face. I would recommend fishing this fly dead-drift under low-hanging riparian trees. They also make a superb dropper off another "terrestrial" of the shaded forest, the adult crane fly.

Small streams with low-hanging vegetation often experience large numbers of Lepidoptera larvae.

Patterns

Falling Ophelia

- **Hook:** Dai Riki 300, 10-14
- **Thread:** 6/0 chartreuse, olive, or tan to approximately match body
- **Body:** Olive, yellow, green, or chartreuse, deer hair
- **Ribbing:** Thread to match body

Small streams with low-hanging branches are prime locales for inchworm larvae imitations. I like the classic look of deer hair, but it certainly does not float as well as foam. The fly should be visible on the surface, though you may want to fish it as a dropper behind an even more visible ant imitation, especially in rough water. On many Eastern small streams, this is an essential pattern in May.

Leaky Little Boat

- **Hook:** Dai Riki 300 or 305, #10-16
- **Body:** Green or yellow foam
- **Legs:** Grey ostrich herl (optional)
- **Ribbing:** Pearl Krystalflash

This pattern basically replaces the Falling Ophelia, but works in a bit rougher water or if you don't want to use a light-wire hook. It is also a bit flashier, which can prove effective if fish have a little more time to inspect the fly and need a bit more convincing. The ostrich flanks allow the pattern to match the legs of a variety of inchworms and caterpillars that descend into trout streams.

Noah Drowning Ophelia

- **Hook:** Dai Riki 135, #12-14
- **Thread:** (optional)
- **Thorax:** Brass bead, preferably painted the color of the body.
- **Body:** Ultra chenille chartreuse, tan, yellow, green (melted at ends)

This fly is an easy one to tie and fishes well as a standard nymph or as a dropper off a larger terrestrial. While "dry" inchworm imitations are fairly common, the larvae do sink rather quickly making sunken larvae imitation important for small stream aficionados.

Net-Winged Midges (Blephariceridae)

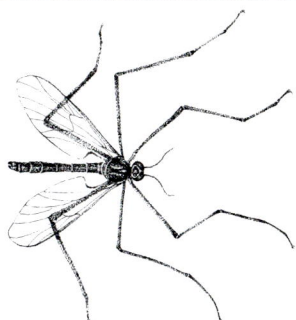

The Insect

While this book covers many unknown insects of crucial importance to North American trout, it also takes on a few totally "mystery bugs." The net-winged midge is one of those bugs that sandbags even experienced anglers who have never heard of the critter. Rarely the foremost bug on the minds of trout anglers, Blepharicerids can at times prove important. In a study on California's famed McCloud River, they composed almost 5% of the diet of adult trout, which was about fifth in overall importance—nearly as common as *Baetis*! Lumped with Diptera net-winged midges serve as minor, but significant, components to trout in swift, mountain streams throughout the montane west and Appalachian east.

With claws and suction discs, Blapharicerid larvae can cling to rocks in the most turbulent currents.

Trout and Blapharicerids cohabitate in the seams of pocketwater.

Jeff Morgan photo

Besides their local importance, I chose to talk about these bugs because like many other creatures, their common name leaves a false image in the angler's mind. Blepharicerid larvae don't look like chironomids or "midge" larvae. Their flattened body looks more like a sowbug than a "midge." The large (10-14mm) grazing larvae crawl over cobble-sized rocks, and equipped with a camouflaging dark olive, brown or gray hue. The larvae move about (and are preyed upon) mostly during the late spring and early summer. The pupae attach to rocks in the same habitat as the larvae, usually in June or July, emerging soon thereafter. Adults fly off and prey on smaller insects, returning shortly to lay eggs on wet rocks along stream edges. As they lay eggs in rough, fast water, many females commonly drown and end up in the drift.

Why are Blephariceridae important to trout? Their relevance coincides with their preferred habitat: stream margins ("seam water" in fly-speak). Not accidentally, trout share their habitat preference. Net-winged midge larvae populations also tend to appear in dense clusters (upwards of 1000/ per square meter of substrate), making them particularly important to trout immediately downstream. Finally, their large size makes them a much better prey resource than the more common, but tiny, chironomid. The wise angler will carry a few imitations of Blephariceridae larvae, especially in the early season.

THOUGHTS ON IMITATION

While I stammer to think of an occasion where I have found trout selective to net-winged midges, I can think of numerous occasions on mountain streams where specific imitations outfished Hare's Ears and other standard attractor nymphs that "dumb" small stream fish allegedly feast upon.

Any net-winged midge larvae needs to be weighted, so that you can fish it deeply in their swift, margin-water habitat. The larvae are most important to trout in the spring and early summer; rarely in the fall. While I prefer dark grey for imitations, black and dark brown imitations also can wok well. Other than color, make sure the nymph is "grubby" looking and in the size 12 to 16 range.

While emergences of these insects are locally dense (as the larvae and pupae live in patchy communities), rarely do the fish turn selective. A Lil L' Pupae 2002 or any black or dark chironomid pupae in the size 12-16 range will suffice as an imitation. The water is fast and the fish cannot afford to be too uppity. It pays to have some of these larger midge imitations whenever you fish streams, as it is easy to get bogged down with tiny midges and forget about the big ones.

Concentrate your efforts with these patterns in seam water where fast and slow water intermingle. Fortunately, in fast small streams, this is where most trout can be found, which is why adding these imitations to your repertoire may help boost your success.

PATTERNS

RAGMAN LARVAE

Hook: Dai Riki 070, #12-16
Weight: 4-8 wraps .010 lead wire, flattened with a pliers
Body: Dark gray (almost black) dubbing, loose
Collar: Black Peacock Ice Dub
Ribbing: Medium black wire or clear mono ribbing

The weight on this pattern is as essential as the fly needs to descend through the swift water to the bottom where the larvae live. A black beadhead can help the fly sink down quicker, which is important in pocket water habitats.

LIL L' PUPAE 2002

Hook: Dai Riki 135, #12-20
Body: Peacock Krystal Flash
Wing: 3-4 strands Pearl Krystalflash (short)
Thorax: Peacock herl or Arizona peacock dubbing
Head: White foam.

This pattern, while designed in smaller sizes for smaller riverine midge emergences, fishes excellently in larger sizes for the net winged midge. While on lakes we fish large midge imitations all the time, on streams many anglers get skittish about fishing midge imitations that are much larger than size 16. This pattern fishes will up to a size 12, as long as you fish it in the same seam water where net-winged midges abound.

Phantom Midges (*Chaoborus*)

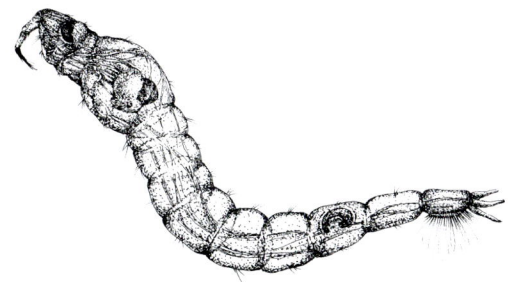

The Insects

While most anglers have simply overlooked many of the insects in this book, the Phantom Midge is not as much ignored as it is confused with another trout food, the chironomid. But, any doubt that trout consume phantom midge larvae in obscene quantities can be calmed by merely consulting a few stillwater predation studies. In one study done on a Washington Lake where Lahontan cutthroat were planted in previously fishless lakes, D.W. Chess, *et al.* wrote:

> "Of available prey, trout preferred *C. trivittatus* and subsequently nearly eliminated *C. trivittatus* during this study. Trout switched to other macroinvertebrate prey in the fall of 1988 only when *C. trivittatus* density was near zero…Late instar *Chaoborus* have large eyes and large bodies increasing the visual detection by fish…"

In the same study, phantom midge larvae were more important to trout than all other food resources combined in the spring (80% of diet) and were still the preferred food source in the fall. On other waters, *Chaoborus* larvae are so heavily harvested by trout that some species of phantom midge (such as *C. americanus*) cannot viably co-exist with fish! Besides scientific literature, numerous British and Irish angling writers document trout feeding heavily on phantom midge larvae and pupae.

What makes phantom midges as, if not more, important than chironomids on many waters? First of all, *Chaoborus* are not simply "clear" chironomids. While almost all midge larvae squirm on the bottom amongst the substrate, predatory *Chaoborus* larvae swim throughout the water column, only occasionally taking refuge in the substrate during the daytime when trout predation is a threat. They also have a conspicuous coloration: transparent, with hints of either white or yellow, with large black eyes. Some almost appear luminescent—though they are not—under proper light conditions. Most species undergo a major migration to the surface in the evening in order to intercept *Daphnia* movements, making phantom midges an available prey item at sunset. Finally, *Chaoborus* propel themselves in search of their *Daphnia* prey with a jerky, lashing wiggling of their bodies. Oh, did I forget to mention that they also appear in dense populations?

On an acidic pond restocked with trout in New York, *Chaoborus* densities reached 400/m^3, while the next most common insects were backswimmers, at a whopping density of 1.4/m^3.

Most anglers (including myself for years) who conduct stomach samples simply assume that *Chaoborus* are chironomids. Their transparent color resembles the empty shucks of emerged chironomids, so many anglers think they are just empty husks of trout prey rather than the real deal. However, these insects differ significantly from chironomids, and knowing the differences in appearance and behavior will add more than a few fish to your season totals.

Chaoborus exist in large and small stillwaters throughout North America, appearing in almost every state and province north of Mexico. Their toleration of a wide variety of pH, water clarity, and alkalinity conditions allows them to live in anything from the warmest Florida bass hole to alpine lakes in the Canadian Rockies. The larvae range from 7-12mm at maturity, and as mentioned above, take on various shades of opaque white, opaque yellow, and totally clear. They resemble chironomids in body shape and proportion. As mentioned in the earlier passage from the Chess study, the large eyes, large size, coloration, and movement all make these insects prime targets for trout.

Locating *Chaoborus* and the trout that feed on them can challenge the angler, as most species of *Chaoborus* larvae migrate daily throughout the water column. *Chaoborus* larvae spend most of the day deep—between five and ten meters below the surface—usually in the same open water habitats as *Daphnia*. At first thought, most would assume that trout feeding during mid-day would never encounter *Chaoborus*—this is not the case. During the hot summer months, trout may spend most of the daylight hours hovering near the thermocline, seeking the abundant oxygen available at those depths. If their conspicuous coloration does not make *Chaoborus* visible to hungry trout, their vigorous movements might help. It was found in a study by G.F. Pope that, "larger trout were found to be more serious predators of *Chaoborus*." This is most likely because larger trout hung in deeper water near the thermocline in the summer, where the only sources of available food were *Chaoborus* and *Daphnia*.

As the sun starts to fall, *Chaoborus* larvae migrate towards the surface to feed on *Daphnia* at depths of three to ten feet. Phantom midge larvae remain near the surface throughout the night, returning to their deep-water confines between 2:00 and 4:00

am (so there is little morning action for the angler). Some spectacular fishing can be had during these migrations, but it takes faith to fish them, as most of the trout feeding remains invisible and undetectable under the surface of wide expanses of open water.

If there were a costume award among the aquatic insect fraternity, phantom midge pupae would certainly win the award for scariest mask. The "face" of a phantom midge has a menacing look more fit for a Poe short story than an aquatic bug. *Chaoborus* pupae, while living for only a couple days, hang out near the surface breathing atmospheric oxygen via tubes in their thorax. They don't move much, loitering near the surface and feebly wigging when disturbed. At this stage, they are also quite vulnerable to trout predation. According to some researchers, the pupae, during their short existence, may become the preferred food of trout. It doesn't take an academic researcher to tell an angler that few things sound better than an "emerger" that takes four days to emerge!

The adult stage of the phantom midge, like most other midges, is of virtually no importance to anglers. The adults do not feed and have a shorter life span than their near-cousins, the mosquitoes. For recommendations on imitating the adults, see the previous section on adult chironomids.

THOUGHTS ON IMITATION

When fish key into *Chaoborus*, they can prove as selective to them as any other trout food. I have encountered several occasions where trout fed on *Chaoborus* larvae to the exclusion of everything else. One instance at a popular western stillwater stands out.

It was a cool, but sunny, spring day and the fishing was typically difficult. I experimented unsuccessfully with several patterns before trying *Chaoborus* imitations, which worked about as well as a gill net. About ten other anglers fished in the general vicinity, and they couldn't seem to match my success despite using very similar chironomid imitations. They shouted over "How deep?" Despite my inclination to slightly mislead when "competing" on the water, the action was too hot not to share. I answered with the correct depth— "ten feet." They all fished their flies from fifteen to five feet with no success. They then asked "what size." I bellowed "size 12." All saw unchanged results. Finally, I heard "What color?" "Clear," I yelled back, waiting for the inevitable follow up questions. Invariably, this was greeted with befuddled looks, and from one boat I heard an excited shout, "Ah, a Disco Midge!!" A few tried the Disco Midge and found it no better than anything else. At this point, I had landed about twenty trout to the sum total of four for the other ten anglers around me—I don't usually do this well, so I soaked up the glory for an hour. Some anglers, wholly convinced I was lying at this point, wanted to call me on it. They rowed over to closely inspect my rig and technique to see if I subtly slipped a salmon egg on my hook between casts. I showed them my orthodox two-fly rig and they were surprised that I was telling the truth: a tiny indicator ten feet above two different clear *Chaoborus* larvae patterns. I gave them a few patterns to use, and within twenty minutes they were well on the way to surpassing my total.

It is common to assume that a Disco Midge can fool trout feeding among an abundance *Chaoborus* pupae. Sure you could tie one on, but you could also use a Wooly Worm with similar results. What anglers need is a pattern that appears neither pearly nor white, while avoiding thick thorax common to many chironomid pupae imitations.

A clear insect presents obvious challenges to the fly tier. A bronzed steel hook is rather difficult to transform into a transparent insect. The key is selecting clear materials so that the final result obscures the dark colors of the steel, especially when submerged. The Phantom Larvae #12 & #20 serves as a viable imitation—while hook is still invisible, the plastic creates a semi-translucent effect in the water. A lightly dubbed body also can work, though a dubbed body can easily become too thick or too white, since a truly clear dubbing material is difficult to locate.

A tiny scud hook (#18-20) with an extended body of clear Larva Lace ribbed with pearl Krystalflash, can also match the semi-clear body of the natural *Chaoborus*. When tied properly, the larvae will be 10 mm long (about the size of a #14 standard hook). This creates an effective imitation, especially when tied with clear monofilament thread (like Uni-Mono).

Sometimes fish strike aggressively at pearly or whitish patterns. This usually takes place in the hour just before sunrise or just after sunset. I am not sure of the reasons why, but patterns of this shade generally produce less fish than truly "clear" patterns during the daytime.

Numerous studies note the "large black eye" of the *Chaoborus* and its role in focusing trout attacks. In the course of fishing patterns with and without black eyes, I haven't seen much difference between patterns with a black eye (usually painted on) and those without. The discrepancy probably stems from the fact that a black spot is far more prominent on the truly clear naturals than on our less-than-clear imitations.

One of the difficulties in imitating *Chaoborus* is locating the depth where trout feed on the larvae. With the tendency of *Chaoborus* to roam around throughout the day in search of *Daphnia*, larvae may exist at various depths, making it easier to blindly prospect with imitations. However, rather than just haphazardly casting around, I like to target areas where *Daphnia* populations, trout populations, and *Chaoborus* all overlap like a Venn Diagram. Physical structure, such as points or cliffs where fish are likely to hold at "suspended" depths, are the perfect locations to try *Chaoborus* imitations. However at times, *Chaoborus* can thrive on flats between four and fifteen feet deep. As when targeting *Daphnia*-feeding trout, cooperative efforts by multiple anglers accelerates the discovery of the holding depth of trout preying on *Chaoborus*.

On days with a light chop on the water, simply casting flies out under a tiny indicator and letting them just bob with the waves and current can be the best technique to imitate Phantom Midges. The rolling, agitated surface will give the flies just enough of a dancing motion to motivate strikes. Many anglers detest this kind of "bobber" fishing, but for larvae active in the middle of the water column, nothing is more realistic or effective.

Chaoborus pupae imitation is straightforward—with long, light leaders and flies fished directly in the surface film. Of course, attempting to imitate a neutrally-buoyant emerger with clear materials is all but impossible. I prefer CDC patterns that tend to hold the fly just under the surface with the thorax grazing the meniscus. These patterns can be slowly jiggled to imitate a strug-

Lake points near deep water allow trout, Daphnia, *and Phantom Midges to intermingle.*

Jeff Morgan photo

gling, pre-emergence pupa. Remember that *Chaoborus* pupae hang at the surface (fleeing during distress) for several days so there doesn't have to be a hatch or even actively rising fish to warrant their use. Oftentimes, when you see a plentitude of smutting rises on a flat lake surface and no adult midges anywhere, *Chaoborus* may be the choice target.

Chaoborus, along with *Daphnia*, offer answers to the many problems fly anglers encounter on stillwaters throughout the hot summer months of July and early August. But before you can have success with them, it is critical to unlearn the myths that all stillwater trout feed exclusively on chironomids, leeches, and damsels in six feet of water!

Patterns

What to Match
Color: It is tough to match clear, but get as close as you can.
Movement: Be it through tying style or retrieve, movement is an essential key with any predatory insect.
Cover Water: Unlike chironomids, phantom midge larvae can be anywhere from the surface to the bottom and suspended in deep open water.

What to Avoid
Fishing the Larvae too Shallow: Try them deep for oxygen-seeking, suspending trout.
Fishing a "Rising Pupae": Keep imitations static in the film.
Fishing Disco Midges: Hell, while you're at it, try a Royal Coachman!

O.G. Phantom Midge

Hook: Dai Riki 135, #12-14
Thread: White 8/0
Body: Pearl Krystalflash
Ribbing: Clear monofilament
Thorax: White or pearl dubbing
Head: Pearl bead
Gills: White CDC

This is the original pattern I used for phantom midges I like to fish it in deep water or during the early morning and late evening hours. It still works, but a more clear pattern fishes far better.

The Stranger

Hook: Dai Riki 125, #12-16
Thread: White 8/0
Body: Clear monofilament over white thread
Collar Hackle: White CDC
Thorax: Pearl flash dubbing
Head: Black Peacock Ice Dub, one or two wraps

Another fine *Chaoborus* pupae imitation that seems to work better in low light, due to the contrast that the black wrap of dubbing adds to the pattern. Fish this fly rapidly under a float, along with one or more other phantom midge imitations

Phantom Larvae #12 & #20

Hook: Dai Riki 135, #12-16
Thread: Clear monofilament
Body: Clear plastic strips
Ribbing: Clear monofilament
Head: Clear or pearl glass bead
Eyes: Black paint (optional)

A perfect example of how simpler can be better, this fly was a stripped down model of the previous pattern. On many lakes this fly greatly outfishes the "original phantom."

Continually *Chaoborus* Emerger

Hook: Dai Riki 125, #12-16
Thread: White 8/0
Body: Clear plastic
Ribbing: Pearl Krystalflash
Thorax: Pearl dubbing
Wing case and gills: White or light dun CDC
Forward Wing: White or light dun CDC, shuttlecock style

This fly, while not the perfect solution, is certainly serviceable. I like to fish it on deep (8-12 feet) flats, totally static with as little movement as possible. Occasionally I will "swim" the fly like a disturbed natural wiggling for safety, but only when I am desperate.

Chaoborus Soft Hackle

Hook: Mustad 3906, #12-16
Tail: Sparse light partridge
Abdomen: Clear plastic
Thorax: Pearl sparkle dubbing
Hackle: Light partridge or white pigeon neck feathers

While there is no "emergence rise" with *Chaoborus* pupae, the pupae do spend a couple days perilously near the surface and vulnerable to fish. When in danger, they wiggle about to escape, but are rarely successful. This fly should be fished either with a slow hand twist just under the surface or with a team of wet flies, loch-style.

Scuds (Amphipoda)

The Amphipod

As most anglers know, wherever you find good populations of freshwater shrimp (scuds), you will find trout eating them. Most anglers consider scuds as the ultimate growth food, like creatine for trout. Their reputation for growing fat trout is so well recognized that foreign shrimp were introduced into dozens of streams in Northern Ireland to help increase the growth of salmon and trout. I've heard of stocking fish, but the stocking of *fish prey* suggests that every angler should be prepared to understand and imitate scuds wherever they exist.

Over 800 worldwide species of freshwater shrimp inhabit lakes and streams, but the variety present in trout-supporting waters is far more modest. In fact, two species, *Hyalella azteca* and *Gammarus pulex,* by far are the dominant species in American trout streams and lakes. Renown for their aggression and activity, *G. pulex* often eliminate native shrimp species (as well as native aquatic insects) where they are introduced. This hyperactivity makes them a prime target for hungry trout.

It should be mentioned that scuds do not appear in every trout water, and in fact, they probably exist in only 8-10% of American trout streams, and perhaps 20% of American trout stillwaters. So while they are remarkably significant where they occur, one should find them before imitating them.

Fortunately, anglers can easily collect and identify scuds in the field. Distinguished by their laterally flattened bodies, seven pairs of legs, and curled appearance when collected and held in hand, most scuds range from 5-20 mm in length at maturity, and range in color from dull grays to dull olives to dull browns, though some can be various hues of purple, dark brown, and even reddish. Differences in diet, age, and temperature will affect the overall hue of scuds. Many species also show a pronounced difference in color between their backs and legs, with backs often much darker than their legs.

Since scuds never leave the water, trout feed on them throughout the year. However seasonal stages in their life cycle make scuds far more vulnerable to trout than other foods. Scuds do have a particular breeding season, which might range from February to September. While mating depends on water temperature and elevation, it often coincides with spring. This breeding period,

Scuds normally exhibit an opaque coloration best matched with muted olive, gray, yellow, or tan imitations.

while highly variable overall, is highly synchronous on a particular body of water. On alpine lakes, it has been shown that breeding takes place roughly at ice-out, with young scuds being released from the marsupium (egg sac) about two to four weeks later. Since the scuds have a life cycle that lasts about a year—with one breeding season a year—we can safely assume that scuds grow throughout the year, starting small in the summer following hatching, and they grow larger through the next spring. This is evidenced by the reduced importance of scuds in the summer and early fall, when the year-old scuds die and the young scuds are still too small to be of value to larger trout. While the summer and fall will find some larger scuds still kicking around, they are less common than in the spring.

The conspicuous movement of freshwater shrimp accounts for part of their popularity with trout. In streams, no trout prey drifts more actively than freshwater shrimp—scuds undergo a diurnal drift rate that puts all other forms of aquatic life to shame. Scuds swim well and their confidence shows. In rivers, swimming usually takes place in the small gaps between vegetation or rocks. In lakes, scuds often swim moderate distances by keeping low to the substrate, routinely only a few inches above it. They can be found actively swimming throughout the day and night in both lakes and streams.

Anglers commonly erroneously assume that scuds swim on their backs. Most books recycle this folk biology, but in reality, most freshwater shrimp swim on their *sides*. Dr. Norm Anderson chided me thoroughly over this little factoid when I submitted the first draft of my undergraduate thesis, where I boldly and repeatedly proffered the unsubstantiated "fact" that scuds swim on their backs. This was the first time I realized that "scientific facts" provided by angling books may not be true! When swimming, scuds often fully extended their bodies while laying on their sides—probably in order to more efficiently utilize their many legs.

While swimming motion is important when imitating scuds, the reactive behavior of scuds during the approach/attack of a fish is an even stronger feeding stimulus for trout. Like many other kinds of prey, trout ignore scuds that remain motionless. Scuds absentmindedly ambling around lake and streambeds, however, are prime targets for attacks. When a predator approaches, many scuds will play dead—go motionless and sink to the bottom. These are the ones that survive.

Other scuds form an arched "C-shape" to make themselves appear larger and more difficult for smaller fish to ingest, much like a cat arches its back and hisses when you let a puppy loose nearby. Other scuds rapidly "jump" around, distancing themselves from the predator, then go into the "C-shape." All this does is get the trout to drool and become even more enraptured by the little scud—for as much as a 12mm long crustacean can arch, it will never be too big for a hungry trout! In a study that compared these behaviors, scuds that took this defensive response were almost uni-

Scud abound in rich tailwaters, especially the first few miles below a dam.

Jeff Morgan photo

versally eaten." In view of the fact that these defense responses are performed only in the vicinity of fish, they are best imitated when targeting sighted trout in shallow water.

A common misconception among progressive anglers concerns the bright orange "egg sac" on female scuds. Some anglers have mentioned a yellowish-gray brood pouch that can be visible on female scuds and "egg sacs" are appearing on more and more patterns these days. Yet, after collecting many scuds throughout the year, I found I often collected more of the "egg-laden females" (albeit with a more orangish color) during the non-spawning season than during the short spring breeding period.

Alas, after a bit of research, I found that the "egg sac" was neither an egg nor a sac. It is actually a parasite, *Pomphorhynchus laevis*, which infects scuds as a means of reaching their final host, fish. The parasite often turned part or all of the scud a bright orange or orangish-yellow, and thus gave the appearance of an "egg sac" to many anglers.

If you think all this mushmouth parasite-host Latin bullcrap means nothing to success on the water you couldn't be more wrong. It has been shown that when offered equal numbers of infected and uninfected scuds, fish will feed "significantly more often" on the infected scuds. To prove that color was the trigger, and not other parasite-caused behavior changes, researchers painted an orange blotch on healthy scuds and painted gray over the orange blotches on infected scuds, and the orange painted scuds were still consumed at a much higher rate. Another researcher mentioned that, "There can be little doubt…that trout and infected *G. pulex* will make contact, and that trout will prey selectively on the infected gammarids."

Trout feed on these alternative scuds via a process known as "oddity selection," where an abundance of abnormal prey among a prey community cause a more intense and selective feeding response. This might partially explain why some trout will rise to a Humpy during a Trico spinner fall, while any number of Trico imitations fail.

While angling writers often praise the trout's culinary preference for scuds, in many cases, trout actually ignore abundant scuds. In a 2000 study in Ireland, brown trout fed on scuds at a much lower rate than they appeared in the drift. In other situations, trout may continue to feed on hyper abundant scuds, but angler success with scud imitations slows down. The reason for this is pretty simple and the ramifications for the angler are significant. Like a dense spinner fall, scuds can be so numerous and available that trout can afford to select according to size, color, behavior, and distance. It is not that the trout are not eating scuds; they just eat ones that fit specific criteria. This kind of ultra-selectivity is also common when feeding on *Baetis* nymphs and simuliid larvae, which along with scuds are by far most common drifting critters in any stream where they exist. The angler should recognize when trout are selective and be prepared to imitate scuds as closely as possible or else attempt to match another food resource.

Thoughts on Imitation

Anglers have long relegated scuds to rudimentary imitation. Almost any small standard nymph pattern, not already classified as a "mayfly," "caddis," or "midge" imitation, was reasoned into,

Scud imitations should utilize some flashy material to match the hard exoskeleton of a scud.

by default, a scud imitation. Patterns as far removed as the Zug Bug and the Tied-Down Caddis have all at one time been defined by convenience as scud patterns. By the 70's, the modern "scud" fly with the plastic shellback and picked out fur dubbing became the standard model and has been passed down to us today with few changes, save color and material variations.

Like the patterns, scud fishing theory has long been simplistic. "Two sizes and two colors [of the standard pattern] is all you need. If the fish are eating scuds, they'll take them. If they won't take those, pattern change won't help." As scientific evidence comes into clearer understanding among more anglers, the adherence to this axiom is slowly eroding.

First of all, size is *not* irrelevant. In the fall and early winter, the vast majority of the scud population in a body given water is smaller than in March-June. This calls for smaller patterns. I have been extremely successful with tiny scud patterns (size 18-24) fished in the fall on a wide variety of rivers and creeks. While it was hard gaining corroborating evidence from other anglers, since virtually *nobody* fishes scuds smaller than 18, I have had a number of my tying clients buy them religiously for several seasons in a row, indicating that they either work or they are routinely dropped and lost streamside. I prefer the former explanation!

On small scuds, stay simple! Just a few twists of hare's ear/antron blend dubbing, a flashy shellback, and a fine copper rib will suffice. On tiny scuds, size 20 and smaller, I also omit the tail and usually don't pick out the dubbing much (legs on scuds of this diminutive size are virtually transparent). These flies are quickly, cheaply, and easily tied. While trout may feed extensively on small scuds, these imitations fool fish because they are realistic and *different*. For late season trout in heavily pressured streams, where I have used most of my small scud flies, the "different" factor may play as big a role as imitation of an abundant natural food.

Color, as the biological information suggests, can be a key trigger for scud-feeding trout. I believe so strongly in the "orange-spot" parasite evidence, that I am currently converting most of my scud patterns to incorporate this vital feature. Old patterns are getting a yellowish-orange spot of paint on their sides, while new patterns of all styles have a wrap or two of bright dubbing in the middle of them.

Other than the parasite, the majority of scud patterns should be tied in various muted shades of olive, gray, or tan. Scuds are quite opaque, so whatever color you use, make sure it is not a strong hue. Pink and orange scuds can be very effective at times. However, when any fly that imitates a relatively rare food (like bright pink "dead" scuds) is overused by large numbers of anglers, it is easy for fish to eliminate that potentially dangerous food source from their diets. On Oregon's Crooked River, where pressure over the past decade has risen exponentially, the Orange Scud, the preferred (nay...the *only*) fly to use in the early 90's, now only catches a fraction of the fish it once did.

Movement is another key for scud patterns. We know we can get a fly to ride upside down by weighting it, but how to get a fly to ride on its side like a natural scud? This problem is surprisingly tricky, considering we all have tied many flies that inadvertently run on their sides! One of the reasons you simply don't want to tie a scud sideways on the hook, is that the obscured hook (because of the picked out legs) certainly improves your odds against tough fish. To make scud pattern ride on its side, tie a strip of lead wire to one side of the hook and glue it in place. Then construct the fly as usual, and hopefully it all goes swimmingly. That was bad, I apologize. Tying the fly sideways on the hook shank can suffice if you don't want to take this extra step, though you want to use a straight-shanked hook.

Many of the scud patterns here are tied with lightly-curved hook shanks, but I always carry a few with radically curved shanks to imitate the "death feigning" c-shaped scuds. These patterns should be used almost exclusively on sight-fishing on stillwaters. I have used them with great success, in of all places, crystal clear Florida springs for picky bull bluegill.

You'll notice that one of the listed scud patterns pattern utilizes dubbed deer hair over a thin foam underbelly. The resulting fly has a neutral buoyancy, which allows you to fish among shallow vegetation without having to face the Catch 22 of an artificially fast retrieve or perpetually dredging weeds. This fly fits a much-needed void in modern scud imitations.

Effective scud imitation requires close attention to the retrieve. Slow, hand twist retrieves are almost always the best choice in lakes, but they are not the only options. As I mentioned earlier, I like to visually target fish with scud imitation. Often I will cast a scud out, let it sink to the bottom to rest motionless until a cruising fish approaches. Then with about five one-inch strips, I "jump" the fly up off the bottom (per the defense response discussed above). I then let the fly resettle like the natural. Fortunately, the fly rarely reaches the bottom before the fish slams it down.

When a trout is seen slowly following a retrieved scud, first slow the retrieve—most of the time we retrieve scuds and other trout foods too quickly, which is why the trout follows it closely, curious how such a slow bug all of a sudden acquired Superamphipodian speed—then "kill" the fly. If the trout doesn't take the pausing scud, give it the "jumping" action. Usually the trout will give a favorable response.

Do not underestimate the importance of scuds in stillwaters, especially alpine tarns and highly-alkaline desert lakes.

Jeff Morgan photo

Patterns

Keys to Match
Parasites: Trout prefer parasite tinted scuds.
Buoyancy: If all your scuds are weighted, you are limited to fast retrieves
Go Small: When trout eat #20's why fish a #14?

Keys to Avoid
Upright-Floating Patterns: Would an upside-down mayfly imitation work?
Bead Heads: Scuds don't have "air bubbles"!
Eyes: If you can barely see them, neither can the trout.

Dubbed Deer Hair Scud

Hook: Dai Riki 135, #12-16
Under Body: Thin gray or tan foam (color is not too important, as it should be covered with dubbing)
Body: Dubbed deer hair (olive, dun, pink, orange)
Egg Sac: Orange Ice Dub
Back: Clear Body-Stretch
Ribbing: 4X monofilament

This is one of my favorite scud patterns, one look and you'll know why. It looks great and fished superbly. The more chewed up the fly gets, the better it performs. The foam underbody and deer hair makes the fly nearly neutrally buoyant, so you can slowly twist along unhurriedly, mimicking the dawdling natural. One of the greatest problems with bead-head or weighted scuds is that they must be fished too quickly. This fly avoids that problem.

Bud Dickman's Scud

Hook: Dai Riki 135, #10-14
Body: Pink, Orange, or Olive Estaz, trimmed top and sides

If you don't mind thousands of tiny Estaz flecks all over your tying area, this fly is a breeze to tie. It can either be weighted with a lead wire underbody or just left unweighted. I have to admit, it isn't my favorite pattern, but it does work well in cloudy water conditions. The fact that you can tie a dozen of all three colors during one episode of The Simpsons is a redeeming quality.

Cockwill Shrimp

Hook: Dai Riki 135, #12-20
Body: Blended seal substitute, squirrel, and SLF dubbing
Ribbing: Fine copper wire

British expert Peter Cockwill devised this simple shrimp imitation, and it works well over the pond as well. Tied in its smaller sizes, this pattern will fool pressured fish and clear water, perhaps because it offers less flash than most standard scud patterns.

Standard Swiss Scud

Hook: Dai Riki 135 or 300, #12-18
Tail (optional): Hungarian partridge feather fibers, to match body
Shellback: treated Raffia to match body, top can be painted with waterproof marker
Body: pale sparkle dubbing (olive, gray, tan, orange, pink) to match naturals
Parasite Mark: two wraps bright orange/yellow dubbing, or small drop of orange/yellow model paint.
Ribbing: 6/0 thread, 4X monofilament, or fine copper wire.

This is one of my favorite scud imitations. Muted in color and limited in flash, it is excellent on slow or stillwaters where fish prove selective and circumspect. I have caught many beautiful browns sight-nymphing this to brown trout on Pennsylvania's Big Spring Creek.

Sidewinder Scud

Hook: Dai Riki 135 or 300, #12-16
Under Body: Piece of lead tape (the matchbook kind used for nymphing)
Tail (optional): Hungarian partridge feather fibers, to match body
Shellback: treated Raffia to match body, top can be painted with waterproof marker
Body: pale sparkle dubbing (olive, gray, tan, orange, pink) to match naturals
Parasite Mark: two wraps bright orange/yellow dubbing, or small drop of orange/yellow model paint.
Ribbing: 6/0 thread, 4X monofilament, or fine copper wire.

While most writers note that scuds swim on their backs, many scuds swim on their sides. This fly imitates that behavior superbly. This is less a fly for rivers than stillwaters, where proper imitation of scud motion is important.

Aquatic Snails

The Mollusk

Like leeches before them, black flies today, and *Daphnia* well into tomorrow, anglers have a long history of overlooking snails. Even prominent advocates, like Gary Borger, who love to fish snails themselves, have been rather modest in their endorsement of snails as an imitable food source. Despite lackluster support from the angling lobby, when snails flourish they can be a significant food resource for trout in both lakes and streams.

Trout certainly are not the pre-eminent consumer of mollusks. Carp, suckers, and whitefish (all with downward-facing mouths perfect for plucking snails from the bottom) all likely consume snails at a greater pace than trout do. Yet, if any doubt exists regarding the seasonal and local importance of aquatic snails to trout, one simply needs to browse the scientific literature on snails and fish predation. One of the best resources is Robert Dillon's *The Ecology of Freshwater Molluscs*, which has a wonderful chapter on the predation of aquatic snails. Not less than thirteen pages of this text is devoted to the important role mollusks play in the diets of trout, sunfish, carp, and other game fishes. Dillon is not the only snail advocate. In another study of an Icelandic lake, a respectable 15% of the char diet was aquatic snails. In a study of trout in mountain lakes, Trojnar attempted to explain away the significant average quantity of snails in the trout diet by explaining that "a few large specimens feeding almost exclusively on snails probably biased the results."

Many professional studies have also found trout *streams* where snails make up almost 40% of the trout diet! Perhaps the most notably study was presented in a paper by Lynn Kaeding that examined the trout diet in the Firehole River. On the legendary Firehole, where anglers worship *Baetis* and *Ephemerella* mayflies like minor Hindu gods, aquatic snails were found in 82-86% of the trout sampled and contributed 26-38% of the total quantity of food consumed by trout, both significantly higher percentages than all the mayflies combined! If snails mean that much to trout on a stream with such exalted glamour hatches, no angler should be surprised to find trout on their local waters feeding on snails.

Aquatic snails have a body that even novice anglers recognize. With their spiral, coiled, or spiral-conical shell, and a muscular "foot" (used for transportation) that can be extended or withdrawn into the shell for defense, the aquatic snail faces few aquatic competitors. In addition to the prominent foot, an

With a complicated mix of head, body, horns, foot, and shell, snails are best matched with impressionistic imitations.

aquatic snail has two horns, which support its eyes. The colors of aquatic snails will depress the innovative tier—they appear in an array of dull quasi-browns, grays and blacks. Snail size ranges widely, from two to seventy millimeters in length. Their size also depends on location, with smaller specimens generally abundant in calm, calcium-rich waters and larger specimens inhabiting the wave-beaten shores of larger lakes. It is generally accepted that trout don't feed heavily on snails larger than fifteen millimeters. This may be due to the fact that trout lack the powerful crushing jaws needed to crack the thicker shells of these big snails.

Where are snails most common? Streams and spring-fed lakes with high calcium carbonate levels abound with snails, as calcium carbonate is the limiting factor in shell construction. In this sense, scuds and snails prefer the same type of habitat, so when you find one in abundance, keep a wandering eye on the other. Anglers will rarely find snails in acidic waters, and almost never where the pH is lower than 6.2. Dissolved oxygen also functions as a critical factor, since snails and trout both prefer oxygen-saturated waters.

Snails love lake shallows with minimal wave action and few sweeping currents. Cobble bottoms offer a permanent base for algae growth (unlike sand or small pebbles), creating an ideal habitat for aquatic snails. On large windswept lakes, snail populations thrive on leeward shorelines, where winds rarely dislodge vulnerable creatures like snails. If the winds reverse, however, snails may be dislodged by the millions, leaving them floating on the surface with their foot attached to the underside of the meniscus. At other times, snails hang in this manner while feeding on algae trapped in the meniscus. Either way, trout will prey upon snails that lay inert at the surface.

Substrate preference among snails is varied throughout the order, but often species-specific. Some species love thick watercress, while others cannot coexist with plants but love mud, while others cannot move over mud and prefer large rocks or logs. It is too complex to document all the minutiae regarding snail habitat here, but locating the preferred snail micro-habitats on the water you fish will serve you well in the long run.

Trout predation on snails is a highly individualistic behavior. While the average trout on a particular stream may only consume 1-3% of their diet in the form of snails, that average of 1-3% may result from ninety trout consuming no mollusks and fifteen trout whose diet is composed of 30% mollusks. This explains the "boom and bust" productivity of snail imitations, and what makes many anglers wary of experimenting with them.

Trout feed on mollusks in two ways: grubbing and catastrophe. When "grubbing," trout cruise the bottom—snout down—and simply pluck the snails off the bottom. Grubbing lacks the grace of sipping mayflies, but it gets the job done. This is an easy feeding mechanism to recognize on the stream. However, remember that besides mollusks, trout "grub" on black fly larvae, aquatic worms, caddis larvae, scuds, and many other critters. If you pump a fish and find snails, and you are not sure where the trout ate them, look for debris. Often, the stomachs of grubbing fish are stuffed with gravel and indigestible plant material. Grubbing often is an individual feeding technique, so tailor your presentation to a particular observed trout and do not assume that because it worked on one trout it will work on all of them.

The other way trout consume snails is through "catastrophe"—when a disruption to the substrate causes a mass eviction of snails. The catastrophe situation is important to anglers because a large percentage of the trout population focuses on an otherwise rarely available food source. The most important period for snail-feeding trout is when waves pummel the shore of a large lake, stirring up the substrate, and causing floating snails to pepper the surface. I saw this for years as a child on Oregon's legendary Crane Prairie Reservoir. When after the midday winds subsided, trout would lazily slurp the nutrient-rich snails laying infirm at the surface. Other catastrophe situations might include flood conditions or when anglers, horses, or children trample through the water upstream of your fishing site.

In drift posture experiments with sixty mollusks of several species (I have neither the ability nor the inclination to identify them more accurately), none extended their foot when drifting. While again, this may be affected by their unwilling eviction from the bottom, it certainly is enough to steer me away from constructing a foot for drifting snail imitations on streams.

Like with crayfish and baitfish, larger fish tend to feed on mollusks more than smaller fish. This holds for many species of fish, as larger fish have a stronger digestive tract that can more efficiently break down the hard shell of the snail. Trout also tend to focus on softer-shelled mollusks, since they have trouble digesting their harder-shelled ilk. These softer-shelled mollusks, as previously mentioned, may also drift further and float better than other snails.

Unfortunately, one of the more common snails in American trout waters (and growing even more common daily) is the New Zealand Mud Snail. This tiny, 2-4mm black snail feeds by grazing on algae and can often outcompete *Baetis, Epeorus, Glossosoma* and other important grazing insects. While competition is a problem, the fact that trout cannot digest mud snails is an even bigger one. On rivers like the Firehole and upper Madison (and a growing number of streams throughout the West), this snail decimated *Baetis* populations. BWO's are not the only victims. Rocks once covered with *Glossosoma* cases are now adorned with these little evil black specks. Washing boots and waders between fishing trips will help prevent the spread of this serious threat to our trout streams.

Finally, on a side note, pumpkinseed sunfish and redear sunfish, which have specialized pharyngeal teeth to crack snail shells, may consume more mollusks than any other gamefish. The numerous studies on pumpkinseeds and redears have shown that these panfish consume an astounding quantity of mollusks. I started mixing in some snail patterns with my spring panfishing excursions and have been pleasantly surprised. If I moved to the Deep South, besides taking up the regional cuisine of NASCAR and Copenhagen, I would definitely target big pumpkins with snail patterns.

Despite this elaborate discourse on snails, remember they remain only locally important for individual fish. Several New Zealand studies outlined instances where snails choked the stream in drift samples, while trout largely ignored them. Snails aren't always critical, but one should anticipate the particular circumstances where they can be. Remember that like all Oddballs, snails always seem to be important when one is least prepared to deal with them!

Thoughts on Imitation

Snails don't move fast. This well-known factoid has been pounded into us all since we are children, right? Why then do we construct weighted snail patterns that require a steady retrieve to keep them from hanging up on the bottom? When fishing snail patterns, the best thing you can do is leave them alone. This calls for floating patterns, regardless of whether you are fishing them deep or in the surface film.

The most common snail imitations utilize a single body material—chenille, deer hair, or foam—with a soft hen hackle, to create a simple pattern. There is nothing wrong with simple patterns, especially for snails, but they must be in the right location. For floating snail imitations, I have found that patterns that hang just under the surface (imitating a snail with its foot in the meniscus and shell hanging down below) are most effective. All-deer-hair or all-foam patterns float high, often partially above the surface. But when saturated with water, or after they catch a fish, these patterns slowly sink. I prefer using a combination of materials, so that I can saturate one part so that it sinks, leaving the buoyancy of the other material to keep the fly tight to the surface film.

There is a time and place for weighted imitation: when trout are clearly grubbing on the bottom. When pursuing these kinds of fish, it is important to pick out a fish slowly cruising the bottom, grubbing its way along. Cast a pattern about ten feet ahead of a fish, let the fly sink to the bottom. Let it be. If the trout is actually feeding on snails, then it will almost certainly consume the fraud. If the fish isn't feeding on snails, your fly won't even get the dignity of inspection. When trout aren't immediately interested in a snail imitation, resist the temptation to twitch or swim your pattern. If you saw a terrestrial snail dart off in six-inch pulls, you would probably also assume it was demonically possessed. Not only will the fish refuse the pattern, a "swimming snail" will also make the fish warier to future presentations.

Weighted patterns can be as simple or as complex as you like, though little middle ground exists between the two styles of patterns. A simple pattern just uses a ball of Woolly Chenille over a lead underbody. The chenille provides an excellent segmented shell look, with little tier effort. If you want to add a "foot" to the

After a storm, foam lines provide a visual clue as to the location of floating snails.

Jeff Morgan photo

pattern you could easily superglue one on, though most research has shown that the snail remains in the shell when drifting.

Since trout tend to consume smaller snails, I rarely fish an imitation larger than a #10. My preferred range of imitation is size 12-16. On lakes where I suspect snail feeding, I like to start with a size 12 floating imitation. Only when sight-fishing to stillwater trout cruising the shoreline and grubbing the bottom will I unleash weighted imitations.

For stream snails, I have settled on a size 16 imitation, usually in olive, brown, or black. The color may not be critical, but I have found that some colors fish better than others at times. Size 16 imitations effectively cover your bases: if the snails are about that size, you're in business; if the trout prefer larger snails they tend to forgive smaller imitations rather than more rotund ones. One should also plan to fish snail imitations in streams below wading anglers, who dislodge them while walking around. Stream snails are best fished dead drift, otherwise they should be used static on the bottom, targeting fish visibly cruising and picking them off the bottom. Remember that trout in streams may mistake a snail pattern for a cased caddis, so be aware and switch to a cased caddis pattern if you think that is the primary target of the trout.

How big of a role do snails play in my fly boxes? Not a starting role, to be sure. On lakes, I may carry a half-dozen each of four patterns, unless I fish a lake with trout known to target snails, when I usually carry more. On rivers, my normal boxes carry a couple of both weighted and unweighted patterns. Having a handful patterns for snails, crayfish, aquatic worms, *Daphnia*, black flies, cicadas, and other seemingly "random" food sources only takes up half of a miniature fly box. While that box may only be opened a half dozen times a season, it may account for a half dozen situations where you conquered a problem that befuddled the rest of the anglers on the water.

Patterns

Keys to Match
1. **Floater:** They are easy to see and eat when they are hanging in the surface.
2. **Size**: Most snails are not huge, especially in streams.
3. **Carry Some in Rivers Too**: While most trout graze on snails, drifting snails can be important.

Keys to Avoid
1. **Movement:** There is a reason for the cliché "at a snail's pace."
2. **Weighting:** If you don't want your snail skipping through the water like a damsel nymph, don't make them sink!
3. **Excessive Sparkle**: Snails are rather boring critters, so make their colors reflect their disposition.

Floating Snail

Hook: Dai Riki 300, #12
Shell: Spun olive or brown deer hair
Foot: Brown or black foam

This is a superb pattern to imitate a floating snail in the surface film. When a pattern is composed of a single material, it is difficult to make it float properly. If you squeeze a little water into the deer hair shell and grease up the foam, the foam will lie in the surface film and the shell will hang down. Be sure to fish this pattern static with as little movement as possible.

Raggedy Snail

Hook: Dai Riki 305, #12-16
Under Body: Black foam
Body: Olive, brown, or black woolly chenille
Hackle: Soft brown hackle

This fly fishes well in both rivers and streams. Its buoyancy makes for an excellent surface pattern, but it can also be fished on a full sink line for a static, "suspending snail" presentation near weed edges. This pattern doubles as a viable imitation of stockier versions of dragonfly larvae.

Cone Snail

Hook: Dai Riki 300, #12-18
Body: Black or brown craft foam, wrapped to create "cone" look
Foot: Peacock Ice Dub blended with seal substitute, dubbed loose.

Another pattern that can be fished in both rivers and lakes, the Cone Snail imitates a whole other guild of snails than do the other imitations. It can also be weighted for deeper presentations in rivers, where the pattern can also double as a cased caddis imitation.

Sow Bugs (Isopoda)

The Insect

Compared to the rich literature on scuds, angling experts and academia have paid little attention to aquatic sow bugs. Few entomological texts give these lowly critters more than a couple sentences, and surprisingly few journal articles have taken on this unique arthropod. Most fly fishing references mention sow bugs as an aside, if at all. Outside of Pennsylvania's spring creek region, few fly shops discuss and carry imitations of the critter that more anglers recognize from their gardens than their favorite trout stream. Despite their modest publicity, sow bugs can contribute greatly to the trout diet and thus are worthy of more careful consideration than we devote to them.

On some of our legendary Eastern spring creeks, sow bugs have long been known as the important "other" scud. In the West, however, thriving populations of sow bugs remain unheralded on productive scud-rich tailwaters. Even on streams trumpeted for their scud-activity—like Oregon's Crooked River, where sow bugs outnumber scuds in some sections—most anglers, guides, writers, and shops remain oblivious to their presence.

At first glance, many will claim that sow bugs look like scuds. Quickly, the differences become obvious. Sow bugs are dorso-ventrally (top to bottom) flattened and their seven pairs of legs extend at an angle from their belly. They use these legs to crawl along the substrate or weed growth, but, the legs are ineffective at helping the scud to swim. Sow bugs most often have dark, slate-gray backs and whitish bellies, yet the color combinations can mix up black, dusky, or brown backs with yellowish or creamy bellies. On almost all bodies of water, one species of sow bug will compose the entire population, so colors and sizes should be relatively constant on a particular body of water. Speaking of size, at maturity, most sow bugs range from 10-18 mm in length.

Sow bugs generally have a one-year life span, with reproduction occurring sometime between March and September, coinciding with the "spring season" on a particular body of water. This differs significantly from terrestrial sow bugs, which can have upwards of a four-year lifespan. The annual reproductive cycle, as with many other aquatic insects, leads to a waning importance to trout over the summer months, when tiny, immature sow bugs predominate.

Sow bugs revel in the slow, unpolluted water of springs, creeks, and small ponds. I used to tell my guiding clients, "only look for sow bugs when you find scuds," but this isn't always the case. Sow bugs are rarely found in large streams or large lakes, even when scuds thrive. Sow bugs occasionally crawl about waters totally absent of scuds, especially on rocky spring creeks with limited weed growth. In general, however, look for sow bugs in good "scud" habitat. Slow water with plenty of weeds is like a salad bar condominium for these little critters. Besides weedy waters, sow bugs can abound in streams with plentiful leaf litter strewn about the bottom of shallow pools and eddies. Hidden in the leafy margins, these sowbugs are missed by anglers who sample by only "kicking riffles."

One sure thing about sow bugs: they live in patchy communities. In small rivers, sow bugs become concentrated in the thousands where swift waters slow down. According to R. W. Pennak:

> "Striking masses, or aggregations, of *Asellus*, consisting of scores to thousands of individuals have been observed in small streams. Such aggregations are thought to be formed chiefly as the result of reactions to current velocity. The migration of some individuals upstream as far as possible, or if the current is too swift, being washed downstream until they are able to maintain a footing has the net result of concentrating the isopods in a segment of the stream where the current is neither too fast nor too slow."

Sow bugs are quite flat with legs better suited to crawling and clinging than swimming.

Below these areas, obviously, sow bugs can be critically important to trout!

Slow, weedy streams do not hold a monopoly on sowbug populations. In lakes, they can also be significant components of the trout diet. In England, "cress bugs" and "hog louse" are reported to be a major source of food on a number of ponds and small reservoirs. Here they may amble amongst the weedy shallows, where trout graze on them directly or stir up the weeds and then feast on the dislodged sow bugs. Sow bugs can also be important in many American stillwaters. In a study of Echo Lake in Maine, intended to research trout predation on other fish, the researchers found that the isopod *Asellus racovitzai* composed 47% of the trout diet over a two-year period, and were most important in the winter and spring months. Why winter and spring, but not summer? Trout predation heavily reduces adult sow bug populations by spring, so after June, freshly hatched juveniles dominate the sow bug population; it is not until the next winter that they reach a size to be a viable target for trout foraging.

Like scuds, sow bugs have a parasite that can make them more susceptible to hungry trout. The parasite *Acanthocephalus* is responsible for turning sow bugs a lighter color and changing their behavior. The blotchy, lighter coloration is a parasitic technique to make the sow bug more likely to be eaten, so that the parasite can get to its final host, the fish. It works. In a 1978 experiment, the light sow bugs were consumed at a greater rate (37 vs. 22) than normal ones on a light substrate, and on a dark substrate, they were consumed almost exclusively (45 vs. 6)! The significant difference was due partially to color and partially to the fact that the infected sow bugs acted like they were on crack: swimming everywhere, trying to crawl out of the container, and basically not using any of their natural avoidance techniques. This parasite generally infects larger sow bugs (10 mm in length). If you collect some samples where there are a few light sow bugs, I would implore the use of a light-colored imitation.

Anglers often miss sow bugs in their samples because most sow bugs live just a few centimeters under the substrate. Protected from currents, they are not generally available to trout. However, when anglers walk through the water, they disturb the substrate kicking up sow bugs galore. At these times, as well as following flooding, dislodged sow bugs move about seeking cover and these clumsy swimmers can elicit a feeding frenzy among trout.

Where sow bugs are present, they provide a rich source of easily obtained food for trout. Because of their mutual ecological preferences, sow bugs and exceedingly large trout often coexist. Knowing isopod habits and habitat does not pay dividends of many fish on many waters, but knowing them on the rare occasion you encounter them, pays dividends of large trout.

Thoughts on Imitation

On a website, I saw a hotly contested debate whether fish differentiated between scuds and sow bugs on a popular western river. Person A's reasoning went like this: As sow bugs were more numerous than scuds, and everyone (a conservative estimate) fished scud patterns, logic would contend that sow bug patterns would be more effective. Person B's reasoning went like this: the river was quite murky, and there is "virtually no difference" between a scud and a sow bug, so just stick with scuds. To resolve this dispute, I would say, let the fish decide. The same website, one year later, abounded with posts on the effectiveness of sow bug patterns.

There are a few cress bug/sow bug imitations out there from eastern anglers and British fly craftsmen. Many patterns are more or less dubbing wrapped around the hook and picked out on the sides. This can often be all you need, though I prefer a slightly more sophisticated imitation.

Awkward tumbling is the usual behavior of drifting sow bugs. Considering the anatomy of such a flat critter, this should not be much of a surprise. This drifting causes the sow bug to alternatively flash its dark back and light belly. I have fished a number of imitations for sow bugs, and generally the most effective were flat with a dark back and light belly and achieved a similar fluttering effect while drifting.

To create a flat body, take a standard size 12-16 nymph hook (the only three sizes I use for sow bugs) and wrap the body with five or six wraps of .20 lead wire. Then flatten the lead wire with pliers and super glue the flat lead. The super glue helps keep the flattened wire together and prevents crumbling after a fish or two chews them up. I have tried lead tape rather than pinching lead wire flat, but the tape is too pliable to support the body and it will collapse ofter a couple trout.

Once you have a number of flattened, weighted bodies, how you tie the fly is really up to your imagination. I like a basic white-dubbed fly with a dark gray scud back, ribbed with 4X clear mono. Once tied, pick out the sides a bit for legs and you're finished. It is an easy, realistic, and effective imitation.

Occasionally, a buoyant imitation is effective just above weed beds in ponds or slow rivers. With this variation, omit the lead underbody and dub a body with white or cream-colored deer hair. I usually keep the same dark shellback and clear ribbing, but a grey foam back can be effective too. With the deer hair, dub a moderately thick body, then flatten it the entire pattern by pulling over the shellback on top and use some strategic scissor action on the bottom.

You should concentrate your sow bug efforts in slower runs of weedy streams. I usually fish mine under an indicator, more to regulate depth to signal strikes. Perhaps the most deadly way to fish sow bugs is sight-fishing them to trout holding in the weed-choked margins of spring creeks. Though the opportunities to execute this technique successfully are rare. Trout feeding in this manner can be incredibly spooky, but they are dwelling in perfect sow bug habitat, and if you put an imitation in front of them while remaining undetected, they usually take with little hesitation.

To fish sow bugs in lakes, use a floating line, long leader, and a small (no. 4 or no. 6) round split shot a foot or two ahead of your fly. This allows you to fish your fly extremely slowly above the weed beds. This is a fine science. You want a split shot heavy enough to sink your fly quickly, but then settle on top of the weeds when at rest. Too heavy a split shot punches through the weeds, and you're constantly ripping it free, making your nymph skip and shoot along in quite an unnatural manner. If you use a sinking tip line, you can be forced to retrieve too quickly, lest the sink-tip similarly becomes mired in the weeds.

Patterns

Keys to Match
1. **Broad, Flat Body:** Use flattened lead wire for this effect.
2. **Legs Extended Out, Not Down:** Pick out the *sides* on all patterns, not the bottom.
3. **Gray/White Contrast:** Be flashy!

Keys to Avoid
1. **Beadheads:** Again, sow bugs don't have air bubbles.
2. **Too Wide:** You want your fly to be broad, but not the shape of a dime.
3. **Overlooking Sow Bugs:** If you won't forget them, the trout won't forget you.

Shaver's Sow Bug

Hook: Dai Riki 300, #12-14
Under Body: .20 lead wire, 6-7 wraps, flattened and super glued
Body: White sparkle dubbing (even pure clear antron works well) or light gray dubbing
Back: Gray or Clear Body Stretch
Ribbing: 4X clear monofilament

This is my standard sow bug imitation, and it fishes well wherever I have encountered sow bugs. Simple to tie, this is a great fly for rivers, especially when you are forced to fish just below a wading angler.

Deer-hair Sow Bug

Hook: Dai Riki 300, #12-14
Body: Dubbed white or cream deer hair, trimmed top and bottom
Back: Gray Body Stretch
Ribbing: 4X clear monofilament

I like this pattern because its buoyancy allows it to be fished just above sow bug-rich weed habitats. If the fly is not flat enough for your tastes, you can always tie on a flat piece of hard plastic (best cut with an razor) to help broaden the profile.

Foam Sow Bug

Hook: Dai Riki 300, #12-14
Under Body: White sheet foam, trimmed to 1mm thickness
Body: White sparkle dubbing, picked out on the sides
Back: Gray sheet foam, trimmed to 1 mm thickness
Ribbing: 4X clear monofilament

Another light, buoyant pattern for fishing the weedy shallows of lakes where sow bugs can be surprisingly abundant. The Foam Sow Bug, like the other imitations, is a breeze to tie. When using it in winter or early spring be sure to fish it slowly, as the naturals are not very active during the cold weather.

Infected Sow Bug

Hook: Dai Riki 300, #12-14
Body: Gray or creamy white sparkle dubbing
Flash: Strip of pearl mylar tinsel
Ribbing: 4X monofilament

This fly is like a beginner's primer for dubbing, but can be effective if fish are not picky about their sow bug imitations. Unfortunately, most places where sow bugs exist, so do large trout. And in most places where large trout exist, so do anglers. This pattern sees its success rate drop quickly as trout get more and more pressure from basic imitations.

Water Boatmen and Backswimmers (Corixidae and Notonectidae)

The Insects

Water boatmen (and their close cousins, Notonectidae, or backswimmers) are common aquatic insects easily recognized and encountered by anglers and non-anglers alike. These insects abound in the shallow margins of most stillwaters, as well as slow-moving stretches of streams. Corixids can tolerate saline or brackish water, and ocean currents may even transport estuarine species to nearby islands, which the little critters then colonize. Corixids kick around in the highest Sierra-Nevada alpine tarn to the warmest desert lake, though I still have never found large numbers of these insects in what most would consider a quality trout stream. However, the cosmopolitan habitat preferences of backswimmers and their affinity for shallow margins makes them important not just to trout, but to bluegill, pumpkinseed, bass, and a wide assortment of other fish.

Don't wait to locate backswimmers in the water before imitating them. In one study, backswimmers were almost totally absent from lakes containing fish. Migratory

Water boatmen prefer weedy shallows.

When at rest, water boatmen and backswimmers must cling to the substrate or else they float to the surface.

Chapter V: The Prey 133

backswimmers fall prey to fish within minutes of plopping through the water's surface. The not-to-subtle "plop" of an arriving backswimmer likely attributes for the speed in which trout pounce on them. Due to their susceptibility to predation, backswimmers prefer weedy margins where they can quickly dive into the safety of the vegetation.

Water boatmen are some of nature's best biathletes—equally adept at flying through the air and kicking through the water. The ability to fly is a crucial adaptation (for them, the fish, and the fisherman), allowing corixids to migrate between waters, particularly in the fall when their native locale may be drying up. It also allows them to populate lakes that may not harbor a population earlier in the season. Due to their migratory patterns, backswimmers may thrive in a lake for a few months, and then disappear just a couple months later.

Corixids mate in the spring, often forming large aggregations in the shallows. Trout may feed heavily on these congregations, though with the abundance of other forage available during this season, trout may focus on chironomids, *Callibaetis*, or damselflies instead. Unlike many species, Corixids take on increasing importance as the season draws to a close. During the early and midseason, the dragonflies, damselflies, caddis and *Callibaetis* emerge, leaving only small, immature aquatic stages for trout to prey on. By the fall, Corixids are one of the largest aquatic insects available to trout. A trout's final few cruising loops of the year almost inevitably result in the deaths of dozens of corixids.

These insects range in size from six to twelve millimeters in length, and have dark olive or brown backs (forewings) and a lighter cream, tan, or very light-olive belly. Many have yellow, olive, or cream patterns on their forewings. A few species have bright red eyes, others have black eyes, but regardless of color, they are quite pronounced. Their two rear pairs of long, oar-like legs lined with brushy hairs that provide their namesake easily distinguish water boatmen from other aquatic insects. These powerful organs propel the boatman around in short quick bursts. Water boatmen and backswimmers are easily distinguished because backswimmers swim on their backs, with their abdomens facing the surface.

Corixids usually reside in the upper foot or two of the water column, for they lack gills and must penetrate the meniscus to acquire atmospheric oxygen to breathe. They also can take a little bubble with them to suck on while they cruise along under the surface. With the added luggage of this air bubble, the bodies of these insects can be so buoyant that they must swim when submerged, otherwise they float to the surface. Many water boatmen battle this buoyancy by grabbing hold of aquatic vegetation in order to rest. Both corixids and backswimmers love the weedy shallows that line the margins of many lakes, for it provides food, shelter, and rest for them. The inside weed edge is the most important location in a lake to imitate water boatmen and backswimmers.

Insects of the order Hemiptera feed on a wide variety of foods, depending on the species. Most Hemiptera have a needle-like sucking mechanism which allows them to suck the innards out of any insect that wanders too close. Corixids feed primarily on plant material, though prey for many aquatic Hemiptera (including Notonectids) includes midge and mosquito larvae, freshwater shrimp, even small tadpoles and young fish. Note where these prey items are concentrated: shallow margin water.

Backswimmers and water boatmen tend to "dive-bomb" the surface in order to penetrate the meniscus, landing with a distinct splat similar to a beetle or hopper. Some research entomologists actually have found these insects dive-bombing the windshield glass of a stationary car, likely mistaking the shiny surface of the windshield for water. Anglers should note this behavior. I have had times when slapping a water boatman pattern hard on the water was like ringing a dinner bell for the trout.

Thoughts on Imitation

The first thing that comes to mind after reading the biology of these insects is that they carry a bubble of air on their body wherever they go. This would obviously warrant some serious flash in the imitation. Pearlescent glass beads, Flashabou, and mylar sheeting are all possibilities that the angler should be willing to incorporate when tying imitations. The use of sparkle dubbing is also a good idea to add more light-catching ability to your imitation.

The next things that come to mind are those big legs that propel these bugs through the water. A picture perfect burnt plastic leg that remains motionless during the retrieve is less productive than a simple piece of Super Floss that pumps with each strip of the line. Remember, water boatmen have legs that point forward while at rest, so imitations that incorporate this feature are better imitations of the natural (and it doesn't take any longer than it takes to tie perpendicular-set legs). Legs that point forward at rest give the fly a more realistic motion when stripped through the water.

The last thing that comes to mind with backswimmer imitation should be the first. When these insects stop swimming they rise straight up. This should warn you NOT to use beadheads or lead when tying imitations. Foam or spun deer hair will provide the buoyancy needed to properly imitate the motion of the natural insect. By using floating materials and creating a buoyant fly, under most conditions, you will catch three times the fish that a sinking imitation would produce.

In the fall, cruising trout often look for the "splat" of a diving Corixid. A fly with a pearlescent glass or plastic bead to imitate the trapped air bubble can give the fly just enough weight to create a meaty plop on the surface. As a glass or plastic bead is not oppressively heavy its slow sink can be masked with a choppy retrieve. Imitations of water boatmen and backswimmers should be fished in short, two to six-inch strips, with a brief pause between strips. This kind of retrieve can replicate the jerky motion of the naturals. Use a slow sinking line when imitating these insects; a floating line will not allow buoyant patterns under the surface, and a fast sinking line will drag the flies too deep. The prime location to fish imitations of these bugs is on the inside edge of a weedbed. Because the inside weed line often lies in two to four feet of water, focus on this area during the low light of sunrise and sunset when trout are most comfortable in the shallows. These insects don't like to venture far from weeds (since they offer food and a place to rest), and they are rarely found deeper than three feet below the surface. If you fish these flies in open or deep water, you may be sufficiently discouraged to never try them again. If you fish them in the proper manner and in the proper places, you may spend all winter tying up more imitations of these "miracle bugs."

Patterns

Keys to Match:
1. **Leg Movement:** A pronounced leg action is key to successful patterns.
2. **Flash!!!:** This is one of the "flashiest" insects you will encounter, so be liberal with the sparkle!
3. **Dark/Light Contrast:** These critters have dark backs and light bellies (or vice versa) that contrast more sharply than nearly any insect you'll find.

Keys to Avoid:
1. **Heavily Weighted Patterns:** Rising naturals + sinking imitations = fishless days.
2. **Stiff Patterns:** Leave the goose-biot legs for stonefly nymphs.
3. **Skinny Bodies:** These insects can be rather squat, so make sure to include some bulk.

Water Boatman

Hook: Dai Riki 300, #12-14
Shellback: Lacquered turkey quill
Air Bubble: pearl or clear glass bead
Legs: Black or Olive Super Floss (half of one strand)
Body: WAPSI White Dubbing Enhancer

This is the pattern I use most often because of the nice plop it gives on the surface. Occasionally in shallow water, you'll see the reverse "v" of a trout (or bluegill or bass) shooting over to the fly the moment it strikes the surface. Despite the weight provided by the glass bead, this fly is not a fast sinker. I like to fish this fly at a rather steady pace, so that it's modest sinking tendencies are not revealed to the fish.

Floater Boater

Hook: Dai Riki 300 #12-14
Under Body: White foam strip wrapped around the hook shank
Over Body: Pale olive, or pale olive/cream blend sparkle dubbing
Legs: Olive pheasant tail
Shellback: Mottled Thin Skin

When fish are picky over boatman patterns, this one seals the deal. When paused during the retrieve, this fly will rise like a natural water boatman. Tie it in olive, tan, or brown, and fish it on a sinking line and a leader just about double the length of the depth. This way the fly can tap the surface on pauses and dive with each short strip.

Krystal Backswimmer

Hook: Dai Riki 300 #12-14
Body: WAPSI White Dubbing Enhancer (perhaps mixed with a bit of cream or pale olive rabbit dubbing)
Air Bubble: Strip of silver mylar tinsel, from rear of the fly to the legs.
Legs: Split Brown or Olive Super Floss (part of one strand)
Shellback: Rootbeer and Peacock (or Black) Krystal Flash (tied under body), blended and soft-epoxied.

This pattern is a superb imitation of a backswimmer and not all that difficult to tie. The shellback, tied under the fly, renders irrelevant the need to weight the fly so that it rides upside-down. The mixing of the two colors of Krystal Flash results in a surprisingly realistic shellback. While the strip of tinsel may look awkward to humans, it imitates the underwater flash of the air bubble better than any other material.

Index

A
algae 15, 17, 88, 111, 127
alewives 30
Ants 9, 12, 14, 15, 17, 19, **23**, 24, 25, 26, 27, 98, 100, 106, 114
Aphids 15, 17, 24, **27**, 28
Au Sable 11

B
backswimmers 9, 12, 14, 21, 52, 118, 133, 134
Baetis 12, 15, 18, 55, 58, 64, 112, 115, 123, 126, 127, 134,
Baitfish 6, 9, 12, 28, **29**, 30, 32, 33, 36, 37, 38, 39, 40, 41, 44, 45, 46, 47, 62, 88, 89, 108, 127
bass 5, *35, 36, 37, 40, 53, 54, 73, 86, 88, 89, 91, 98, 111, 112, 117, 128, 132, 133, 137, 142, 164, 167*
Beetles 9, 11, 15, 17, 18, 19, 23, **48**, 49, 52, 53, 54, 92, 98, 99, 100, 102
Black Flies 6, 9, 11, 14, 15, 19, 25, 55, 56, 57, **58**, 59, 126, 127, 129
bluegill *7, 72, 90, 93, 112, 125, 133, 135*
Borger, Gary 126
brown trout 17, 18, 19, 23, 29, 30, 33, 35, 97, 107, 123, 125
BWO (See *Baetis*)

C
Caddis 6, 7, 9, 11, 12, 13, 14, 15, 17, 19, 25, 31, 42, 49, 52, 55, 56, 57, 58, 59, 60, 64, 69, 70, 73, 78, 86, 91, 97, 108, 123, 127, 129, 134
Caddisflies 7, 11, 13, 97
Callibaetis 6, 12, 81, 108, 134
Cascade Flying Ant 23-26
Cascades 25, 39, 85, 91
CDC 25, 26, 28, 53, 58, 59, 66, 67, 69, 70, 71, 79, 86, 99, 100, 101, 112, 119, 120
Centipedes **60**
Chaoborus 12, 44, 61, 63, 88, 108, 111, 117, 118, 119, 120
Chernobyl Ant 25, 98
Chironomids 6, 12, 14, 19, 21, 29, 55, 58, **61**, 62, 63, 64, 65, 66, 67, 68, 69, 76, 81, 91, 107, 108, 111, 112, 116, 117, 118, 119, 120, 134
cicadas 9, 129
Crane Flies 6, 9, 11, 12, 14, 17, 18, 19, 25, 55, 60, 61, 62, **76**, 77, 78, 79, 80, 113
Crayfish 9, 14, 19, 37, 55, **72**, 73, 74, 75, 127, 129
cutthroat 17, 31, 42, 44, 79, 88, 102, 103, 117

D
damselflies 62, 65, **81**, 84, 85, 85, 91, 92, 93
Daphnia 6, 9, 11, 12, 19, 28, 44, 46, 55, **87**, 88, 89, 90, 108, 118, 119, 126, 129
Deer Flies **102**, 103
Delaware 23
Deschutes 11, 13, 57, 77
Diptera 17, 23, 55, 61, 63, 76, 115
Dragonflies 7, 81, 84, 85, **91**, 92, 93, 94, 95, 134
Dylan 55

F
fish eggs 6, 11
Fly Patterns for Stillwaters 14
fry 6, 30, 31, 32, 33, 34, 35, 36, 41, 42, 45

G
George Harvey 25
Glossosoma 15, 127
Golden Stones 12,
Grasshoppers 7, 9, 11, 14, 17, 18, 23, 25, 48, 49, 57, 66, 72, 74, 91, **96**, 97, 98, 99, 100, 101, 102, 108
Green Drakes 12

H
Hemiptera 17, 134
Hoff, C.L. 24
Honeybees **106**,
hoppers 11, 23, 25, 48, 57, 66, 74, 96, 97, 98, 99, 100, 101, 102, 108
Horseflies 99, **102**, 103
Hymenoptera 17, 23, 106

I
inchworms 6, 17, 21, 87, 99, 108, 113, 113, 114

L
Ladybugs 15
LaFontaine, Gary 7, 11, 13, 97
lakes (See *stillwaters*)
Leech 9, 12, 14, 19, 21, 37, 74, 75, 89, 91, 92, **107**, 108, 109, 110, 119, 126
Lepidoptera 17, 113, 114
Letort 9, 25, 99, 101

M
Mahogany Duns 7
mayflies 7, 9, 11, 14, 17, 23, 39, 42, 48, 49, 55, 59, 64, 70, 79, 86, 93, 97, 107, 113, 123, 125, 126, 127
millipedes 19, 60
Mosquitoes 9, 55, 91, 103, **111**, 112, 118
Moths 113

N
Net-Winged Midges 55, 114, **115**, 116

O
Oligochaeta 19
Oregon 19, 23, 24, 31, 32, 36, 39, 48, 73, 91, 92, 107, 124, 127, 130

P
Phantom Midges 55, 108, **117**, 118, 119, 120
PMD 6, 9, 12, 53, 55, 77

R
Raffia 25, 28, 59, 67, 75, 79, 95, 103, 106, 125
rainbow trout 18, 19, 23, 31, 32, 46, 55, 88
rainbow smelt **44**
reservoir 12, 30, 32, 34, 36, 39, 46, 49, 54, 61, 65, 72, 80, 81, 88, 92, 107, 111, 127, 131
Rhyacophila 15, 59, 73
Rowley, Phillip 14, 61

S
Salmonflies 6, 7, 11, 12, 14, 57, 91, 93
Scuds 6, 9, 14, 19, 28, 66, 89, **121**, 122, 123, 124, 125, 127, 130, 131
sculpin 15, 30, 36, **41**, 42, 43, 45, 73
shad **30**
Sierra Nevada 25
small streams 11, 12, 19, 24, 67, 92, 94, 98, 138, 139, 140
Snails 3, 126
soft hackles 11, 120
Sow Bugs 6, 9, 14, 62, 130, 131, 132
stillwaters 6, 7, 9, 11, 12, 14, 19, 29, 30, 31, 32, 34, 44, 49, 52, 61, 62, 63, 64, 70, 79, 81, 84, 85, 88, 91, 92, 93, 94, 95, 107, 108, 109, 112, 117, 118, 119, 121, 124, 125, 129, 131, 133
Sticklebacks 36
stoneflies 6, 9, 11, 13, 15, 16, 42, 48, 73, 77

T
tailwater 6, 12, 59, 62, 84, 130, 122,
Terrestrials 9, 11, 12, 14, 16, 17, 18, 19, 23, 25, 26, 27, 28, 29, 48, 49, 57, 59, 60, 72, 76, 77, 96, 97, 98, 99, 100, 102, 106, 112, 113, 114, 128, 130
Tetramorium caespitum 24
Trico 12, 23, 65, 86, 123
Trout and Salmon Fry 30
Tui Chub 39

W
Washington 24, 44, 45, 88, 117
Wasps 25, 98
Water Boatmen/Backswimmers 9, 12, 14, 21, 52, 55, 107, 118, **133**, 134, 135
Western Hatches 13
Woolly Buggers *12, 74, 108*

Y
Yellowstone 11, 25, 31, 77 79, 85, 97, 98, 99, 102, 103

Z
zooplankton 14